Media-Made Dixie

Jack Temple Kirby

Media-Made Dixie

The South in the American Imagination

Revised Edition

The University of Georgia Press

Athens and London

Revised edition © 1986 by the University of Georgia Press
Athens, Georgia 30602
All rights reserved
First published in 1978 by Louisiana State University Press.
The paper in this book meets the guidelines for
permanence and durability of the Committee on
Production Guidelines for Book Longevity of the
Council on Library Resources.

Printed in the United States of America

90   89   88   87   86   5   4   3   2   1

Library of Congress Cataloging-in-Publication Data

Kirby, Jack Temple.
Media-made Dixie.

Bibliography: p.
Includes index.
1. Southern States—Historiography.   2. Southern
States—Civilization.   3. Mass media—United States—
History. I. Title.
F208.2.K57   1986   975'.04'072   86-11236
ISBN 0-8203-0885-4 (pbk.: alk. paper)

To the memory of
WILLIAM DAVID PALMER
(1879–1958)

Contents

Preface to the
Revised Edition

Almost a decade has sped by since those salad days of early 1977, when I wrote the epilogue to the first edition of *Media-Made Dixie*. Jimmy Carter's administration was underway, the television serialization of Alex Haley's *Roots* had just been broadcast, and Billy Carter was on the brink of peddling his own brand of beer and "Red-Neck Lobbyist" T-shirts. Larry L. King had recently declared in *Esquire* that "We Ain't Trash No More!" and I, too, believed in those fabulous moments that a new era had dawned. So at the end of the eighth chapter and in that epilogue, I euphorically surpassed my evidence that yankees had accepted the South at last, and rushed on to predict Dixie's imminent demise as a distinctive region.

Some scholarly reviewers ignored my rash conclusion in favor of predictable second-guessing of selections for emphasis, nitpicking, and/or stubborn misunderstanding of the modest intentions I had set down in the preface. Reviewers in southern newspapers, however, could see little else. Like mine, their livelihoods and hobbies are what John Shelton Reed calls dixiology; and they thought they saw a brother insanely urinating in the campfire. Reed, the columnists, and the southern masses nonetheless kept the fire burning, and now I publicly repent: I actually saw (and felt) the flames all along. So this revised edition properly and (I hope) clearly separates the matters of image and perception, which are the business of this book, from sociology, which is not.

The new ending may be rash, too, however, Once more I have attempted to interpret historically events very recent and still unfolding. This is always risky. In a few years I may bear fresh lumps and bruises, but my hide is toughened for that eventuality. I fully expect to discover that I missed details and misweighed some of the proportions of recent media happenings. Yet I remain such a hopeful creature. Despite persisting nonsense and occasional name-calling, reminding one that silliness and misunderstanding go on, the eighties have presented some remarkable events in real life and in the media. It is these I choose optimistically to emphasize, for they seem to point to what I have always wished for: popular objective understanding and appreciation of the South and its people, and the reconciliation of regions and races. Why not the best of possible worlds?

Were I to rewrite the first seven chapters I would make only minor adjustments. Somehow I neglected, for example, Lillian Smith's *Strange Fruit*. It belongs in "The Visceral South," or maybe the "devilish" chapter following. I believe, however, that this and a few other oversights brought to my attention are in effect treated by inference, at least, via my chronological typology of popular images. Still, I apologize to champions of all books, plays, movies, and television shows that may unjustly be slighted. Another matter concerns the great novelist, Frank Yerby, who became my correspondent in 1978. Yerby objected to my neglect of his post-1970 works, and to my description of him as "a southern black man." On both matters I believe we are reconciled. Few novels other than best sellers are considered here, by design. It is a shame that the American public has not patronized Yerby's later work so well as before, for in my opinion (and that of more learned critics), they are even better than his best sellers of the forties and fifties. It is true, too, that Yerby has not been a "southern" man for a very long time; and having become a European, he no longer shares the arbitrary American concept of race. He is not, in other words, "black," but of mixed racial ancestry. I hope some day to find opportunity to write more fully about Frank Yerby and his fiction.

Finally an acknowledgment of my debts: George Tindall liked this book before it was published the first time, and that still means a great deal to me. Frank Trippett wrote a generous review in *Time* that brought forth a torrent of letters from former students, long-lost friends, strangers (such as Thomas Newsom of Valdosta, Georgia, who sends me clippings and insights), and from John Shelton Reed, who has become a valued friend and stimulating colleague. As much as John Reed and I have disagreed over dixiology, his works inform this updating much to its advantage. Reed also joined James Cobb, Clarence Mohr, Charles Wilson, and others in promoting the creation of this new edition. Then Malcolm Call, director of the University of Georgia Press, became all a writer might desire in a publisher—professional, supportive, and eager. Last but maybe most important, my teenaged children, Val and Matt, read Alice Walker's *The Color Purple* with me, watched Steven Spielberg's version, along with other movies on my mind, and talked sensitively about them all. That they agree with my interpretations is no small relief. Some of us are blessed with creditors.

J. T. K.

Oxford, Ohio
March, 1986

Acknowledgments

Miami University has supported this study in many ways: a summer research grant; subsidies for film rentals; a light teaching load one fall so I could write; the aid of an eager library staff; and the help of a succession of graduate assistants who gave more than they were paid for—Earl W. Crosby, Steven E. Anders, Robert A. Spaier, and Robert E. Kimmel. The American Philosophical Society provided two grants to support travel to libraries in the South. By no means the least of my benefactors, Ann Bulleit Kirby scoured *TV Guides* for fugitive movies I never would have seen, and she tried to check my obsessive southern self-consciousness in evaluating the films. She is a tough-minded yankee.

This book is dedicated to my maternal grandfather, a South Carolinian who was never reconstructed despite all the literature of reconciliation during his lifetime. An avid and emotive baseball fan, he rooted for any team opposing the New York Yankees during their years of glory in the forties and fifties. So far as I could tell, this was because of their name and because they always won.

Oxford, Ohio   J. T. K.
March, 1977

xiii

Preface

History High and Low

For ignorance is the first requisite of the historian—ignorance which simplifies and clarifies, which selects and omits, with a placid perfection unattainable by the highest art.

Giles Lytton Strachey[1]

Historiography means the history of historical writing, primarily academic. (The term also often includes historical methodology and philosophy.) The subject of the American South has been covered quite well by scholars. The Old South and slavery, the politics of southern sectionalism, the Confederacy, Reconstruction, and the so-called New South with all its subsubjects—have received lavish attention.[2]

This attention, like that given other subjects, has traditionally been delimited by professional boundaries. At most, historiographers consider a subject's contemporary polemics; then they proceed to examine scholarly progress to their own times. Pervading the scholarship is an assumption that once the generation involved in an event has passed on, scholars control communications and understanding about the event. Thus historians have constructed without serious reflection or criticism a pyramidal model representing the transmission of historical knowledge: At prestigious history departments hypothesizing dons develop research and publish monographs and syntheses that break interpretive barriers. Their graduate students carry the work to lesser parts of academia like good disciples, adopting their old mentors' textbooks and anthologies for use in their own classes. Enlightened undergraduates in turn transmit the word to high school and elementary students when they have become teachers. New knowledge seeps down to the base of society. During the past thirty years historians have frequently reminded each other that they are part of society and that their interpretations are affected by factors of time lapse, current events' relevance to historical subjects, and historians' own ideologies and idiosyncrasies. Yet the pyramidal model has survived along with the largely professional limits on sources of historical understanding.[3]

In this book, academic historiography since about 1900 provides a reference point for the main object of inquiry—*popular* historical images of the South since the advent of feature movies and annual best-seller lists. The objective of this study is first simply to survey this imagery in the mass communications media: films, best-selling fiction, documentary books and films, popular (*i.e.* nonacademic) histories, school texts, music, and television. Some attention is also given to radio, drama, sports, and to advertising through the printed and television media.

Since the objective is to survey imagery that was/is popular, my test-principle for selection and emphasis has been that of the "free marketplace." So whatever the artistic or scholarly merit of a novel, movie, or TV program, if it sells well (has good box office, survives the Nielsen ratings), it is significant in representing mass taste, perception, and understanding.[4]

Many worthy artifacts of Americans' fascination with Dixie, which would almost inevitably be included in literary anthologies or filmographies, will receive scant notice here. During the 1920s, for example, few people bought or read such artistically significant poetry magazines as *The Fugitive* and *The Double-Dealer*. As for scholarship, the great southern sociologist Howard Odum reported that his *Journal of Social Forces* had but twelve subscribers in the entire state of North Carolina. Eight were Chapel Hillians; seven of these members of Odum's Sociology Department.[5] So then, here Erskine Caldwell rates more space than William Faulkner and Ellen Glasgow; Claude Bowers more than Ulrich Bonnell Phillips and C. Vann Woodward; *Nashville* and *W. W. and The Dixie Dance Kings* more than Jean Renoir's *Swamp Water* and *The Southerner*. On the other hand, the organization of the book is basically chronological; therefore the ascendancies and demises of interpretive models (or genres) must be set in a context that always includes meritoriously significant works. When historical frameworks are thus laid, readers should be able to relate, for example, such major literary works as Glasgow's *Barren Ground* (not very popular) to Caldwell's *Tobacco Road* and *God's Little Acre* (enormously popular), and then in turn to Professor Frank L. Owsley's *Plain Folk of the Old South* (obscure).

Two descriptive conclusions affecting the pyramidal model of knowledge transmission have resulted from this research. First, from the 1890s to the mid-1930s the pyramid is almost wholly nondescriptive as an explanation of the origins of either specific historical interpretations or of vague genres which reflect the South's status among American regions. If any usage of the pyramidal form is applicable, it would be in the inverted position, with "ivory tower" scholars *receiving* interpretations from the masses and supplying footnotes. Second, from the mid-thirties onward—to the credit of the professionals—academic historians have usually been about a decade or more ahead of the popular media. *Ahead* means the abandonment of neo-Confederate sentimentality toward slavery and post–Civil War paternalism in race relations, for example, and the adoption of a neoabolitionist treatment of the Old South and the human rights cause since 1865, along with sympathetic portrayals of the white poor as well.

In place of the pyramid, I offer an alternative geometric model for knowledge transmission, the circle. Academicians, filmmakers, fictionalists, and television people are nearly all part of the rather amorphous American middle class, sharing many experiences (including public education) and values. Forming a sort of circle with most other people, they continually broadcast information and images to each other as well as to "the masses." It would seem, then, that about the circle's circumference transmission would continually flow in both directions at once. Nonetheless, an important distinction remains for scholars. While living on the circle, they are usually disciplined to the ideal of objectivity; and perhaps more important, as subsidized professors they usually do not compete for money in the communications free market. There remains a certain reality for the old pyramid, then. But as suggested above, this limited shape appears with regard to southern historiography only after about 1935.

An important assumption in this book is that there are heavy historical implications in many communications that are not directly intended as "historical." Examples are "contemporary" novels (Caldwell's, many of Faulkner's, the "sharecropper realism" of the twenties), contemporary films (Renoir's *The Southerner*, Altman's *Nashville*), and advertising in most media. In such cases I approach historiography by way of primitive semiotics. (*Semiotics* is loosely defined as the "study of symbols.") Contemporary novels (old and new ones) are often governed by historical assumptions, whether or not the author has raised them to his/her own consciousness and revealed them openly to readers. Sympathy for the southern rural poor in the sharecropper novels and films of the twenties and early thirties reflect also an assumption of historical "legitimacy," worth, and dignity for the common people, in stark contrast to the "white trash" tradition in fiction and history. In examining advertising I have looked for pictorial representations which in context reveal historical interpretations. Thus whiskey advertisements set in the genteel South, with docile blacks serving up the booze, convey a great deal about the history of the ruling class, slavery, and race relations. Assuming that advertisers wish to identify their products with positive imagery, it would appear that such advertisements reinforced an understanding about the Old South which I call sentimentalist and neo-Confederate. Still photographs in 1930s documentary books have been perused in much the same manner as the sharecropper novels.

Because popular historiography and semiotics are seldom precise and do not systematically and empirically document their historical messages, I have used the term *genres* rather than *interpretations* to describe the various sets of images of the South. *Genre* in popular culture studies and filmography usually means a broad subject field, such as "western," "cops and robbers," "horror." Here, the parallel "southern" would encompass the entire book. Instead I use *genre* to describe interpretive styles within the broad subject. *Neo-Confederate*, for instance, is the popular genre counterpart of the academic Dunning School of Reconstruction historiography and Professor U. B. Phillips' history of slavery. *Gothic* encompasses the Caldwell-Faulkner treatments of white common folk, in contrast to sharecropper realism. *Neo-abolitionist* includes both popular and scholarly liberalism in black history and race-relations imagery and scholarship, and a certain cynicism toward white southern elites.

Why do genres change? Thomas Kuhn, author of *The Structure of Scientific Revolutions*, suggested that scholarly interpretations change when irreparable fault lines produced by both changing social environment and empirical evidence render existing theories irrelevant and/or intolerable.[6] No doubt popular genres change for much the same reason. By the 1970s, for example, it was virtually unthinkable for Hollywood to make a western without black characters and/or noble Indians. Popular feeling and understanding of western history would not permit otherwise. An additional reason, going beyond Kuhn's theory, is the factor of familiarity. According to one student of popular genres, familiarity "breeds contempt" sooner or later. Hollywood or other free market communicators experiment (frequently aided by market research) until they find a successful genre. Success induces repetition and imitation. The market becomes surfeited and boredom sets in. Then for practical business reasons genres will be changed.[7]

Such business considerations must be combined with the elements of prevailing values, social environment, and the state of scholarship to produce a formula for popular historiographical change. Even then no general rule of proportionate influence may be assigned to the elements individually. Sometimes, too, the felicitous influence of good scholarship and liberal social environment may lead the free market communicators past realism into fantasy and worse. A case in point is Hollywood's treatment of Afro-Americans. From the 1920s until the late 1940s, blacks were humiliated in the "tom," "coon," and "mammy" stereotypes. In 1949, building upon liberal scholarship and the recent war against Nazi bigotry, several sympathetic films were released. During the fifties "race" movies about Joe Louis and the Harlem Globetrotters were produced by white companies for the mass audience. In the early sixties the genre was extended to neoabolitionist dramas set in the South. By then Hollywood had discovered that whites would tolerate aggressive black males ("bucks") and that urban black audiences were an enormous market which would support yet more "militant" films. Thus was born "Blaxploitation," fantasies such as *Shaft* and *Superfly*, in which ghetto heroes operate beyond "white" law, make fools of whites, get rich, and sometimes defend their people against the "honkeys." Black audiences were apparently delighted, but black and white liberal activists and scholars, who had pressured Hollywood for social comment in the forties, fifties, and sixties, were appalled. Productive social energy, they protested, was being diverted and drained into the darkened cul de sacs with the marquees outside.[8]

Finally, by *South* I mean mainly the white majority. Americans typically intend *southerner* as descriptive of whites only, unless they are distinguishing between blacks by region—then they are "southern Negroes," not southerners—and this book is about Americans' perceptions. But of course black southerners have played a vital role in the South and in whites' consciousness of role and region; so I have tried to account for the black South both in proportion and justice, too.

Chapter 1

Griffith, Dunning, and "the Great Fact of Race"

It's like writing history with lightning!
Attributed to Woodrow Wilson,
upon seeing Birth of a Nation, 1915

In the second half of the nineteenth century the pervasive image of the American South was negative. Despite spirited efforts by Romantics, proslavery propagandists, then by postwar sentimentalists, the abolitionist tradition prevailed. The South was brutal and backward, un-American. The reconciliation of the sections began slowly in the 1870s and finally necessitated the historical rehabilitation of the white South as part of the bargain of emotional reunion. Gradually, the abolitionist tradition that slavery was barbarous, was turned upon its head: slavery became a benign, paternal system that was unfortunately incompatible with other American institutions. Reconstruction —a trauma within the memory of many in 1900—became a foolish, tragic misadventure instead of a noble conclusion to the abolitionist crusade.[1]

All that remained at the opening of the new century was further synthesis and thorough broadcast. Coincidentally, several broadened or new mechanisms of information dissemination had appeared to facilitate generalization. One was the growth of higher education and the professionalization of history. By 1900 hundreds of young men (and a few women) were earning doctorates in American graduate schools, writing scores of publishable dissertations, and going

1

D. W. Griffith, 1914

THE MUSEUM OF MODERN ART/FILM STILLS ARCHIVE

out to teach undergraduates their and their mentors' new "progressive" interpretations. Many of the undergraduates themselves became teachers in the expanding secondary and elementary schools, where they, presumably, further disseminated new historical information. Meanwhile book publishing in the United States expanded to such an extent that *Bookman's* sought an accurate measure of mass sales. In 1897 the first annual best-seller list appeared, and in 1914 more books would be published in the country than in any year thereafter until 1953.[2] As we shall see later, southern historical subjects were prominent among those directed at the new markets.

An entirely new mass medium of communication in the new century was the motion picture. After some years of technical experimentation in the United States and western Europe, the movies became commercial, truly "mass" in their appeal, and sophisticated in technique. The American industry was organizationally helter-skelter in the progressive era, and credit for the development of the medium cannot be briefly attributed. But of the great innovator-impresarios of the age, David Wark Griffith (1875–1948) was the colossus (to employ a Hollywoodism). The great Soviet filmmaker Sergei Eisenstein, who is often credited with the invention of mature cinematic montage, himself identified Griffith as his master. "Griffith invented Hollywood," wrote another observer.[3] He was one of the great communicators of all time, and for reasons biographical and chronological, Griffith has very special significance in popular southern historiography.

Griffith was Kentucky-born and self-consciously southern. Son of "Roaring Jake" Griffith, a florid, stentorian Confederate cavalryman, he absorbed the lore of the Old South and Lost Cause from his flamboyant father and from the embittered milieu of a late nineteenth-century border area. As a teen-aged dry goods store employee and bookstore clerk in Louisville, he decorated his boardinghouse bedroom walls with a portrait of his uniformed father, a Confederate flag, and a concocted family coat of arms modeled after the ancient royal Welsh Griffiths. Decades later G. W. "Billy" Bitzer, the director's ace cameraman, thought of Griffith in middle age as southern. In faraway California or in Mamaroneck, New York, Griffith liked to have near him actor Henry Walthall, a fellow southerner who played "the Little Colonel," Ben Cameron, in *Birth of a Nation*. According to Bitzer, Walthall exhibited a "sort of lazy Southern laxity" which endeared him to everyone, but particularly to D. W., who needed Walthall's "touch of home . . . to relax."[4]

Southerner Griffith had a sense of historical mission, too, which he often emphasized along with his concern with "authenticity" of detail. As early as 1911 he made a Civil War film for the Biograph Company, *The Battle*, in which he employed actual period artillery as well as authentic uniforms and other artifacts.[5] As an independent producer setting out to make *Birth of a Nation* in 1914, Griffith became, in Bitzer's view, charged with sectional purpose. "This was not just another picture. . . . He was fighting the old war all over again and, like a true Southerner, trying to win it or at least to justify losing it." Griffith "*lived* every minute" of the production, "blaming the carpetbaggers for seeking to profit from the South's sufferings and glorifying the clansman for rescuing those fair flowers of the South," the belles, from black men's storied aggressions. He personally selected the horse to play Lee's Traveller. "It had to be just the dappled gray," recalled Bitzer. "You'd think we were back in 1864–65. Of course, in Griffith's mind we were." [6]

Griffith found a ferocious collaborator in Thomas Dixon, North Carolina-born preacher-author-promoter, whose novel *The Clansman* Griffith adapted as format for the second half of *Birth*. Dixon arranged showings of the epic for his friend and college classmate, President Woodrow Wilson, and for a former klansman, Edward Douglass White, Chief Justice of the United States. Wilson pronounced the film "like writing history with lightning," and White, a man of notorious cold reserve, melted with nostalgia for "the days of '76." To Wilson's secretary, Joe Tumulty, Dixon averred that "the real big purpose back of" *Birth of a Nation* was "to revolutionize northern sentiments by a presentation of history that would transform every man in the audience into a good Democrat!" Better yet, "every man who comes out of one of our theatres is a Southern partisan for life." Dixon felt compelled to exempt only the northeastern radicals and the liberal, interracial NAACP—"the members of [Oswald Garrison] Villard's Inter-Marriage society who go there to knock." In New York, Griffith was obliged to excise from the film several of the more inflammatory chase-rape scenes. But the famous sequence in which actress Mae Marsh ("pet sister" of hero Henry Walthall) leaps to her death rather than submit to the sex-crazed black soldier, Gus, remained. In reply to claims by NAACP official Morefield Storey that the picture distorted history, Griffith cited as his authorities Woodrow Wilson's *Division and Reunion* (1889), James Ford Rhodes' seven-volume *History of the United States from the Compromise of 1850* (1896–1906), and Walter L. Fleming's *Civil War and Reconstruction*

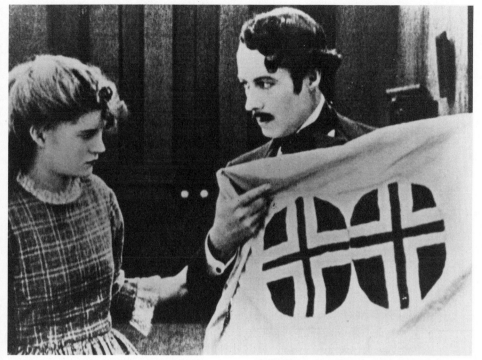

Birth of a Nation: the *"Little Colonel" (Henry Walthall) reveals
his Klan costume to his "pet little sister" (Mae Marsh).*

in *Alabama* (1905). The director offered Storey ten thousand dollars
if he could prove historical error, then ignored Storey's and *Crisis*
editor W. E. B. DuBois' counterscholarship.[7]

Historian DuBois had written of Reconstruction for the *Atlantic
Monthly* in 1901, again in his famous *Souls of Black Folk* (1903);
and as recently as 1909 he had read a paper before the American Historical Association entitled "Reconstruction and its Benefits." On
the eve of the release of *Birth of a Nation* another Afro-American,
former Mississippi congressman John R. Lynch, published his autobiographical *The Facts of Reconstruction*. DuBois, Lynch, and a few
whites (such as Albion Tourgée, former carpetbagger and civil rights

activist) maintained an interpretation of Reconstruction essentially the same as that "revisionism" prevailing in the 1960s and 1970s: federal policies had not been "radical" enough to complete reform in the South; land ("forty acres and a mule") should have been distributed to freedmen; there were few black officeholders in relation to black population; whites (sometimes Democrats, too) were principally responsible for corruption, nationwide; in most states Reconstruction was shortlived and mild in its effects; and despite failures, Reconstruction accomplished important reforms such as establishment of equality before the law and free public schools.[8]

But in 1915 Griffith and Dixon rode a historiographical and political juggernaut which swept all before it. In the 1890s white southerners had undertaken the formal separation of the races and the disfranchisement of black citizens—the undoing of Reconstruction. The campaign was accompanied by an intense historical didacticism directed to the nation. The burden of the southern version was that the "tragedies" of the Reconstruction era demonstrated blacks' civic incompetence and inaugurated a dangerous interracial propinquity ("social equality") which threatened the integrity of Anglo-Saxon racial stock. The region would never achieve peace and public honesty while blacks continued with the franchise, inviting corruptionists of both colors into politics. The Supreme Court validated the legal mechanisms of the racial settlement in 1896 and 1898, accepting the historical interpretation justifying segregation and disfranchisement.

Just then, too, the United States became an imperial power with overseas colonies of nonwhite peoples. During young Griffith's precinematic career as an itinerate actor, Americans debated the "place" of colored colonials, finally deciding that they were both unassimilable and unfit for citizenship. They would be ruled and "cared for" by those ordained by God to hold dominion. The racial settlement at home, with its justification in a neo-Confederate interpretation of Reconstruction, gave the imperial decision an airtight logic.[9]

Walter L. Fleming, whom Griffith cited for support in his historical dispute with the NAACP, belonged to the second generation of conservative writers on the South and Reconstruction. Wilson and Rhodes, whom he also cited, had earlier painted the broad strokes. So, too, had many nonprofessionals. In 1901 the *Atlantic Monthly* printed a series of articles on Reconstruction, including DuBois' and one by Wilson. Among the other contributors were two Alabamians, the novelist-politician Hilary Herbert and the clergyman–child-labor reformer Edgar Gardner Murphy. Both wrote indictments of black and white Radicals and insinuated parallels between the conservatives who overthrew Reconstruction and disfranchisement. The *Atlantic Monthly*'s series was concluded by Professor William A. Dunning of Columbia University, who was Fleming's mentor. Dunning's essay was restrained in tone, but its burden lay with Herbert, Murphy, and Wilson rather than DuBois.[10]

Dunning was a northern man of southern sentiments who believed that an objective, "balanced" history of the Civil War era required the southern white point of view. He was an American patriot who sought reconciliation of whites North and South. A racist like most whites, he sacrificed blacks to the nationalist cause. Fleming was a bright young Alabamian who was among the first of a generation of southerners to attend Dunning's famous seminar and write histories of southern states during Reconstruction. Fleming's dissertation on Alabama was the first issue of the so-called Dunning School. Enormous in size and copious in detail, it seemed the last word on one of the important former Confederate states where Radicals controlled government for a considerable time. Fleming supplied charts and lenghty lists of figures which amounted to, it was thought then, an incontrovertible case against the Radicals. His passionate interpretation, however, was not new at all, but an exhaustive elaboration of what Herbert, Murphy, and countless nonprofessionals had already maintained.[11] Such, indeed, was the case with most of the Dunning School histories.

Griffith's epic of the war and its aftermath, then, amounted to a completion of a great historiographical tour through the media of the day. The academics of the Dunning School elaborated an interpretation rooted in the traditions of the southern white conservatives, who relived the period while reordering race relations in the 1890s and 1900s. From these grass roots the interpretation was adapted by scholarly generalists such as Wilson and Rhodes. Dunning, Fleming, and company supplied the fine work. Carrying their predilections into the archives, they conferred upon the neo-Confederate version the imprimateur of scientific methodology. Dixon, meanwhile (whose *Clansman* appeared the same year as Fleming's first book), had maintained that intense popular contact, dramatizing his novel for the stage in 1907 and carrying the word to all parts of the country.

What Griffith and Bitzer accomplished was the brilliant adaptation of the southern interpretation to a new medium that could reach theretofore undreamed of multitudes. Few people read the Dunning histories; and while *The Clansman* was a best seller (Number 4 in 1905, about a quarter million copies), movie theaters drew millions. Griffith's audacity in presenting a production so long, and his and Bitzer's spectacular technical innovations, made *Birth* the unforgetable source from which countless Americans learned their history. As late as the 1930s, while both *Birth* and Griffith faded from currency in popular culture, they began to assume a sort of hallowed status which lasted until well after World War II. Indeed, as recently as 1972, Griffith's principal biographer took pains to declare that *Birth* was a "fantasy" and not documentary. And in early 1975 Joseph Henabery, who played Lincoln in *Birth*, protested in the pages of the New York *Times* that "Griffith was not a bigot." To Henabery, unlike the biographer, the director merely "presented true events." [12]

Griffith was no scholar. He was instead a rather spontaneous man —"all heart" as Bitzer put it—eager for that which tugged at nonintellectual white Americans. He made movies which reflected popular understanding rather than instructed it. *Birth of a Nation* magnified convictions already there; it was a saga *dé jà vu*: Dixie was glorious, fallen, raped-but-redeemed. The white South suffered defeat for error, humiliation for Yankees' blindness, but through the agony forged a reconciled, united, and sad-but-wise nation. Box office receipts told Griffith and his contemporaries that Americans in all regions wanted to be entertainingly reinforced about the saga, about the Old South's society and about the qualities that made the heroes of the Civil War era. From the very start of his film career, Griffith responded.[13]

The American Mutoscope and Biograph Company was just making the transition from production of peep shows for the viewer-cranked mutoscope machines to "feature" films for theater audiences, when the rangy Kentucky actor "Larry" Griffith came to work early in 1908. Within a few months Griffith became one of Biograph's directors, then the principal director who staged nearly all the company's movies. The films he made averaged five hundred to a thousand feet in length, playing ten to twenty minutes each. The production schedule was hectic. A feature was usually shot in a day, three at the most; and often several productions were scheduled simultaneously, with all indoor shots taken one day on hastily improvised sets, all outdoor action the next. Scenarios came from almost anywhere: plagiarized blatantly from literary classics, or from other companies' films, or from the stage; or they were submitted by fans and actors. Griffith wrote some, improvised on all he directed, and frequently worked without a written script at all. Scenarists for most Biograph films are today unknown, for until 1913 no one—writer, actors, directors—received screen credits. Some are known, however, from company pay and production records and from written memoirs. In addition to Griffith they include actress Mary Pickford, newsman and sometime-director Stannard E. V. Taylor, George Hennessy, and Emmet C. Hall. The last two each wrote more than one Civil War scenario. But neither Hennessy nor Hall (nor anyone else ascertainable) seems to have specialized in sectional or racial themes, or to have had special personal reasons for an interest in the South. Known scenarists wrote scripts on a variety of topics, including the war, contemporary urban drama, and also farce. Griffith once cynically referred to such film-making as "grinding out sausages"— giving the public back its poor taste, factory style. Despite the fact that some of the short Biograph films had considerable artistic and technical merit, and despite Griffith's own southern identity, scripts and themes were cleverly chosen for the market of the time. These pictures' commercial success justifies their designation as important artifacts not only of popular taste, but popular historical under-standing.[14]

As such, Griffith's southern movies reflect arch racism and his-torical naïveté, even if one makes allowances for the overacted ste-reotyping and oversimplification common to twenty-minute silent dramas. Griffith presented only two Souths: the mountain South—alternately innocent-idyllic and bloodthirsty-feuding; and the Flat-land South—peopled almost entirely by haughty aristocrats and faithful darkies. There is no middle South (despite his and Dixon's use of "Piedmont" for the South Carolina town in *Birth of a Nation*) —no white yeomanry, professional class, native merchants, herds-men. He omitted the vast majority. Mountain whites are simple and honest because they live in nature, but they do not forgive very read-ily. Low-country gentry are languid, paternalistic, and incredibly brave (whether male or female). There are no antebellum free blacks and very few unfaithful slaves. (Even in *Birth* faithful retainers are at least as numerous as dangerous, uppity freedmen.) Negro characters were usually played by white actors who knew precisely how to fawn, weep, or jive on directorial cue.

Griffith repeated two broad value messages in the Civil War pe-riod films: North-South reconciliation at the expense of blacks—the same as in *Birth*, writ smaller; and Dixie as a superior breeding ground for physical courage. The dramatic nexus connecting the themes paralleled the literary peacemaking of the 1880s-1890s.[15] In order for the sections to be reconciled and the nation to be strong, the war was depoliticized and reduced to a grand exercise in machismo: the yankees won because they were brave, but mainly because of numbers and superior industrial might. The white South's enduring compensation (in addition to a free hand in race relations after the nineties) was solemn national recognition for the bravery of the men in gray. Of course, majestic "Marse Robert" E. Lee symbolized the courageous integrity and soldierly bearing now conferred upon sons of the South generally. The doomed Old South thus won immortal-ity in literature, both high and low. Dixie became the hedonistic, im-practical, decadent-yet-noble soul of the industrializing society of the new century. Griffith, regal son of Colonel "Roaring Jake," a phy-sical, hell of a fellow himself and as sentimental as any American, was consummately well suited and situated to emote both reunion and rebel masculinity for the eager public. There was no incompati-bility between Griffith's art, his emotional spontaneity, and excel-lent business.

Griffith and his scenarists found the border states—especially Griffith's own Kentucky—the perfect historical setting for sectional reconciliation dramas. *The Guerrilla* (released November, 1908), one of the director's early efforts at Biograph, emphasized goodness on both sides as well as the dependability of southern slaves. Yankee outlaws don Confederate uniforms, and one of them, masquerading as a colonel, terrorizes Dorothy, who is enamored of a handsome Union soldier, Jack. The endangered girl sends her faithful black re-tainer through the lines for help, and though shot and harassed by yankees, he finds Jack, who comes to Dorothy's rescue.[16]

In Old Kentucky (September, 1909) was a melodrama of a family divided. Son George goes Union; Robert (Henry Walthall) goes rebel. George captures Robert, who escapes to their mother's protection: much bitterness. In the postwar finale, tattered Robert, clutching the Stars and Bars, arrives home, and peeping in the window unseen, observes the warm welcome being accorded brother George, who is well tailored, triumphant, and carrying the American flag draped over one arm. Sadly turning away, Walthall is spied by Uncle Jasper, faithful retainer, who steers him into the bosom of his family again. At the dissolve the brothers, still bearing flags, clasp hands.[17]

In the Border States, "Or a Little Heroine of the Civil War" (June, 1910), was a fast-paced tangle of adventure and sentiment. A Union soldier leaves his battle-area home, wife, and two small children. A little later a Confederate patrol is bushwacked nearby, and one of the wounded rebels drags himself to the yank's house. At the well he finds the little daughter, who shields him. Meanwhile, the Union-ist father goes on a dangerous mission through southern lines, is wounded, but makes it home with the rebels hot on his trail. The daughter remains with him while the other child goes for help. Then the rebels arrive. The father-soldier burns his secret papers as they break down the door. The Confederate in charge is none other than the same man recently aided by the girl. Enraged over his failure to obtain the Union secret papers, he prepares to dispatch the wounded yankee, when the daughter intervenes. The Confederate recognizes her, spares her father, then protects him from his wrathful comrades. Forgiveness and humanity win.[18]

Before the year was out Griffith made another, simpler, movie about hiding enemies. *The Fugitive* (November, 1910), subtitled "Showing the Extreme of a Mother's Tenderness," was set in the Virginia mountains, although the characters and theme are rather flatlandish. Two young men, both named John, go into regiments on opposite sides. Union John kills Johnny the rebel in combat, but in a retreat around the old neighborhood, seeks shelter with—none other than the dead Confederate's mother, who does not yet know of her loss. A compassionate soul, she hides the yankee in her fireplace. Searching rebels inform her of her son's death. In despair she is tempted to give away her hidden guest. But as an act of reconciliation she finally decides to continue protecting the Unionist.[19]

Twice more, after *Birth of a Nation*, Griffith dealt with sectional reconciliation themes. His next-to-last picture, *Abraham Lincoln* (1930), starring Walter Huston as Lincoln, emphasized at considerably more length the same conciliatory mercy Griffith attached to the president in *Birth* (wherein Lincoln was called "Great Heart"). More extraordinary was *The Girl Who Stayed at Home*, a potboiler released early in 1919. A contemporary drama set in France during World War I, the film included an ancient, unreconstructed Confederate émigré whose heart finally softens at the sight of yankees suffering along with southern boys in the trenches. Making peace at last, he lowers the Stars and Bars he has defiantly flown outside his foreign home, and raises in their place the Stars and Stripes.[20]

For all his generosity to yankees in films of reconciliation, Griffith made peace largely on southern terms. Like the pacifiers of the postwar generation, he accepted slavery's demise and the failure of southern independence—but little else. Yankees were obliged to acknowledge the splendor as well as the decadence of the antebellum social system. Gus and other dangerous blacks in *Birth of a Nation* notwithstanding, the darkies were faithful, and quality folks respected obligations. It seemed a shame that it all had to end.

Swords and Hearts (August, 1911), for instance, was a complicated love-war story. Dashing Confederate Hugh Frazier is loved by Jennie, one of the few humble whites Griffith presented. Hugh, however, is engaged to a cool, aristocratic hussy, Irene. Toward the conclusion of the war, Jennie saves Hugh from the yankees. But meanwhile her father, a rare scalawag type, is killed leading an attack on the Frazier mansion. His followers burn the place and murder Hugh's father. Irene deserts Hugh, as he has seemingly become penniless. Hugh finally perceives her cupidity and turns at last to Jennie. Then, lo and behold, Old Ben, the Frazier retainer, turns up with the family strongbox (presumably filled with non-Confederate money), which he had saved from the flames and the Fraziers' social enemies. Not only is Jennie's love redeemed, but the Fraziers' paternalism is justified and emancipation made a rather silly irrelevancy.[21]

Griffith's greatest paean to paternalism and the faithful darky was an ambitious two-reeler which Biograph officials released in January, 1911, as two separate but sequential movies, *His Trust* and *His Trust Fulfilled*. In the first reel a departing Confederate charges Old George with the protection of his wife and small daughter. Lee Dougherty, the Biograph press man who wrote bulletins for films, described George as "the old trusted body servant, whose faithful devotion to his master and his master's family was extreme to the extent of even laying down his life if required." The Confederate is killed and his sword is returned to hang over the mantel. Later, a fire destroys the dead master's house, and Old George rescues widow, daughter, and sword, bringing all three to his own tiny cabin for safekeeping.

In *His Trust Fulfilled* Old George is financing a higher education for the daughter, now a young woman. But his money gives out. The girl cannot continue, and George, lest he fail his trust, is tempted to steal. His good moral training forbids this, however. Meanwhile, a male English cousin has observed everything unseen and, impressed with George's integrity and loyalty, secretly assumes the costs of the girl's schooling. Later, love blossoms between the cousins and they wed. Griffith crosscut from his shot of the happy nuptials to a view of Old George, "tears of joy streaming down his black but honest cheeks." The second reel dissolved with George, back in his humble cabin, fondling his late master's saber.[22]

Three other Civil War pictures celebrated military machismo as a primary southern value. *The Honor of His Family* (January, 1910) was a chilling tragedy of pride. "Old Colonel" George Pickett cares for nothing but the honor of his "haughty military family." Son George, Jr., goes off to extend the record, but terrified by his first combat, flees home. The aged colonel, citing the enormity of his off-spring's offense, shoots his son and secretly carries the body back to the battlefield, where he lays it out, sword in hand, facing enemy lines.[23]

In *The House with Closed Shutters* (or "The Price of Cowardice," August, 1910), Charles Randolph, scion of another haughty southern family, goes to war carrying a flag sewn by his noble sister, Agnes. Given secret dispatches to deliver, Charles instead sneaks home without accomplishing his duty, and drinks himself into a stupor. Agnes dons his uniform, tucking her hair under his hat, and delivers the dispatches in his name. Returning, she is caught in a battle, fights heroically to save her flag, but is killed. All believe the sweet death to be Charles'. So to protect the family's male honor, the mother closes the shutters, and Charles remains inside, "dead" the rest of his life.[24]

The Battle, or "An Influence that Makes the Hero" (November, 1911), was the story "of the transforming of a pusillanimous coward into a lion-hearted hero by the derision of the girl he loved." During an engagement near his fiancée's home, a young soldier runs and cowers before her. She scorns him. He takes courage, and in a technically daring sequence for 1911, drives a powder wagon through a gauntlet of bonfires and exploding charges to rescue his comrades.[25] Thus the war for union and freedom became playground and proving ground for American—particularly southern—manhood.

Griffith's other South was not so sectionally or racially loaded, although flatland Dixie stereotypes crept in occasionally. His southern Appalachia was principally the scene of the nature idyll, frontier simplicity—nostalgia with a southern accent for turn-of-the-century Americans. Perhaps city-trapped moviegoers took some solace in the truism that nature is the scene of considerable savagery, too. Kentucky-Virginia novelist John Fox, Jr.'s *A Mountain Europa* (1899) and best-selling *Trail of the Lonesome Pine* (1908) had already tapped the popular potential of romance and feuding in the mountain setting.[26] But Griffith, owing to his birth and inclination, would probably have found his way to the hills, anyway.

The Feud and the Turkey ("A Romance of the Kentucky Mountains," December, 1908) blended hillbilly fratricide with a little flatland Dixie sentimentality. A bitter feud between two families does not prevent love between a girl and a boy from opposite sides. They elope, carrying with them into impoverished exile two elderly blacks, Aunt Dinah and Uncle Daniel. A child is born. Then Christmas comes with hard times for the young family and their retainers. Dinah prays for a turkey. Daniel fails to get one on a hunt; so, succumbing to what whites allowed was instinct, he steals a turkey—from none other than Colonel Wilkinson, patriarch of one of the clans and father of the runaway groom. Tracking Daniel, the colonel confronts the Appalachian Romeo and Juliet; danger looms. But the patriarch's fury melts at the sight of his grandson. The purloined bird becomes the entrée for a joyous reconciliation feast.[27]

The Mountaineer's Honor ("A Story of the Kentucky Hills," November, 1909) exploited John Fox's mountains versus flatlands genre. A silly, impetuous hill girl (Harum Scarum) is compromised by a slick character from the valley. Her brother hunts down the slicker and shoots him. The sheriff arrives, taking the brother. But in order for her son to escape the ignominy of a hanging, the mother slips him a revolver, which he employs to execute himself in a more honorable fashion. Harum Scarum is so contrite that a simple "mountain poet," who has always loved her, forgives her past. They depart together at the dissolve.[28]

Southern states' haste in outlawing liquor resulted in some precocious prohibition dramas. *The Revenue Man and the Girl* (September, 1911) matches a moonshiner's pretty daughter and a tender-hearted revenuer. In a raid the agent's partner kills the moonshiner. Love sours and the daughter vows revenge. A member of a local vigilante posse, she stealthily approaches the leading man and prepares to mete out mountain justice. But just then her pet dove falls by the agent, who humanely helps it back to flight. Her vengfulness vanishes and she helps her lover escape danger.[29]

Love in the Hills (October, 1911), billed as "A Tale of the Tennessee Mountains Where Strangers Are Unwelcome," was an inane melodrama. A girl has two local suitors, one a shiftless fiddler, the other a "manly fellow." A big-city flatlander enters the picture and nearly sweeps the girl off her feet, when the manly hillbilly runs him off and reminds the girl that cities and flatlanders are no good. She sees the light again, and the poor fiddler remains hapless. For a change, in *A Feud in the Kentucky Hills* (October, 1912) a flatland education apparently rendered one mountaineer tenderer and more virtuous. Pitted against his crude brother for a girl's love, he bravely refuses an invitation to mayhem. But a feud complicates everything, and in the end tenderness gets the girl anyway.[30]

Griffith used the bitter strife of the "Black Patch" tobacco wars of 1905–1909 as a setting for *The Rose of Kentucky*. The complex struggles of farmers and the monopolistic American Tobacco Company are only incidental to a love story, but Griffith and his scenarist apparently had no sympathy for the radical Kentucky and Tennessee farmers attempting to countervail the Duke conglomerate. A tobacco "planter" adopts a pretty, homeless girl and grows to love her. However, feeling himself too much her senior, he encourages her toward his younger partner. But when radical night riders attack the tobacco barns, the younger man "shows the yellow streak." The girl rejects the unworthy fellow in favor of the planter-benefactor, who proved courageous.[31]

Griffith's Dixie was homey in the highlands, decadent in the tidewater, but virtuous, courageous, and rather violent throughout. It was a useful South. Imperialists, reactionary paternalists, reformer-

segregators, nature-lovers—all found something pertinent and rein-
forcing. But in an age of eugenics, racial separatism, xenophobia,
and the "new" immigration of Catholics and Jews, Griffith's, Dunning's and their contemporaries' use of the South was only one key
to reconciling the past with the new world. Ethnicity—the larger
sense of what Professor Dunning called "the great fact of race"—was
the matrix of pluralistic society's identity; and contrary to Israel
Zangwill's myth of a harmonious "melting pot," most Americans
seemed to understand that sensible social history explained white
dominance and permanent ethnic separation and hostility. Griffith's
film portraiture of the other American races and white ethnic groups
sets the new southern historical imagery in its proper national
context.

After Griffith became one of Biograph's principal directors in
1908 he made many movies in many genres, including a spectrum
which exploited the American fascination with race. Of the enormous total of short films he directed before *Birth of a Nation*, ten
were Civil War subjects in which blacks were featured to some degree; a half-dozen treated Kentucky-Tennessee mountain themes
with blacks as occasional parts of the landscape; there were two
"Chinese" movies; and an undetermined number concerned Mexicans in the American Southwest, urban Jews and Italians, as well as
California Spaniards.

Although silent films tended to exaggerate stereotypes, Griffith
did not brutalize white ethnic minorities. Sometimes he was generous. In *The Greaser's Gauntlet*, for example (August, 1908), the main
character, José, is "a handsome young Mexican" who momentarily
goes astray, but in the end justifies the trust and moral training invested by his saintly mother. Other Mexicans might be brigands,
drunkards, and/or murderers, but Anglo-Saxon cowboys might be
brigands, drunkards, and/or murderers, too. The environment, rather
than ethnicity, explains the behavior of bad guys. At worst "greasers,"
Spanish aristocrats—Latins of any class—are congenitally more
"hot blooded" and passionate than paler Anglos.[32]

East Side Jews and Italians appear in predictable roles: Hebrews are ingratiating and parsimonious; Italians passionate, violence-prone, and somewhat improvident. But in portraying these minorities, Griffith used the stereotype as a vehicle for exposing despicable urban housing and social conditions, or more often, in telling a sentimental story. In *Italian Blood*, for example, a Mafia connection threatens the love of a father and daughter, but in the end it is the nuclear family which triumphs.[33]

Orientals did not fare so well. In *That Chink At Golden Gulch* (October, 1910)—subtitled "A Chinaman's Sacrifice through Gratitude"—Charlie Lee is a hero of sorts: "a saffron-skinned Pagan, his soul is white and real red blood pulsates his heart." A white man rescues him from danger. Later, at the climax, Charlie cuts off his sacred queue in order to use it to tie the hands of a villain. He collects the $5,000 reward, but gives it to his white patron, only to disappear so to escape the shame of having no queue. *The Fatal Hour* ("A Stirring Incident of the Chinese White-Slave Traffic"; August, 1908) had not even a quasi-hero of yellow hue. Pong Lee, indeed, is "a Mephistophelian saffron-skinned varlet" who victimizes white women. Of course he is done in by whites in the end.[34]

Years later, after his rise to fame with *Birth of a Nation* and *Intolerance*, Griffith made a tender, beautiful film about a Chinese-white love affair. *Broken Blossoms* (1919) starred Richard Barthelmess as a humble Chinese boy and Lillian Gish as his doomed fifteen-year-old love object. Barthelmess' character was stereotyped—a bent-humble, flowery-exotic creature. But he personified virtue when counterpoised against Gish's murderous boxer father, hypocritical English missionaries, and a broader occidental society which bred intolerance and countenanced violent death. In the end the lovers suffer the fate miscegenators (even chaste ones) must—death. But Griffith eloquently placed the blame upon western bigotry, not miscegenation itself. In this remarkable film the great director, so much a creature of white culture, rose to damn it. It was an extraordinary lapse, understandable only in the context of the epidemic revulsion of World War I's slaughter.

Important as black, yellow, and white ethnic imagery were in

Griffith's time, he and his contemporaries were far more deeply engaged in Indian motifs. Here only two weak parallels with portrayals of blacks seem possible. First, in a few films (usually early frontier action dramas) red men are mindless beasts who savagely attack and probably rape, as well as shriek and scalp. Second, while Indians were viewed as fully capable of functional evolution (unlike blacks), and while they were a noble race (unlike blacks), they were just as unassimilable with white society. Griffith and his contemporaries shared the eighteenth century's appreciation of Indian culture and "nobility." And unlike filmmakers of the 1930s through 1950s, Griffith was not preoccupied with themes of Indian savagery subdued by heroic white cavalry. But unlike Thomas Jefferson and so many eighteenth-century whites, Griffith and his scenarists forbade a happy red-white amalgamation. In this sense some Indian pictures form part of the literature of segregation.[35]

One of Griffith's earliest films was *The Call of the Wild* (October, 1908), which featured an attractive character called George Redfeather, a Carlisle honor graduate and football hero. Taken under wing by white Indian agent Lieutenant Penrose, Redfeather falls in love with Penrose's daughter, Gladys. But Gladys spurns him on racial grounds. Lamenting that he is "good enough as a hero, but not as a husband," George suddenly hears "the call of the wild," tears off his "white man's" clothing, dons Indian duds, and mounts up for the plains. Now a confirmed white-hater, he encounters Gladys out riding and captures her, intending harm. Gladys eloquently reminds him of another call, however—that of the Great Master in the Sky. George, defeated again, this time by conscience, releases her. *Finis.*
A Romance of the Western Hills ("Civilization as It Appealed to the Indian Maiden"; April, 1910) was one of the first films Griffith and Bitzer shot in California. Here an Indian girl is tempted by white tourists to assume white ways. Adopted by a paleface couple, she becomes enamored of their nephew, a collegiate cad who breaks her heart. He prefers marrying "one of his own race." The maiden returns to her people, and a young brave vows revenge for the insult. Brave grapples with white cad, Indian maiden pleads for cad's life,

white girl sees through cad at last. *Finis*. The lesson, according to press man Lee Dougherty, was that "civilization and education do not improve to a great extent the social status of the poor redskin." Such is the burden, too, of *The Chief's Daughter* (April, 1911), in which a white prospector wins the love of an Indian maiden, but "cruelly casts her aside" when his white sweetheart arrives from the East.[36]

Heredity ("The Call of the Blood is Answered"; November, 1912) was as explicitly antimiscegenation as *The Call of the Wild*, although the characters and plot are quite different. A renegade white trader buys a squaw, who gives birth to their son. The boy grows up with Indians, and as he approaches manhood, "the racial difference between father and son is felt." Son finally repudiates father after discovering that the trader has sold bad whiskey and inferior guns to the tribe. The evil white dies, and squaw and son are reclaimed "by their own." The good-Indian bad-white arrangement of *Heredity* is in marked contrast to the film treatment of Indian-white relations a generation later. And the treatment of Indians as noble, dignified individuals certainly contrasts with the black beasts and "toms" of Griffith's Civil War movies. But that Griffith and company considered the boy in *Heredity*, who was half Caucasian, to belong to the Indians—"their own"—is comparable to the mullato-equals—"black" logic of white Americans. In this sense white thinking as reflected in popular movies was consistent with the rationale of the age of segregation.[37]

Griffith, a self-conscious southerner and frank racist, was an extraordinary director. However, he was not an extraordinary bigot for his time. The American (not just southern) film-going public demanded these subjects, and Griffith was ever the responsive businessman-dramatist. Compared with a few vicious movies made by his competitors—e.g., *Coon Town Suffragettes* and *In Slavery Days*—Griffith's treatments of blacks could even be called restrained.[38] Portrayals of orientals were stereotypic, but ranged from cruel to honorific. His Indians were nobler than redmen would appear again until the mid-1960s.

Klan vengeance on Gus, "the renegade negro." From Birth of a Nation.

After *Birth of a Nation* Griffith seldom showed blacks on celluloid, although twice he offered startling vignettes. *The Greatest Thing in Life* was a war propaganda picture he made in 1917 with official British cooperation. In one scene a southern white soldier (Robert Harron) crawls to the side of a mortally wounded black soldier who has been crying for his "mammy." The white comforts him, and to the outrage of some viewers, kisses the black on the cheek. Some students of film have interpreted this as a sign of the director's sensitivity to liberal criticism of *Birth*. To Griffith, however, the scene was in no way an atonement for Gus in *Birth*. He had heard an unsubstantiated story of such an incident in the trenches, and he wrote it into the script himself as "a bit of 'business'" for the audiences. Five years later, in *One Exciting Night*, Griffith had a blackfaced white actor perform comic fright antics in the midst of a thunder storm.[39] The Kentuckian remained quite unreconstructed.

Griffith was never repentant or apologetic for his racial portraiture. His America hardly demanded such. Even his greatest epic, *Intolerance* (1916), ostensibly a tract against bigotry, avoids color altogether in favor of labor relations, the persecuted Huguenots, and ancient history. Most Americans (the protesting NAACP notwithstanding) shared Griffith's attitudes and his insensitivity toward racial minorities, especially Afro-Americans. With him, they simply relished dramas of the white man's triumphs, sensing few of the ironies.

Chapter 2

Claude Bowers
and the Establishment

The . . . scheme of having little groups dominate the interpretation of history . . . is dying hard.
Claude Bowers, 1930

Claude G. Bowers (1878–1958) never attended college, but wrote a
shelf of histories. He wrote little that was new and founded no school
of interpretation, yet more than anyone he educated Americans on
their early national period, the age of Jackson, and on the Reconstruction era. His two most famous books, *Jefferson and Hamilton*
(1925) and *The Tragic Era* (1929) narrowly missed winning Pulitzer
prizes. Both did make national best-seller lists, and both are cur-
rently available in paperback and are still selling. Bowers was a lion-
hearted partisan, an unabashed presentist, and an unapologetic racist. Relevant lessons and popular entertainment were the mighty
stuff of his writing. He was one of the greatest communicators of historical understanding the nation has produced.

Bowers' effective use of melodrama with twentieth-century readers derived from his nineteenth-century rearing and tastes. Born
near Indianapolis, Bowers moved with his mother to the city when
Claude was twelve, following his father's death. Mrs. Bowers earned
their humble livelihood as a milliner and dressmaker. Claude went
to Shortridge High School, found a corps of demanding teachers,
met engaging friends, and exploited to the utmost the cultural opportunities of a provincial capital. In school he devoured literary

23

classics and famous orations, and excelled as an orator. At English's Opera House, night after night, he "delighted," "wept," "cheered," "thrilled," and was profoundly moved by touring singers, dramatic troupes from the East and Europe, and by imposing public figures. Learning was an emotional experience, a cause for exuberance. Reading classics compelled him to emote afterwards. Lecture points led to joyous debate with friends far into school nights. Following a performance of *Othello* by actor Robert Downing, Bowers confided to his diary, "I feel that I have learned more tonight than ever before during so short a period." Such enthusiasm in knowledge and company, and a compulsion to confront issues in argument, endured through Bowers' long life. His memoirs, written in the 1950s, contain much of the air of the high school diaries, with nearly as many "thrills" and "amazements" per page.[1]

Before him on English's stage in the nineties paraded the most eloquent partisans of the time: Robert Ingersoll antagonized and challenged Hoosiers with agnosticism. General John B. Gordon ("the grandest of the Southern Orators") spoke on "The Last Days of the Confederacy" (Bowers was thrilled). Booker T. Washington enthralled his audience for an hour and a half. William Jennings Bryan lectured "like a cavalry charge." And young Albert J. Beveridge (whom Bowers knew socially, too), championed imperialism.[2]

Claude's father's family were pre–Civil War immigrants from the South, and they were Democrats; but as a teenager Bowers was under the influence of his mother's family, who were Republicans (nee Whigs). Mrs. Bowers' father enlisted in the Union army at age forty and was killed at Missionary Ridge. In 1896 young Claude favored Iowa's William B. Allison for president over William McKinley, whom he considered a high tariff extremist and a tool of Wall Street interests. Bowers favored moderate protection, retention of the gold standard, and generally a party stance for the good of the "masses." Bryan enchanted him, but Illinois' Democratic Governor John Peter Altgeld frightened Bowers. (He was "an awful power—for evil . . . an ideal revolutionary advocate.") Already, however, his conversion to the Democrats was underway. His civics lessons and the most attractive oratory he heard had wedded him to "the equality of all people" and a set of concepts soon to be called "progressive." Already, at age seventeen, he held a romantic image of democracy at the dawn of the century, now threatened by antipopular forces. By 1898–1899 he was a Democrat. Dangerous Altgeld was out of the way. Bryan, spokesman of farmers and small business, was his man.[3]

Finishing high school, Bowers worked briefly for the Democratic Indianapolis *Sentinel*, then moved to Terre Haute, where he wrote for the *Gazette* and dabbled in district politics. In 1904 (only eighteen months after his arrival) the party nominated him for Congress—a sacrificial lamb against an entrenched Republican. But he conducted a spectacular show as an orator; audiences were stunned by the enormous voice resonating from his boyish face and small frame. Indiana Democrats would call him back again and again for rollicking, tub-thumping convention keynotes, long after he had left the state for national journalism, politics, and acclaim as a historian.[4]

Bowers' first visa to the East was an appointment as secretary to U.S. Senator John Worth Kern, who had defeated Beveridge in 1910. A fervent Wilsonian, Bowers was for the next six years an eyewitness to the climax of progressive politics. To him (writing in the 1950s), the Payne-Aldrich Tariff of 1909 had marked the "high tide of privilege." Wilson's tenure broke "the long sordid tradition" and "marked the beginning of a new and more progressive period in our history." Kern's defeat in 1916 sent Bowers back to Indiana as editor of the Fort Wayne *Journal-Gazette*, the state's largest Democratic paper. Having already tested himself successfully as author with *The Irish Orators* (1916) and a loving biography of Kern, Bowers stayed up nights in his office and wrote *The Party Battles of the Jackson Period* (1922), a long but quick-paced paean to the old hero. The eloquence of his partisanship for Democrats past and present drew the attention of New York *World* editor Frank Cobb and Arthur Krock, *World* writer. Krock met Bowers in Indianapolis and hired him, and Bowers was off to the East for good.[5]

New York was nirvana to the gossipy, hyperactive, social-climbing Hoosier. From his office high above city hall, under the Pulitzer

COURTESY LILLY LIBRARY, INDIANA UNIVERSITY

Claude G. Bowers at work, ca. 1930

Building's golden dome, he looked down on the fabulous ticker-tape parades of the twenties, consulted with colleagues Krock, Herbert Bayard Swope, Heywood Broun, and Walter Lippmann, and sallied forth to dine with Theodore Dreiser and to talk politics with William Gibbs McAdoo, Al Smith, and his greatest idol, Franklin D. Roosevelt. When everyone else had retired he wrote books. *Jefferson and Hamilton* appeared, then a potboiler called *The Founders of the Republic* (1927), and then *The Tragic Era*—all before the decade was out. The books brought Bowers money, travel, honorary doctorates, and more notice from politicians. In 1928 he delivered a thundering keynote address, broadcast nationally on radio, to the Democratic National Convention in Houston. He moved closer to Roosevelt, campaigned on radio and rostrum in 1932, and in 1933 he went to

Spain as ambassador. Following his recall in 1939 he was sent to Chile, where he served fourteen years, finally returning home in 1953.[6]

All the politicking did not stay his pen. *Beveridge and the Progressive Era* appeared in 1932. *Jefferson in Power*, a sequel to *Jefferson and Hamilton*, came four years later. In Madrid he also wrote *The Spanish Adventures of Washington Irving* (1940). *The Young Jefferson* appeared in 1945, and in 1950 he published *Pierre Vergniaud: Voice of the French Revolution*. During his last five years he wrote accounts of his ambassadorships, *My Mission to Spain: Watching the Rehearsal for World War II* (1954), and *Chile Through Embassy Windows, 1939–1953* (1958); his autobiography; and numerous pamphlets and shorter pieces. On his seventy-eighth birthday he exulted to his diary: "I sit at my typewriter writing books, articles and speeches as forty years ago, and get just as much thrill out of my work now as I did then."[7]

Throughout his career Claude Bowers invested his boundless energy and vivid imagination in an ideal of citizenship—"Jeffersonian liberalism"—which he adopted as a teenager and young man. Jeffersonianism ("liberalism" or "democracy") was never carefully defined. It meant "equality for all," although Bowers certainly never believed Afro-Americans fit for equality. It also meant enthusiastic popular participation in politics and openness and integrity of political practice. Like so many others of his generation, he wished fervently to throw out "bosses" and elect models of disinterested civic responsibility. He was against "the interests," or "special privilege," and for "the people." He visualized "class" antagonisms with ideological consistencies in America, and damned "aristocrats" who "blackguard Jefferson," Jackson, or FDR for championing "the people." But just as his liberalism opposed plutocracy, it opposed socialism and other radicalisms against private enterprise. Bowers wrote in 1900 that "Jeffersonian Democracy" did not preclude large accumulations of wealth *honestly* acquired. His mentality—or heart —was with rural and small town America, the small businessman, and the striving farmer. Laissez-faire was his ideal, but in order to

check plutocracy's foul play he would fight for governmental regula-
tion. He was the consummate "middle" American.[8]

The civic ideal and the history served and controlled each other.
Both were animated by a combativeness born of Bowers' conviction
that historical writing was manipulated by a closed establishment
comparable to the economic "interests." In this belief he belonged to
a host, mainly midwesterners and southerners, who in the 1890s and
1900s seized the initiative and rewrote American history. Charles
Beard, Frederick Jackson Turner, Vernon Louis Parrington, Ulrich
Bonnell Phillips, and the southern students of William A. Dunning
—among many others—declared that American democracy was bred
and continually reborn in the frontier experience, that special privi-
leged interests had always sought to control the masses, and that,
contrary to the eastern abolitionist tradition, southern slavery had
been a relatively benign institution. Thus in the age of Bryan, populism, and angry provincialism, the East was put down along with its
patrician amateur historians who had always disdained the out-
lands.[9]

The rise of "progressive" history was in part too a professionalization of historiography. The provincials who rewrote the past were
Ph.D. bearers with teaching posts. Most of them wrote poorly, though.
(Beard and Parrington were exceptions.) Claude Bowers was probably the greatest nonprofessional of the progressive historians. Above
all he was a flamboyantly effective communicator. He conferred eloquence and passion upon what the dry professors researched, and he
arched back to the grass roots deep prejudices and soaring ideals.

The Jefferson and Jackson books embodied Bowers' view (shared
with the professionals) that American history is a sort of seesaw,
with progress and backsliding, reform and reaction, ennui and re-
awakening. Americans were divided between liberals (progressives)
and conservatives, or good guys and bad. The Manichean contrasts
were perfect for the drama he loved. Bowers maintained this version
of the past to the end of his life.

In his memoirs he recalled writing *Party Battles of the Jackson
Period* specifically to refute "conservatives." "The very conservative

school of historians," he wrote in the fifties, "had been condescending toward Jackson himself and his long overdue crusade against the embryo plutocracy" of his day. "Jefferson's election in 1800 had definitely determined that ours should be a democratic republic," but then began the backsliding: over "the years the people had lost sight of fundamental principles," Jackson's "historical mission" was to "reawaken the democratic fervor." [10]

Jefferson and Hamilton was a flashy exercise in the same liberal drama as well as an idealistic statement of progressive citizenship. Jefferson trusted "the people"; Hamilton, the brilliant administrator, did not. Throughout the 1790s the battle between democracy and plutocratic trusteeship hung in the balance. Jefferson forged a party (lineal ancestor of Jackson's, Bryan's, Wilson's, and FDR's Democratic party, of course), and in 1800 the issue was finally decided. The republic emerged from darkness. Jefferson became the ideal progressive, a good and disinterested man who made politics a clean vocation. In the midst of the Harding scandals and in the aftermath of the Democrats' own disaster of 1924, the Sage of Monticello himself emerged from decades of eastern "conservative" scorn to a pinnacle of national honor. Bowers' new hero FDR oversaw construction of the Jefferson Memorial in the next decade. [11]

Recent revulsion at the prodigious negrophobia and anti-Radical bias in *Tragic Era* has overshadowed Bowers' essentially progressive presentation of Reconstruction. To begin with there was little incompatibility between racism and progressivism. In the South progressivism as a multifaceted reform ethos was inaugurated with the turn-of-the-century racial settlement of segregation and disfranchisement. Whites imposing the settlement invariably referred to Jim Crow and barring blacks from the polls as "reform." They employed an anti-Radical interpretation of Reconstruction as part of the rationale for racial discrimination, too, just as professional historians of the Dunning School were issuing their pro-Confederate state histories. Indeed formal history served the white disfranchisers and reinforced the southern tradition that yankee Reconstructionists were cynical corruptionists, or at best misguided reformers who did not understand the Negro. Nonsouthern white professors either ignored blacks' claim in history (e.g., Beard), or joined vigorously in the rehabilitation of the Old South, some exonerating even the Ku Klux Klan. D. W. Griffith brought such "progressive" history to the screen. Bowers' work was actually only a late restatement, deep in the age of segregation, of an interpretation grown rather old.[12]

Amazingly (to employ a Bowersism) Bowers claimed to be a revisionist, just as in *Jefferson and Hamilton*. Responding to compliments at a congressional stag dinner early in 1930, the author referred darkly to his struggles against "the conspiracies in academic circles against Democratic interpretations of history."[13] A quarter-century later he wrote that researching the book had been "a liberal education in that period," that he "had not set out to prove any preconceived theory of my own," but that his materials led him to "discoveries that sharply challenged interpretations of fifty years"! Bowers' research consisted of a perusal of New York newspapers (no Washington papers), Dunning's *Reconstruction: Political and Economic* (1907), all the Dunning School state histories, and W. L. Fleming's *Documentary History of Reconstruction* (2 volumes, 1906), the *Congressional Globe* and *Record*, and a few conservative southern newspapers. There was no reference to DuBois' pre-1929 writing, nor to John R. Lynch's autobiography and caustic attacks on white historians. He listed but one of black historian Alrutheus A. Taylor's state studies (and Taylor's middle initial is given as "H"). He listed one sole southern Radical paper, the McMinnville (Tennessee) *Enterprise*, for 1867 only. Bowers did not use the personal papers of Johnson, Charles Sumner, Thaddeus Stevens, or many other figures. He did consult with aged Henry Clay Warmoth, former carpetbag governor of Louisiana; and the daughter of Indiana's Radical Senator George W. Julian allowed Bowers to read her father's diary. The only other source he listed sympathetic to the Radicals was Georges Clemenceau's *History of American Reconstruction*. Bowers thought he gained insight into the era by visiting Lancaster, Pennsylvania, "the home of that picturesque old fanatic Thad Stevens." There he heard gossip (which he apparently accepted as fact) that

Stevens had an illegitimate daughter by a "woman Thad knew in Gettysburg before he moved to Lancaster." He also solicited materials on daily life in the white South from the Baltimore historian, Matthew Page Andrews. Andrews asked officers of the United Daughters of the Confederacy to send Bowers private letters. He received a large box of offerings—"all throwing a white light on the actual living and thinking of the people." Reading the letters, Bowers thought he "really lived as a contemporary through those tragic days." [14]

His claim to revisionism rested broadly on the anti-Radical stance, and specifically on his "discovery" that Radicals "hated" Lincoln (this was sufficient to damn them), and that Andrew Johnson was not a drunkard, but rather a hero who suffered calumny in defense of "the people" and the Constitution. Bowers, like so many students before him, registered only the face value of Lincoln's conciliatory wartime "ten percent plan" and second inaugural, and concluded that had the president lived he would have virtually restored the *status quo ante bellum*, without slavery of course, but certainly there would have been no Negro suffrage, either. Bowers thought the country needed to know "how intensely Lincoln was hated by the Radicals at the time of his death." (Julian's diary shocked him.) Poor Johnson "fought the bravest battle for constitutional liberty and for the preservation of our institutions ever waged by an Executive . . . seeking honestly to carry out the conciliatory and wise policy of Lincoln." But historians had "left [him] in the pillory to which unscrupulous gamblers for power consigned him." [15]

As a young man Claude Bowers shared with his white contemporaries a swelling generosity towards Dixie. Logically, Lincoln's saintly reputation for "malice toward none" and a virulent negrophobia (coincident with the beginnings of the age of segregation) were primary vehicles of sectional reconciliation. Bowers himself captured the spirit perfectly in a 1905 oration before the annual encampment of the Indiana Sons of Veterans. He scorned bloody-shirtism and declared that the Civil War had made "One Common Country." "The Duty of the Sons" (his title) was to overcome bitterness, recognize the manly heroism of the rebels, and celebrate the new nationalism forged by the war and its aftermath. Implicit throughout, as in all reconciliation literature, was the lesson that white southerners were wrong in the war (although "sincere") but right in Reconstruction. The exchange of *quid pro quos* was the contract of reunion. Full of glory, pathos, and paradox, the drama served the progressive historians, D. W. Griffith, then Bowers.[16]

Nor was Bowers' treatment of Andrew Johnson revisionist. As early as 1913 the aged James Schouler, one of the surviving eastern establishment historians Bowers loathed, began Johnson's rehabilitation in the seventh volume of his *History of the United States under the Constitution*. Robert W. Winston published his scholarly *Andrew Johnson: Plebeian and Patriot* in 1928. (Bowers cited the book.) Here Johnson emerged fully as martyr to Radical cupidity, and as latter-day Jeffersonian-Jacksonian voice of the masses. L. P. Stryker's *Andrew Johnson: A Study in Courage* (1929) also appeared early enough for inclusion in Bower's bibliography.

Virtually the only novelty of *Tragic Era*, then, aside from the prose power, was the synthesis of progressive values and imagery Bowers achieved. Republican Radicals were corruptionists representing special interests. (Professor Howard K. Beale restated this thesis the next year in his *The Critical Year*.) President Johnson was the clean citizen of principles (like Jackson and Bryan) who fought for the Jeffersonian-progressive ideal.

Bowers' vaunted struggle with an antagonistic historical profession was as patently mythic as his claim to revisionism. In May of 1930, for example, he was embittered that the Pulitzer committee did not award the history prize to *Tragic Era*. (*Jefferson and Hamilton* had narrowly missed, too, four years earlier.) He raged in his diary: "The old traditional scheme of having little groups dominate the interpretation of history in the interest of the old Federalist and Abolitionist schools is dying hard." Bowers took solace that in only six months the weighty "five dollar history" had sold more than 130,000 copies. But Bowers was well aware that if partisans on the committee discriminated against his partisan history, it was not the professionals, for two New York newspapers reported that a historians' consulting committee headed by James Truslow Adams had voted two-to-one in favor of awarding the prize to Bowers. Indeed he adopted the professors' interpretations wholesale, and more often than not, they were most generous in praise of his serious books.[17]

Professor William E. Dodd of the University of Chicago, southern-born Jeffersonian liberal, read the manuscript of *Party Battles of the Jackson Period* for Houghton Mifflin. Dodd was so enthusiastic that he sided with Bowers in opposition to the publisher's demand that Bowers condense the manuscript from two volumes to one. (Bowers lost anyway.) *Jefferson and Hamilton* has been adopted for use in college classes for decades—recently, perhaps, more for its evocation of the Jeffersonian fetish than as a sourcebook. The immediate responses to both *Jefferson and Hamilton* and *Tragic Era* were good reviews, invitations to colleges and universities, and honorary degrees voted by academicians. President Edwin Alderman of the University of Virginia, who had written some history himself, was extravagant in his expression of gratitude to Bowers for apotheosizing the founder, and of course for telling the *truth*. Bowers was deliciously gratified, too. After *Tragic Era* appeared, he wrote in his diary: "Have more invitations to make commencement addresses in Southern Universities. The list is so appalling I am sure it has few equals." It included the universities of North Carolina, South Carolina, Georgia, Alabama, Tennessee, and Kentucky, plus North Carolina State, Louisiana State, Emory, and Oglethorpe. He delighted in the dilemma of choosing schools and dates.[18]

Teachers accustomed to singling out *Tragic Era* for its racist stridency may be dismayed at its reception among liberal politicians and journalists and reputable historians. FDR, for example, wrote approvingly from Warm Springs, Georgia, that the book "had a very definite influence on public thought." Governor Harry Flood Byrd of Virginia (then very "progressive") extolled: "Why should one read fiction when one can read history in this compelling form." Florida progressive Duncan U. Fletcher (then a U.S. senator) was deeply moved. Fletcher "personally knew Harrison Reed [hapless Republican governor of Florida] and John Wallace [black stooge who wrote an anti-Radical account]. Wallace tells the truth about reconstruction days." Nicholas Murray Butler complimented Bowers upon his physical description of Andrew Johnson, which jibed with Butler's personal recollection. Bowers' friend Arthur Krock justified the "strong prejudices" flaring from *Tragic Era*: "historians who lack them leave their readers without thrill." Lloyd Lewis, another popular nonacademic historian who harbored delusions of battle with professors, praised Bowers' scholarship (he was impressed by printed footnotes), declaring that the references would "see him through" the howls of "orthodox, reactionary" historians.[19]

David S. Muzzey, famous textbook author and orthodox professor of history at Columbia, nonetheless praised *Tragic Era* in *Current History*. In a review which contained three errors of date in the first paragraph, Muzzey emphasized Bowers' mastery of his materials and thorough research. Professional friend William E. Dodd wrote approval in his review of Bowers' "trenchant style," an appropriate means when "a historian must call spades spades"! Henry F. Pringle, Theodore Roosevelt's biographer, wrote: "Here is the 'new history' at its best. It bears the unmistakable authenticity of careful scholarship, hard work, heart-breaking research among musty records and forgotten documents." Professor Burton B. Kendrick, a Civil War authority, confessed his "keen enjoyment of Mr. Bowers' arraignment of the radicals."[20]

Only three white professors were even slightly cool. Nathaniel W. Stephenson, while approving the general interpretation, was offended by the intensity of Bowers' partisanship for Johnson. He "appears at the bar as counsel." Like Stephenson's, Charles R. Lingley's appraisal in the *American Historical Review* debited Bowers for his emotion, and Lingley found serious deficiencies in the research, too. Yet the professor concluded that *Tragic Era* was a fitting capstone for the Reconstruction scholarship begun three decades earlier by Dunning. Arthur M. Schlesinger, Sr., was not impressed with Bowers' research, either, and took him to task for ignoring southern economic progress and the establishment of schools and social services under the Radicals. He also complained that "after a time the reader becomes surfeited with scandal, corruption and fraud." Schlesinger immediately added, however, that "this is not the author's fault; it is history's." He allowed, too, that "Bowers . . . [is] the greatest living American practitioner of what for want of a better term may be called personal history." "It is the art of the motion picture applied to historiography."[21] Schlesinger knew his media.

The only vigorously adverse criticism Bowers sustained came from blacks. An unnamed reviewer (presumably editor Carter G. Woodson) in the *Journal of Negro History* blasted *Tragic Era* as "downright propaganda" "written by an historically untrained politician." He hoped that "the thinking element will take little notice," but "with the efficient advertising machinery now behind this book, it will probably have a large circulation among the gullible of our population. The teaching of history, too," he sadly concluded, "will be rendered more difficult by the sinister influence of such a work written for notoriety and published to exploit the uninformed."[22]

A much longer critique appeared in the *Journal* in January, 1931, in the form of a communication to the editor from aged Republican politician and memoirist John R. Lynch. The letter paralleled his famous roasting of James Ford Rhodes a dozen years previously. Lynch, too, lashed out emotionally: "I do not hesitate to say the *Tragic Error* would be a more appropriate name for the book, because it is a composition of errors, misstatements, misrepresentations, and false assertions." But then he went on, for seventeen pages, and disassembled Bowers' epic—from his value-laden character sketches of blacks, carpetbaggers, and scalawags, to his avoidance of Radical accomplishments and conservative misdeeds, to a host of smaller errors of fact, date, or place. The letter-review was a *tour de force*, heated to be sure, but close to a model of thoroughness—and written by a man who, like Bowers, lacked formal university training. Lynch, born a slave, mocked the "objectivity" of scholars and amateurs alike.[23]

But in 1931 such criticism went unheeded (unheard, too, it would seem) by whites and the profession. In 1935 W. E. B. DuBois published his monumental Marxist account, *Black Reconstruction in*

America, 1860–1880, which concluded with a masterful and indignant indictment of whites' racist, pro-Confederate "Propaganda of History." Shortly, younger white scholars such as Francis Butler Simkins, Robert Woody, and C. Vann Woodward would join with blacks in a vindicating revisionism which came to prevail in the 1950s and 1960s. Bowers himself remained unreconstructed. Invited to Lexington by Professor Holman Hamilton to speak on "The Aftermath of the Civil War" at the Kentucky Civil War Roundtable in 1956, he delivered a rambling synopsis of *Tragic Era*. If he had read and learned little since his return from Chile, he missed ample opportunities: he was friendly with Hamilton and Allen Nevins, and often dined with Nevins before attending the latter's seminars at Columbia.[24]

If Bowers never escaped the narrower, racist confines of his provincial progressivism, there is still much to recommend other aspects of his old-fashioned brand of liberalism. Occasionally he could be scrupulously, even heroically, fair. His relationship with Albert J. Beveridge illustrates Bowers' best.

As an Indianapolis schoolboy in the 1890s young Claude was occasionally in Beveridge's home, and he was a frequent auditor of the handsome Republican's orations at English's and on the stump. By 1898 Bowers had become a Bryanite and vociferous anti-imperialist, and he regarded Beveridge with soaring contempt. Following a GOP campaign speech in which Beveridge extolled America's destiny to monopolize trade in the Caribbean and western Pacific, Bowers wrote in his diary a disdainful critique of the Republican's "true Yankee egotism"; the speech was "a great string of sophistries." A dozen years later he aided Kern's electoral victory over Beveridge. Once Beveridge had retired to writing his weighty biographies of John Marshall and George Washington, however, he and Bowers became friends (even though Beveridge was a "Federalist" historian). Beveridge suggested Houghton Mifflin for *Party Battles of the Jackson Period*, and they exchanged editorial suggestions on their respective works. Following Beveridge's premature death Bowers gained access to his papers and wrote a fine biography, only recently superseded. The research is more thorough than in his other works, and while the tone is respectful, Bowers' attention to detail and his restrained, balanced treatment of Beveridge's spread-eagle imperialism is a solid counterpoint to the melodrama of the Jefferson, Jackson, and Reconstruction books.[25]

Bowers' Democratic partisanship and his disinterested liberal ideal sometimes complimented one another, too. In the same decade he wrote *Tragic Era* he campaigned through his columns in the *World* against the second Ku Klux Klan, which in 1924 ripped the party and in 1928 opposed Bowers' candidate, Al Smith. Bowers "urged that a systematic collection of the 'literature' of intolerance be made and preserved for historians in the future."[26] He wrote without apparent recognition of irony.

His support for FDR's New Deal was without stated reservation. In Spain his impropriety in denouncing Franco's illiberality made his continuance as ambassador an obstacle to the Roosevelt administration's desire to conciliate the dictator. During the late 1940s, down in Santiago, Chile, he wrote his biography of *Pierre Vergniaud: Voice of the French Revolution*. The book was another exercise in Bowers' first love, oratory; but it was also a paean to middle-of-the-roadism: petty bourgeois democrat Vergniaud champions popular government, but in the end is guillotined by the left-extremist Jacobins. On his return to the United States, Bowers blasted right-wing extremism in the heyday of McCarthyism. Speaking before an assemblage of the Indiana Historical Society in late 1953 he warned that enemies of civil liberty "always try to take advantage of the crimes of revolutions to turn back the hand of the clock of democracy" —more of his historical seesaw. "Our immediate mission is to meet the peril of communism with all we have; but it would be a mistake not to guard against creeping fascism." In the midfifties he was also liberal coadjutor of Eleanor Roosevelt, and he campaigned for Adlai Stevenson.[27]

In his autobiography there is no commentary on welfarism, militarism, imperialism, or the party's turn towards the human rights movement. By blindly (or bravely) ignoring inconsistencies Claude Bowers was able to die a Jeffersonian progressive. His progressivism was lovingly nationalistic; and that brand of nationalism, like Griffith's, included an honored place for the white South.

Chapter 3

The Embarrassing
New South

Growing steadily more realistic . . . the Caldwells and the
Faulkners, sternly rooting out not only sentimentality but
even sentiment . . . remained in some curious fashion romantics in their choice of materials—shall we say, romantics of the appalling.

W. J. Cash[1]

Superficially, one of the oddest literary friendships in the early twentieth century was that of Thomas Nelson Page and John Fox, Jr. Page
was the quintessential Virginia gentleman. Born on the family estate
in Hanover County (near Richmond) in the mid-1850s, Page studied
law at "The University" (Jefferson's), retired to letters as early as he
could, maintained a Washington townhouse, and wore a bushy
moustache, turned-up collars, vests, and a large ring on his left little
finger. After 1900 his local-colorist genre was out of style, but Page
continued to prosper as an Old South sentimentalist who wrote
mainly in slave dialect. Page's métier was the short story, and in
1883 he had gained overnight national recognition when *Century*
published his "Marse Chan." It was in this masterful tearjerker that
Page had his black narrator yearn for the homey comforts and fixed
relationships of "de good ol' days befo' de war." "Dem was good ol'
times, Marster, de bes' Sam ever see."[2]

John Fox, Jr., was no patrician and in many respects presents a
southern image the opposite of Page's. As vigorous and outdoorsy as
his acquaintance Theodore Roosevelt, Fox had middling origins and
an often ungentlemanly public reputation. Born to a schoolmaster

and his wife in Kentucky's Blue Grass country during the Civil War, Fox went to Harvard, reported for newspapers, but returned home to nurture a frail body. Prospects of good health and fortune took him in 1888 to a brother's coal mine operations in Big Stone Gap, Virginia, a hamlet deep in the Appalachian southwest, which stretches under West Virginia to Kentucky and Tennessee. There he became not only a successful coal entrepreneur but a rugged naturalist and volunteer constable. His first mountain-theme stories began to appear in the nineties. Experimentations with novels were spaced between journalistic jaunts to Cuba in 1898 and Japan during 1904–1905, covering wars; drinking, guitar-playing, socializing with Roosevelt, Mark Twain, and Peter Finley Dunn; and some quasi-scandalous newsmaking in New York. In 1908 he married a celebrated Viennese Broadway dancer named Fritzi Scheff. They were divorced some time later. Meanwhile his name became (in the words of best sellers' chronicler) "synonymous with 'best seller.'" *Little Shepherd of Kingdom Come* (1903) was tenth on the 1903 annual list, seventh in 1904. *The Trail of the Lonesome Pine* (1908) sold out in a short time and placed third on the 1908 list; it was fifth at the end of the next year. Fox's third and last fictional hit, *Heart of the Hills* (1913), ranked fifth in sales nationally the year it was released. Fox contracted pneumonia at Big Stone Gap and died at fifty-nine in 1919. Among best-selling authors of southern books from 1897 to 1920—his rivals were Page, Thomas Dixon, Mary Johnston, and Ellen Glasgow—Fox was the most successful.[3]

Little Shepherd of Kingdom Come was a Civil War yarn about Kentucky children. There are sectional reconciliation and other themes with heavy implications about the Old South. But most of Fox's fiction concerns the postwar era, his contemporary Appalachian South. There are engineers from the "flatlands"—sometimes his own Blue Grass; hillbilly villains and poets; feuding clans, vigilantes imposing order with justice. From *A Mountain Europa* in the 1890s to *Heart of the Hills* Fox nurtured and exploited pastoral sagas, the nature idyl—a homey upland South which had a powerful pull on Americans in their first age of "conservation." Fox's South, like TR's West, was the noble region of nature where Americans might (if it were not too late already) find the wilderness. In *Trail of the Lonesome Pine*, Blue Grass engineer John Hale, an instrument of polluting streams and ruining mountains, repents: "I'll tear down those mining shacks, float them down the river and sell them as lumber. . . . I'll stock the river with bass again . . . and I'll plant young poplars to cover the sight of every bit of uptorn earth along the mountain. I'll bury every bottle and tin can. . . . I'll take away every sign of civilization."[4]

Page's South was moss-covered and belligerently decadent. Like Griffith's Dixie, Page's Virginia counted virtually no middle class, only courtly-but-tragic ol' gemun, dashing beaux, beauteous belles, and loving, loyal darkies.

However, when in the 1890s Page decided to try a novel about Reconstruction, sentimentality slipped into bitterness and a present-ism bordering upon the vicious. Reconstruction novels in general were failures. The former carpetbagger Albion Tourgée's famous works, *A Fool's Errand* and *Bricks Without Straw*, were exceptions, although hardly deathless. Ellen Glasgow's *Voice of the People* and *Miller of Old Church* were good novels which covered the historical period, but Glasgow was not interested in political horrors or race, so these works do not quite fit the genre. Page's *Red Rock* (1898), the number five best seller of 1899, is not only evocative of the failure rule, but the most influential Reconstruction tale until Dixon's *Clansman* appeared in 1905.[5]

Page had the scions of two prominent Virginia families battle scalawags and carpetbaggers and thwart a black would-be rapist of Ruth Welch, daughter of a yankee promoter. Southerner Steve Allen marries Ruth in the end, achieving symbolic sectional peace. But the burden of *Red Rock* was vigorous yankee-baiting, racism, and vindication of the white South. Well before the Dunning histories and Griffith films, Page had the yankees make the major concessions in creating an American synthesis.[6]

Page fought unsuccessfully against the coarser side of his sectional partisanship; yet he also sought to delude himself and others.

To a friend he wrote that, reading a draft of the novel, "I discovered that I had drifted into the production of a political tract." So "I bodily discarded what I had written" and attempted another draft along "a more serene path." Nonetheless Page "discovered" in his research "that the real facts in the Reconstruction period were so terrible that I was unable to describe them fully." His research included southern white testimony of Negro atrocities in the congressional "Ku Klux Reports" of 1872, and two bitterly partisan Conservative tracts about South Carolina: John A. Leland's *A Voice from South Carolina* (1879) and James S. Pike's *The Prostrate State* (1874), which Dixon would mine again. Page actually superimposed the Palmetto State's decade of tumultuous postwar experience upon Virginia—which had a brief, mild "reconstruction"—without a qualm. Then he lent his personal prestige as well as the popularity of *Red Rock*, to the current black disfranchisement campaign in the South. "I intended 'Red Rock,'" he wrote in 1900, "for a 'composite picture' . . . for the south generally," and he eagerly received plaudits from correspondents who justified, for example, white brutality in the 1898 riots in Wilmington, North Carolina.[7]

Page indulged open hostility toward yankees and Afro-Americans again in a tract entitled *The Negro: The Southerner's Problem*, but seldom after the outbursts of *Red Rock* would he abandon his genteel manner. More characteristically, in 1903 he published a story called "Old Jabe's Marital Experiments," a loving portrait of a dependent Uncle Tom type; and in 1904 came "Mam Lyddy's Recognition," a tale about a faithful mammy who after the war repudiates "free niggers."[8]

Page was a gentleman far more comfortable with benevolent tyranny over house servants than with the ugly physical repression of his own day. He was a serene reactionary out of place in the age of segregation. Yet Page and Fox, the modern southerner, gentle perhaps but never genteel, were fast friends and, in many ways, shared hearts and minds. The South—their love of it and missions to honor and vindicate it—bound them, along with whatever quirks of character and fate existed which are no longer obvious to biographers.

"God bless Kentucky—and Virginia" wrote Fox to Page in 1891; "—and I can't stop there—the South!" Fox pledged himself "to the sole purpose of trying to get a prayer to the heart of every young son of the South to hold to his inheritance—to get rich if he can, but to bring the old past back." Visiting Page in New York, Washington, or traveling the world, the adoptive mountaineer was drawn to tribal origins: "It's no use, Tom—no use. I'm dead against the spirit of things in the East, in England, France, everywhere except in my own land. I know our shortcomings, but there is a spirit with us still that is nowhere else, as far as I know." [9]

And despite his contrasting life-style and fictional genre, Fox several times walked upon paths well trod by Page—as well as countless lesser writers and some of the Dunningite historians. In *Crittenden*, an unsuccessful (artistically and commercially) novel published in 1900, Fox evoked the bitterness of white southerners who experienced war, reconstruction, and alienation. At the soapy conclusion, however, the title character goes to Cuba as an American soldier in 1898 and discovers his nationalism: There "Crittenden, Southerner, died straightaway, and through a travail of wounds, suffering, sickness, devotion and love for that flag—Crittenden, American was born." [10] The terms Fox made for reconciliation were the same, too, as other communicators of his generation: southern white. Americans launching an overseas imperial adventure took solemn recognition of Dixie's experience with Anglo-Saxon dominion. If this were not quite so apparent to readers of *Crittenden*, expansionist Fox made the connection perfectly clear in *Little Shepherd of Kingdom Come*. After the devastating Civil War, Confederate character Chad Buford "was starting his life over afresh, with his old capital, a strong body and a stout heart. In his breast still burned the spirit that had led his race to the land, had wrenched it from savage and from king, had made it the high temple of Liberty for the worship of freemen—the Kingdom Come for the oppressed of the earth. . . . he was going to help carry its ideals across a continent Westward to another sea and on—who knows—to the gates of the rising sun." [11]

In the twenty years before World War I the South, Old and New, following a long siege of calumny, resurged with unprecedented authority and prestige. Fox, Page, Griffith, the historians, and windy politicians (Wilson not the least among them) proclaimed this stature in all the media. At the end of this era, there fittingly appeared Ulrich Bonnell Phillips' monumental *American Negro Slavery* (1918), still respected, but a racist and sentimental treatment by a Georgia-born professor at the University of Michigan. Phillips' slavery was but a "benevolent tyranny"—one not unlike the system Page dimly remembered from his boyhood. But remarkable as this progressive era phenomenon was, it did not last long.

First the South began to suffer the indignity of silence. From 1916 through 1928, not a single book on a southern subject appeared on annual best seller lists. Virtually no notable film concerned the region, either—except Buster Keaton's hilarious (if silent) 1926 classic, *The General*. Here the Confederacy, the war, and the exciting episode when a rebel train was stolen in north Georgia were subjected to grand ridicule. It was a cynical age. W. E. Woodward wrote debunking biographies, the revived Ku Klux Klan that paraded in Washington in 1923 was obviously a national (not merely southern) organization. Worse, in such an age, any southern prestige which might have survived was turned inside out in 1925 at Dayton, Tennessee, during the judicial circus called the Scopes "Monkey" Trial.

Gradually a whole new genre of southern writing took form, and with it, a new American imagery of the region. For lack of a formal designation in the literary histories the genre might be dubbed sharecropper social realism. Novelists, then filmmakers who labored in the field, were sympathetic to the humble white folks; and some were more concerned with social scientific solutions than their art. The realists cannot be compared with John Fox, for their rural South after the war was not idyllic, a refuge from modern tension and industrial turmoil. It was pathetically in need of massive governmental help. Many of the genre writers were consumed with bitterness, too, and in the course of their exposés attacked Page's smug Lost Cause mystique with a gusto akin to Mencken's.[12]

Ironically, if any one writer may be credited with originating this critical realism, it was a quiet Richmonder of Page's own class, Ellen Glasgow. Three of her five annual best sellers were published during the great progressive era consensus which Page and Fox so dominated and typified. Her *The Deliverance* was number two in 1904; *The Wheel of Life* ranked tenth the following year; and *Life and Gabriella* was fifth in 1916. Glasgow undertook as a very young woman to write the social history of Virginia from the Civil War. She was concerned with white people's problems—with tradition, hard times, and class—not with Reconstruction, race relations, and paying homage to the Confederate dead. In *The Deliverance* and in *The Descendant* (1897), *The Voice of the People* (1900), *The Miller of Old Church* (1911), and her best novel, *Barren Ground* (1925), Glasgow wrote of the yeomanry and the "trash" with understanding and considerable accuracy as well as sympathy. Ordinary whites—not planters and plutocrats—were the soul of the culture and the wave of the future. They heroically restored destroyed farms, waged grueling war with creditors and railroads, and rose to political authority as populists.[13]

Readers of Glasgow's yeoman novels who also perused *Time*, the weekly news magazine founded in the mid-1920s, could hardly have assumed that humble southerners triumphed, however. In notable advertisements southern companies, trade associations, and governments vied with one another in portraying white laborers (children of the Populist masses) as degraded and docile. The Atlanta Chamber of Commerce, for example, promised prospective industrialists that "in the South, the worker is your friend . . . efficient, willing, Anglo-Saxon." The Carolina Power and Light Company announced: "you can make it for less in the Central Carolinas," and the Duke Power Company celebrated "willing labor, unhampered by any artificial restrictions on output; native born of old pioneer stock and not imbued by un-American [read "union"] ideas or ideals."[14]

Nevertheless in the twenties a spate of sharecropper novels appeared, just as public concern over poor whites mounted in the incongruous age of ballyhoo. Edith Summers Kelley's *Weeds* appeared in 1923. It told of a spunky Kentucky girl whose spirit and hope are broken after marriage to a luckless tobacco tenant. Dorothy Scarborough, an activist Texas plantation woman, detailed a plan of reform in her 1924 novel, *In the Land of Cotton*. Elizabeth Maddox Roberts in *The Time of Man* (1926) and Jack Bethea in *Cotton* (1928) also blended bitter melodrama with social action formulae. Best known (although artistically inferior to Kelley's *Weeds*) was Henry Kroll's *Cabin in the Cotton* (1931). Kroll, son of a Tennessee sharecropper, won popular recognition because his book was made into a successful film in 1932.[15]

The movie version was a typical "issue" picture of the Hoover and early New Deal years. Director Michael Curtiz starred an aging, pudgy Richard Barthelmess (who had been the young Chinese in Griffith's *Broken Blossoms* in 1919) as Marvin Blake, a bright-but-naïve son of a cotton 'cropper. Marvin is ordered out of high school and back to the fields by planter-boss Lane Norwood; but later, on the advice of his daughter Madge (Bette Davis), Norwood gives Marvin a clerk's job in his country store after school hours. Bette Davis is a designing, party-going, Chesterfields-puffing bitch, who would groom Marvin for matrimony. Marvin is impressed, grateful, seduced —away from his own kind, from rustic simplicity, and from the love of wholesome Betty, a good girl.

Meanwhile Marvin's clerking opens the main plot, class struggle. He gradually discovers that Norwood cheats his sharecropper customers through price gouging and phony accounting. (The worst features of the crop lien-furnishing merchant system which plagued the South are well depicted.) Marvin is caught in the ensuing conflict. An uncle—played well by Griffith's old star, Henry Walthall— is the most uncompromising advocate of "peckerwood" collective bargaining and merciless justice to crooked planters. Norwood orders Marvin to catch "cotton thieves," some of whom are lynched. Then the store burns, with considerable assistance from Marvin's uncle. Norwood's secret and corrupt books appear lost to Norwood's class enemies, but Marvin has kept a duplicate copy. Will he betray his own people out of gratitude to the boss? Madge vamps him into momentary confusion, but Marvin studies the books and verifies the tenants' charges.

The climax is a preposterous denial of all the foregoing, turning a leftist "message" movie into consensus fantasy. Marvin moderates a grand courthouse confrontation in which he "settles" everything without changing anything. Indignantly propounding the share-croppers' grievances, he then turns about and defends not only the landlords' property rights but their "right to charge high interest" because of high risks. Marvin demands only "fair play" and written contracts from Norwood and his cohorts. They agree. The other part of the plot is concluded, too, when Marvin spurns hussy Madge for pure-and-true Betty—pap for class solidarity.

Cabin in the Cotton was virtually an all-white film, even though most actual sharecroppers were black. If class struggle was too dan-gerous for radical solution in Hollywood in 1932, class and racial struggle were utterly out of the question. Thus a few blacks—all obsequious—merely decorate the beautifully photographed land-scape. Standing up to "the man" in the entertainment business was white man's business. This despite the fact that the radical Southern Tenant Farmers' Union of the thirties was interracial, and that the dramatic southeastern Missouri cotton-pickers' strike of 1937 was al-most entirely a Negro affair.[16]

Sympathetic evocations of humble white existence in the twen-tieth-century South made money, and, often, good art, through World War II. Nearly all the new writers, wrote W. J. Cash in 1940, "had decisively escaped the old Southern urge to turn the country into Never-Never Land [;] nearly all of them stood, intellectually at least, pretty decisively outside the legend."[17] The most popular examples were the writings of Marjorie Kinnan Rawlings. A latter-day local colorist, Rawlings moved from Washington, D.C. to north-central Florida, where she bought a home and orange grove and discovered the Florida cracker. Her affectionate stories "Cracker Chidlings" and "Jacob's Ladder" preceeded her first novel, South Moon Under (1933). Then came two best sellers: The Yearling (1938; number one on the list), which also won a Pulitzer Prize; and Cross Creek (fourth on the 1942 nonfiction list), a nostalgic recollection of her backcountry experiences. Rawlings' contemporary southern whites were quaint and superstitious, but proud and independent. The same traits were found in Caroline Miller's antebellum Georgia frontiersmen, whom she celebrated in her Pulitzer-winning 1934 novel, *Lamb in His Bosom*.[18]

Close to Rawlings' genre, and close, too, to John Fox's mountain idylls, were two films made by the French director Jean Renoir during World War II: *Swamp Water* (1941) and *The Southerner* (1945). Neither was great box office, but both have maintained well-deserved critical approval. Renoir, like his Impressionist painter father, Auguste, was obsessed with nature themes, particularly nature's paradoxical bountiful-destructive forces. In the southern hinterlands of the United States he found abundant materials for portraying man's timeless ambivalent relationship with nature.

Swamp Water starred Walter Brennan as Tom Keefer, a wrongly accused man hiding alone in the hostile Okefenokee. Keefer has so made peace with the great swamp's destructive forces that he recovers from a moccasin bite on the face without benefit of civilized medicine. Dana Andrews portrayed young Ben Ragan, a noble, woodsy fellow who discovers Keefer in the swamp and comes to share his values and seek his vindication before the law. Anne Baxter provided romantic interest as Keefer's daughter. Ward Bond played one of the villainous Dorson brothers, who are finally exposed as the real murderers. One is punished by nature itself as he perishes in quicksand. The conclusion is a happy scene of reunion and rustic celebration among fiddles, food, and hound dogs. White southerners are simple, honest people, not to be either ridiculed or reformed.

The Southerner took place in the cotton country, where a plucky sharecropper, Sam Tucker (Zachary Scott), nearly crawls out of his economic slough of despond, when nature in the form of a rampaging river destroys his farm and floods his fields just at picking time. Yet, rather than head for California or lose hope, he exuberantly catches fish from the river with his bare hands, recognizing like Renoir that nature is bountiful, too. Instead of class conflict Renoir presented a cooperative spirit of community among landlords, townspeople, and tenants, all of whom struggle for existence with dignity.[19]

Meanwhile the new realism had undergone a profound metamorphosis. Despite the persistence of local color and nature-idylls which evoked either admiration or sympathy for the white masses, gradually the surreal potential of Dixie poverty, social customs, and history gained dominance in the media. What Ellen Glasgow was to call in 1935 the "Southern Gothic School" appeared.[20]

Like the sharecropper genre, the Gothic novels were born out of the 1920s. T. S. Stribling illustrates the transition. Following the Scopes trial, Stribling, W. J. Cash, and a small corps of southern writers joined H. L. Mencken in brutal satire of the region's ignoble characteristics, particularly the whites' tribal ethos, which Cash was later to call "the savage ideal." Stribling's *Teeftallow* (1926) and *Bright Metal* (1928) ridiculed hillbilly ignorance, violence, and fundamentalism. Like the social realists, he operated beyond and against the sentimentalist tradition of Page. But Stribling did more. His humble whites are anything but sympathetic. They need education and perhaps, first, a sharp whack with a two-by-four between the eyes to get their attention. In the early thirties new greater-than-life elements were added, and Stribling gained reward and national popularity. He won a Pulitzer Prize in 1932 for the first volume of his "Alabama trilogy," *The Forge*. *The Store* (1932) and *The Unfinished Cathedral* (1934) followed. Here he traced the epic rise of James Vaiden from blacksmith to planter, through the course of war and reconstruction, and to the forge again. The tale was well told, but Stribling embellished it liberally with doses of sex and other sensation which might have set Page and his contemporaries to revolving in their graves. Best remembered was James's son's miscegenation, the birth of a mulatto grandson, then the horrific lynching of the grandson provoked by his own grandfather.[21]

By the time Stribling concluded his trilogy he had already been surpassed in the Southern Gothic genre by the two men who would dominate it through the 1950s, William Faulkner and Erskine Caldwell. Mississippi's Faulkner, read carefully, was a good social historian. His characterizations are powerful, and in scene-setting background sketches he excelled. In one short passage from *The Hamlet*

(1931) he told volumes about the frontier and the culture of ordinary whites:

> The people . . . came from the northeast through the Tennessee mountains by stages marked by the bearing and raising of a generation of children. They came from the Atlantic seaboard and before that, from England and the Scottish and Welsh Marches, as some of the names would indicate—Turpin and Haley and Whittington, McCallum and Murray and Leonard and Littlejohn, and other names like Riddup and Armstid and Doshey which could have come from nowhere since certainly no man would deliberately select one of them for his own. They brought no slaves and no Phyfe and Chippendale highboys; indeed, what they did bring most of them could (and did) carry in their hands. They took up land and built one- and two-room cabins and never painted them, and married one another and produced children and added other rooms one by one to the original cabins and did not paint them either, but that was all. Their descendants still planted cotton in the bottom land and corn along the edge of the hills and in the secret coves in the hills made whiskey of the corn and sold what they did not drink. Federal officers went into the country and vanished. Some garment which the missing man had worn might be seen—a felt hat, a broadcloth coat, a pair of city shoes or even his pistol—on a child or an old man or woman. County officers did not bother them at all save in the heel of election years. They supported their own churches and schools, they married and committed infrequent adulteries and more frequent homicides among themselves and were their own courts, judges and executioners. They were Protestants and Democrats and prolific; there was not one Negro landowner in the entire section. Strange Negroes would absolutely refuse to pass through it after dark.[22]

Yet Faulkner's material on the yeomanry flows from a cynical outsider; little compares with John Fox's, Caroline Miller's, or Margery Rawlings' apostrophes. Faulkner's aristocrats are approachably democratic for the most part: he hardly belonged to the cape and sword tradition. And while gentry and yeomanry love the hunt—witness the fox hunt in *Sartoris* (1929) and the first half of his story, "The Bear"—southerners are not particularly ennobled by contact with nature. Indeed the humble folk closest to nature are often pathetic (the Armstids) or greedy and amoral (the Snopeses).[23] Faulkner (Caldwell much more so) also injected—or reinjected—the bawdy theme so appropriate to the American age of Freud. His southerners of all classes, races, and sexes are frequently motivated by, ruined by, renewed by—sex. As a literary historian of poor whites observed, the bawdy theme in writings of the South was introduced early in the eighteenth century by William Byrd II in his delightful *History of the Dividing Line*. Ribald innuendoes and Rabelaisian scenes recurred until about the Civil War. Then the prudish sentimentalists of Page's generation abandoned it.[24] By comparison, the dead-serious sharecropper realists of the twenties were closer to the Victorians than to their own Lost Generation. Faulkner, Stribling, and Caldwell revived sex and the surreal, and the public responded with enthusiasm.

Faulkner's Yoknapatawpha novels, beginning with *Sartoris* in 1929 and including *Sanctuary*, *The Hamlet*, and *The Wild Palms* before the end of the thirties, sold moderately well and brought the writer an entrée into the Hollywood screenwriters' corps (notwithstanding Faulkner's reluctance to enter). Yet no Faulkner novel appeared on an annual best-seller list until 1962 (*The Reivers*). On a list of best sellers which includes both cloth and paperbound sales cumulatively through 1966, only *Sanctuary* (1931; 2,080,985 copies) and *The Wild Palms* (1939; 1,534,371) appear.[25] Faulkner did not win popular acclaim in his own country until after he received a Nobel Prize in 1950. Despite the critical notice, it would seem, the book-reading middle class found Faulkner turgid, puzzling, and "difficult" (to quote many a student in the past decade).

Not so Erskine Caldwell. While his novels made no annual top-ten lists, he attracted enormous attention, and in terms of combined cloth and paperback sales through 1966, he outranks all other writers on southern subjects—and a great many others, too. Thirty-five years after the appearance of *Tobacco Road* (1932), at least 40 million copies of Caldwell's novels and stories had sold. *God's Little Acre* (1933) is the best-selling southern book in history (8,061,821 in 1966), exceeding sales of *Gone with the Wind* by more than a million copies. Twelve volumes of his work, including an anthology edited by someone else, sold at least 1.5 million copies each. Other than his two early books mentioned above (3,455,947 of *Tobacco Road*), Caldwell's books that sold more than 2 millions of copies each included: *Trouble in July* (1944), *Georgia Boy* (1943), *House in the Uplands* (1946), *The Sure Hand of God* (1947), and *This Very Earth* (1948).[26] In the printed medium, Caldwell must be ranked as the most influential communicator about the American South. He has also been, perhaps, the most controversial, particularly within his native region.[27]

Caldwell was born early in this century in rural Georgia, the only child of an Associate Reformed Presbyterian minister and his good wife. The future writer of the grotesque had a happy, secure boyhood under the loving tutelage of a father he adored. In *Georgia Boy* and two autobiographies, Caldwell related warm, even idyllic stories of his upbringing and the tolerant-yet-steady influences of his parents. His father was liberal minded, with progressive reformist sensibilities regarding the plight of the southern poor; and in the ministry which moved the family from Georgia to the Carolinas to Louisiana to Tennessee, Ira Sylvester Caldwell showed his son the grand spectrum of Dixie's social problems. Erskine recalled in 1951 his father's profound sympathy for cotton tenants forty years earlier: Sharecroppers were "as bad off as a toad in a post hole. It's a disgrace that human beings have to live like that."[28]

So Caldwell, according to his own recollection, grew up with a liberal social conscience. In the early and mid-twenties he dropped out of college in North Carolina, tried professional football, attended the University of Virginia, and worked as a cub reporter for the Atlanta *Journal* (where at the same time Margaret Mitchell wrote features and framed up the Georgia epic which would appear a decade

Henry Hull as Jeeter Lester in Tobacco Road, *on Broadway, ca. 1938*

later). Following a rather short apprenticeship in journalism Caldwell heroically—or recklessly—quit his job and headed for the Maine woods, determined to learn to write fiction that would sell. This apprenticeship consumed seven years of painful labor not only at the typewriter, but at the woodpile and in his potato patch. From Caldwell's own account of his hungry years, readers can only conclude that he emerged a rather cynical and clever professional—lean, mean, and bound for victory in the merciless world of literary capitalism.[29]

Tobacco Road launched him upon a career as celebrity which dwarfed John Fox's. The Gothic saga of Jeeter Lester and his lazy-greedy-morbid tribe was dramatized for Broadway by Jack Kirkland, and played to rave notices for seven and a half years. Subsequent novels outsold the first, and Ty Ty Walden and Darling Jill of *God's Little Acre* became popular property, creations made into southern realities. In 1946 *Tobacco Road* was made into a film; other Caldwell stories would be adapted by Hollywood in the future. Meanwhile Caldwell married and divorced several times, most publicly with *Life's* ace photographer, a showwoman in her own right, Margaret Bourke-White.[30]

Critics have disagreed wildly in characterizing Caldwell's work. As early as 1935 Ellen Glasgow disapprovingly dubbed Caldwell and Faulkner founders of a "Southern Gothic School." She despaired at their apparent despair: "What is left of the pattern?" she wrote. "Has Southern life—or is it only Southern fiction—become one vast, disordered sensibility?"[31] Six years later Kenneth Burke, like Glasgow, felt compelled to deny that Caldwell was a "realist." Burke thought him closer to Poe, or the Dadaists—fellow "makers of grotesques"—than to the nineteenth-century English and European social novelists.[32] Shields McIlwaine, literary historian of southern humble whites, called both Faulkner and Caldwell naturalists in that both authors emphasized the supremacy of "animal instincts" in man: hunger and sex. Yet, McIlwaine added, Caldwell endowed some of his human creatures with a nobility implicit in the natural setting: Ty Ty Walden (as perhaps the heavy symbolism of his last name would indicate) has a definite sense of human divinity; and Jeeter Lester's obsession with farming represents an eternally high human value.[33] A more recent student of Caldwell finds him a great critic of the American Dream, a scathingly effective debunker of the promise of reward from rugged individualism. Caldwell thus becomes a political radical of sorts: southern socioeconomic conditions (the environment itself) make a mockery of American values.[34] Malcolm Cowley simply dichotomized Caldwell, leaving the paradox unresolved. Caldwell Number One was a sociologist-reformer (e.g. the Lesters would prosper if cooperative farming with federal support were introduced). Caldwell Number Two was a ribald storyteller without social conscience or aim. Jeeter was no more than an aged woods elf, an American Pan.[35]

But critical perception is not the subject of this book. Popular perception is. And lacking reader polls, firm assertions about the imagistic and historiographical significance of Caldwell's South are impossible. One can, however, deduce certain things—with care; the rest is presented as no more than the impressions of yet another student. First, that so many critics confronted Caldwell as a "realist" may well mean that from the thirties through the sixties, readers assumed that Caldwell's contemporary South was actual. The gruesome photographic portraiture in documentary books (popular with students and the northern middle class), along with federal studies which in 1938 branded the region the "nation's economic problem number one," provide a context in which Caldwell's nonsouthern readers may very logically have assumed his books accurately represented the South and its people. More tangible: in his principal autobiography Caldwell himself mentioned receiving hundreds of anonymous letters which protested his crass "exploitation" of southern rural poverty.[36] Whether Caldwell cynically went about accomplishing just that is probably a question beyond serious investigation. But if indeed most of his readership assumed realism in his works, then one may safely argue at the very least that Caldwell's carefully honed "Rabelaisan method" misled an unsophisticated middle class because, as one observer put it, the bawdy treatment "is out of key with

Anglo-American culture." "One reader," wrote the folklorist John Maclachlan, "searching eagerly for pornographic details, is so bedazzled by those he finds that he sees nothing else." Yet "another is so antagonized and so lost because he regards the guffaw as a poor vehicle for philosophical judgments."[37]

There is no doubt that many southern whites were offended by Caldwell's creations. Assuming that middle class nonsoutherners perceived the portraits as realistic, they lashed out at Caldwell. Leading the onslaught were the Vanderbilt Agrarians, an assortment of poets, novelists, and two historians associated with the university at Nashville. In 1930 these "Twelve Southerners" published an "agrarian manifesto" entitled *I'll Take My Stand*, in which they blasted industrialization, urbanization—the "national" (*i.e.* yankee) way—and presented a pastoral, conservative, religious South as an alternative. The Agrarians had been deeply offended by H. L. Mencken's and Clarence Darrow's gleeful pillorying of Dixie backwardness at the famous 1925 Monkey Trial. *I'll Take My Stand* was a counterattack against them as well as an expression of alarm over the recession of rural values before the onslaught of technology and urban sprawl.[38]

John Donald Wade, most militant of the Agrarians, led the attack on Caldwell. Wade had a near-paranoid obsession with Caldwell's readership and their alleged image of his region. Caldwell's "stories deal with country and village poeple," Wade wrote in 1936, "in short with just the sort of people that sophisticated New Yorkers and would-be New Yorkers—the major part of the book-buying population of America—can at once most envy and marvel over and deplore, with the sort of people best calculated to satisfy at once the current vogue for primitivism and the constant vogue of metropolitan complacency." Wade deplored what he perceived as a cultural imperialism at the expense of ordinary southern whites. "Mr. Caldwell," he surmised, "has apparently persuaded himself and many others, among them the editors of the intellectual weeklies in New York, that Jeeter Lester and his kind are fairly typical of twenty million Southern countrymen." To Wade, Caldwell was a rank panderer who had sold out his own people for money and the acclaim of perverse voyeurs and misguided northern liberals.[39]

Another 1930s controversy which closely paralleled, then included Caldwell, concerned documentary films and books on those same rural poor. First came a lurid book and famous motion picture, *I Am a Fugitive from a Chain Gang*. The book, purportedly an autobiography by Robert E. Burns, was first serialized in early 1931 in *True Detective Mysteries*. In early draft Burns's was a 1920s-style success epic: the hero escapes from a hellish Dixie penal colony, goes underground and straight, and becomes a wealthy Chicago executive. The magazine editors, sensitive to a rising popular interest in social comment documentaries, revised the tale as an exposé of southern corrections. Enter the diabolical southern sheriff/guard in sweaty khakis and of mindless brutality, associated before only with Devil's Island—or perhaps with antebellum overseers. The 1932 film version starred Paul Muni and won box-office success. Not only was the chain gang genre founded—it would thrive through the sixties— but a new perspective (*i.e.* nonfarm) on southern backwardness was introduced.

David O. Selznick cashed in the same year with *Hell's Highway*, exposing the horrors of Georgia's penal system. Selznick concluded with a fanciful solution comparable to *Cabin in the Cotton*'s finale: the governor appears and promises to clean up the mess. Meanwhile the radical *New Masses* photographer, John L. Spivak, made his way to darkest Georgia and developed a spectacular exposé called "On The Chaingang." The portfolio included one of Spivak's most famous pictures, a young black prisoner in striped suit, with wrists chained to ankles, a wooden pole drawn between his arms and knees, and lying hopeless, nearly catatonic, on his side in the broiling sun.[40]

Interest in southern "conditions" (just as Agrarian Wade insisted) was liberal and radical chic during the thirties—much to the embarrassment of many southerners. Priscilla Hiss (Mrs. Alger) always reminded Washington acquaintances who greeted her with "Nice day!" that sharecroppers were not having nice days. Novelist Mary McCar thy recalled New York parties to raise money for the National Share-croppers Fund, where "dreadful" liquor in too-small glasses was served. The federal government probably did more than the private communications media to arouse such sympathy. The New Deal's Farm Security Administration (FSA) sent out its own photographers —many of whom were strongly motivated to evoke sympathy and social action—who generated huge files of widely circulated pictures of hungry people and eroded hills. FSA photo files were open to private makers of documentary books.[41] Others were busy, too, including southern scholars and liberals.

In 1930 the most important negative reactions to *I'll Take My Stand* had come from Professor Howard Odum of the University of North Carolina's sociology department, Stringfellow Barr, a liberal Virginia editor, and scores of other southerners who were oriented toward the social sciences and problem-solving (as opposed to poetry and nostalgia). Odum had earlier founded the scholarly *Journal of Social Forces* which in those years focused upon the South. After 1930 Odum and his colleague Rupert Vance originated a "regionalist" (as opposed to sectionalist) approach to southern problems, which involved careful description of conditions and federal help in reconstruction. Vance's *Human Factors of Cotton Culture* (1929) compiled enormous data on poverty and prefaced his own and Odum's future volumes on the region.[42] The Chapel Hill Regionalists sold few books, but other social scientists gained considerable notice. For example, Arthur Raper's *Preface to Peasantry* (1937) documented convincingly (without the weight of the Chapel Hill tomes) the impending collapse of agriculture in the Lower South. And sociologist John Dollard's 1937 classic, *Caste and Class in a Southern Town* examined race relations and white class structure as well as poverty. Both books are available in paperbound editions forty years later. No doubt much better known to the general public was a magnificent documentary film made for the FSA in 1937 by the master director Pare Lorentz. In *The River* Lorentz's cameras followed the Mississippi downstream from Minnesota to New Orleans, emphasizing the relationship between natural ecology and human welfare. The film was an eloquent message in behalf of the four-year-old Tennessee Valley Authority, and it was presented in movie houses throughout the nation.[43]

But the most popular productions were yet to come. In 1939 the photographer Dorothea Lange with caption-writer Paul Schuster Taylor released a picture book called *An American Exodus: A Record of Human Erosion*.[44] Some of the photographs were taken on the High Plains and in California, but the book was primarily a study of southerners' suffering. The faces are worried and tired; yet they are not Caldwell's and Faulkner's people. They retain dignity and strength.

An American Exodus won notice and good sales, but easily the best-selling picture book of the thirties was Erskine Caldwell and Margaret Bourke-White's *You Have Seen Their Faces* (1937). Bourke-White was the best-known American news and feature photographer of the thirties and forties, a celebrity even without Caldwell. Loose among sharecroppers and Negro worshipers in the Black Belt, she made pictures that seemed to verify Caldwell's fiction. Bourke-White specialized in weird angle shots which produced surreal images. In a black church she crawled down the aisle and lay flat on her side before the pulpit. Caldwell composed captions to accompany the pictures and placed quotation marks around them, presenting them (to readers who skipped the introduction) as the subjects' words. In sharecroppers' cabins Bourke-White rearranged furniture and people in order to obtain melodramatic images. They wished to evoke sympathy and, according to Caldwell, government action. Malcolm Cowley praised Caldwell's captions. However, Bourke-White, in particular, seemed to feel little beyond her artist's preoccupations. She wrote: "When we first discussed plans for *You Have Seen Their Faces*, the first thought was of lighting." James Agee later sneered that, at work among these people, Bourke-White wore an expensive red coat. At one point in their work she and Caldwell offered to pay a couple to pose. They wanted snuff. "So far as we could tell," reported the photographer, "they hadn't any food. . . . They seem to live on snuff and religion."[45]

A reviewer of the picture book for *The Nation* was so depressed that he declared the South was "so sick from its old infections of prejudice and poverty that it is a menace to the nation." This was too much for the Agrarians. Poet Donald Davidson responded this time. His chief complaint—other than that Caldwell profiteered in "turning state's evidence" against his own people—was that Caldwell and Bourke-White seemed to blame the South, instead of the imperial North, for southern travails. Caldwell flailed landlords when they too were exploited by northern creditors and lived barely above the lip of poverty.[46] Of course there was truth in Davidson's analysis, but again the Agrarian counterattack contained more of the *ad hominem* than the empirical.

There were in fact a number of documentary books available which might have countervailed *You Have Seen Their Faces*, from the viewpoint of the Agrarians and other sensitive southerners. In 1935 Muriel Early Sheppard's *Cabins in the Laurel* appeared. A paean to mountain life in northwestern North Carolina, the text and pictures belong almost to the genre associated with John Fox. It was pure idyll—no ugliness, unhappiness, disease. Poverty, if one could call the mountaineers' existence thus, was more a superior, noble lifestyle. The University of North Carolina Press released three small printings.

More pointedly, an antidote to *You Have Seen Their Faces* was Herman C. Nixon's *Forty Acres and Steel Mules*, published also by the University of North Carolina Press, in 1938, the year following the Caldwell/Bourke-White release. Nixon was a Vanderbilt (later Auburn) historian associated with the Agrarians, who happened also to be proprietor of an Alabama farm. Deeply committed to country life and to the practical rehabilitation of the rural South, Nixon preached the consolidation of family farms, mechanization ("steel mules") and diversification of crops. As veteran director of the Louisiana Rural Rehabilitation Corporation, he had, by 1938, moved considerably beyond the romantic reactionary position of the Nashville poets. Yet he militantly announced in his preface that the book was "a hillbilly's view." One group of photographs displayed sturdy, smiling 'croppers with the caption, "Have You Really Seen Their Faces?" Another picture showed black boys frolicking in a swimming hole, with Nixon's comment: "There are health-giving elements in Southern rural life which even ignorance and poverty cannot nullify." *Forty Acres and Steel Mules* remains a valuable source of farm life in the thirties. Riffling FSA files, Nixon selected excellent exhibits of the cycle of life year-round in various parts of the South, black and white. He did not excise the squalor—or the beauty. It was a fine documentary. The shame is, from our perspective, that it was never a "commercial" book and attracted little notice.[47]

Today the volume synonymous with "thirties documentary" is not *You Have Seen Their Faces*, but the remarkable *Let Us Now Praise Famous Men*, by Tennessee-born James Agee with photographs by Walker Evans. It was published by Houghton Mifflin in 1941. Everyone seems to have heard of the book now, and Evans' poignant photographs of the three white Alabama tenant families are so familiar as to be clichés of the genre. Actually *Let Us Now Praise Famous Men* was utterly unlike other documentary books of the thirties and early forties. There are only a dozen or so pictures, and Agee's text is not only more than five hundred pages long, but bizarre. He and Evans went to Alabama in 1936 and spent many weeks with the three families, living in their cabins, sleeping in their buggy beds, eating their pork and cornmeal. (No wonder Agee disparaged Bourke-White's expensive coat.) Agee, somewhat akin to his giant southern contemporary, Thomas Wolfe, poured out all in his text, even his sexual fantasies.

Agee and Evans were not trying to evoke sympathy or even to portray "accurately," in the documentary sense of their age, their subjects. They constructed in actuality a novel, one in which the real people, probably just because they were real, were treated with tenderness and honor, not sympathy. Agee despised the "professional" contrived aloofness and "objectivity" of Bourke-White and most other documentarists. For this reason *Let Us Praise* had been a great success since it was again released in 1961 (after Agee's death), but was a commercial disaster in 1941. *Fortune* magazine had originally commissioned articles on which the book was based, but Harper Brothers, after contracting for the volume, decided not to publish. Five years after the work was completed Houghton Mifflin finally printed the weighty volume. It sold but a few hundreds of copies; the rest of the printing remaindered; and the editor responsible for convincing the company to publish was cashiered.[48]

Let Us Now Praise Famous Men, then, was hardly noticed. But at last, toward the end of the thirties, professional historians became interested and ultimately triumphed in placing the southern ordinary man in proper context. As early as 1930, interest in 1890s populism prompted serious study of the rural environment of common-man protest. At the end of the decade C. Vann Woodward's doctoral dissertation on Tom Watson, the Georgia Populist, illuminated the southern version of the story.[49] Meanwhile Professor Frank L. Owsley of Vanderbilt, one of the Agrarians, his wife Harriet, and his graduate students undertook studies of the southern antebellum yeomanry. Finally in 1949 Owsley's synthesis, *The Plain Folk of the Old South*, appeared. Owsley reaffirmed what had long been known—that sturdy farmers without slaves had been the backbone and vast majority of the white population. He also showed that they lived among planters, were not pressed ever westward; and that they were home-loving, God-fearing, neighborly people. Critics questioned some aspects of Owsley's research, and without doubt there is clearly the mark of Agrarian partisanship upon the work. But Owsley made his way into textbooks, and few but the blindly romantic or surreal could seriously propose again that Dixie had no respectable middle class.[50]

Yet, by the time of *Plain Folk*'s appearance and absorption, the thirties and the Depression were long gone. Owsley, other Agrarians, and local-color sentimentalists could never compete for popular attention with Faulkner, Caldwell, and the liberal documentarists. Considering the successful Hollywood adaptations of the Gothic South in the 1950s and 1960s, it appears safe to generalize that Jeeter

Lester and Flem Snopes were fixed, perhaps never to die. In the thirties, despite Agrarian outrage, the appearance of more realistic documentaries and novels, and finally of good academic history in popular history and imagery, the school of poverty and degeneracy remained accredited.

Chapter 4

The Grand Old South

It's difficult to put over a joke about any of the Southern states. They go best in sentimental songs. Northern states are different. A fellow from New Jersey, Iowa, Kansas, or Minnesota can be funny (except to natives of those states) but if his birthplace, in the plot, is Virginia or Tennessee he has to be a straight man.

I don't know the why of all this.

W. C. Fields, 1934[1]

But I admire and esteem Sir Galahad in spite of all that you and post-war fiction have done to put him out of fashion.

Ellen Glasgow to James Branch Cabell, 1934[2]

The thirties rage for the "real," problematical, and sordid was devoted almost totally to contemporary matters. During those very same years, paradoxically, the popular Old South and Confederacy remained rather much as Page and the nostalgists had left them: a benevolent tyranny over happy, jiving darkies, with florid-but-kind Irish masters, fickle belles, plumed young tragic heroes. There is no reasoning in such a weird bifurcation of Dixies, with the Old mellowing and becoming even more entrenched in legend, the New wallowing in misery and yankee pity. Common knowledge (not research) has it that the Depression generation wanted escape. They found much of it at the movies. The most successful genres of the times diverted attention from reality: westerns, monster films such as *King Kong*, screwball comedies (the Capra movies, the Marx Brothers), expensive "production" musicals—and the magnolia-scented

Old Southerns.³ Such truisms may indeed be true. Another logical explanation for the Dixie fad is sheer public ignorance of history—black history and slavery in particular. And finally, the thirties exposés of the contemporary South may well themselves have accentuated the traditional white sentimental imagery of the Land O' Cotton. This smaller paradox is well illustrated by the case of H. L. Mencken.

The Bad Boy of Baltimore was both an alien esthete from the German-American community, *and* a southerner. (Baltimore had been rather pro-Confederate and remained southern early in the twentieth century.) His mètier was scalding satire, and late in the progressive era, when the great pro-South consensus was just passing its zenith, Mencken put the contemporary South over his merciless burners. In 1920, following several pilot articles, his long essay, "The Sahara of the Bozart" appeared. A magnificent blast at Dixie pretentiousness, it proclaimed the region a sterile desert of the beaux arts. "Down there," Mencken sneered, "a poet is now almost as rare as an oboe-player, a drypoint etcher or a metaphysician." As for other arts, "critics, musical composers, painters, sculptors, architects . . . there is not even a bad one between the Potomac mud-flats and the Gulf. Nor a historian . . . sociologist . . . philosopher . . . theologian [or] scientist. In all these fields the south is an awe-inspiring blank—a brother to Portugal, Serbia and Esthonia." The only expressions not "held in suspicion" were "the lower reaches of the gospel hymn, the phonograph and the Chautauqua harangue."⁴

The brilliance of the invective excused the bald exaggeration and untruth for all but the most defensive. Five years later Mencken went to Dayton, Tennessee, and extended his talents to fundamentalist religion and southern anti-intellectualism. Meanwhile Mencken was joined in spirit in flailing modern Dixie's savage ideal by Columbia Professor Frank Tannenbaum, whose *Darker Phases of the South* appeared in 1924, and by W. E. B. DuBois and other NAACP publicists whose campaigns against lynching gained broad public notice during the twenties. In the South itself Mencken catalyzed, but did not originate, a new critical movement among white journalists and academicians. Howard Odum, Gerald Johnson, W. J. Cash, and Nell

Battle in North Carolina joined the attack on philistinism and proposed realistic reforms at the roots of poverty and ignorance. Julian
Harris (ironically, son of Joel Chandler Harris, the creator of Uncle
Remus) applauded Mencken from Columbus, Georgia; and Virginia's
nonconformist aristocrat James Branch Cabell (virtually the only
southern writer Mencken approved) invited the Baltimorean to his
estate. This joyous corps of debunkers reigned during the ballyhooed
decade, particularly in journalism. Between 1923 and 1929 they
won no fewer than five Pulitzer prizes.[5] They were at home with the
sharecropper realist novelists, and they contributed to the literature,
high and low, of the embarrassing New South of the thirties.

Among the young southern critics, W. J. Cash, Odum, and Gerald
Johnson had few if any romantic illusions about the Old South. Cash
in particular became obsessed with southern history, and his master-
piece, *The Mind of the South* (1941) frontally attacked the cavalier
myth and traditionalist distortions of Old South social structure.
Few people outside academia studied the various "Souths" as Cash
did, however; and while it would be eccentric to assert that anything
about H. L. Mencken was typical of middle-class Americans, in the
context of popular understanding of history it does indeed seem rea-
sonable to offer Mencken's assumptions about the Old South as revealing.

First, Mencken was woefully ignorant of even the basics of southern history. He had fixed in his mind an antebellum Golden Age during which the ambiance, scholarship, and statesmanship of Thomas
Jefferson was the rule. It was "a civilization of manifold excellences,"
he wrote. Not until about 1933 (when his interest in the region had
waned) did Mencken learn to differentiate the Jeffersonian South
(*ca.* 1776–1810) from the Calhounian South (*ca.* 1810–1860). Even
then he remained a captive of the tradition that Old South society
consisted only of planter-aristocrats, slaves, and poor white trash.
Meanwhile he glowed in the company of genteel, fallen Virginians
who came to Baltimore with "good manners and empty bellies." In
such company elitest Mencken was most likely to refer to himself as
southern. In 1930 (the same year, incidentally, of his marriage to an

Alabamian), he published "The Calamity of Appomattox" in *American Mercury*. The yankees' triumph was "a victory of what we now call babbitts over what used to be called gentlemen," he declared. If the Confederacy had won, the South would have become the center of North American culture.[6] Thus the New South was all the more tragic because of lost potential. Surely, if the late Thomas Nelson Page had revolved in his grave at some of the new Freudianism and debunking of his native land, the prevalence of such romantic nonsense as Mencken's would have quieted his rest anew.

There was a curious validation of this Old South imagery in the most popular and respectable United States histories of the period, Charles and Mary Beard's *Rise of American Civilization* (2 volumes, 1927), which was widely cited and adopted as a text in colleges. Liberals who co-opted part of Marx's economic determinist model of historical change, the Beards portrayed the Civil War era as the "Second American Revolution." Here the bourgeois North, representing the rising industrial juggernaut, overcame the semifeudal South, representing the last premodern society in western civilization. There was inevitability to it all. Slavery had to end; the nation had to become strong in the modern sense. In simplifying their sweeping characterizations of the sections, the Beards (who were no Dixie sentimentalists) left too much implicit in the logic of their design. To be "semi-feudal" the Old South might well have corresponded to the cavalier tradition. The North, by contrast, must have borne both sperm and egg for the babbitts of the future. The quasi-Marxist, liberal-chic intellectualism of the late twenties and thirties, then, reinforced the embarrassing New South-grand Old South dichotomy. The mass-media managers, especially the moviemakers, experimented as usual with genre, and discovered for themselves the cash power of that grand Old South.[7]

Musical extravaganzas, so popular throughout the Depression, often were set in the antebellum South. Ringing with banjos and brimming with high-kicking, happy darky stereotypes, the films conveyed an interpretation of slavery basically the same as Thomas Nelson Page's. *Hearts of Dixie* (1929), an early sound picture that virtually pioneered the genre, featured blacks continuing on de ole plantation after the Civil War. There are "coon" hijinks and fawning gestures of "tom" loyalty to whites, as if no emancipation had occurred. The film was produced and directed by whites, but featured three of the most accomplished black actors who accommodated themselves to the only roles available for them in Hollywood: Stepin Fetchit, Clarence Muse, and Mildred Washington. When Negro filmmakers such as Oscar Michaux made "race" movies with all-black casts, they seldom (if indeed ever) set them anywhere near Dixie. But whites found the South irresistible when casting for romances. Director King Vidor, for example, shot the all-black musical *Hallelujah* (also 1929) in Tennessee and Arkansas. *Hallelujah* revolves about a humble religious farm family. Son Zeke goes to town with the crop money, is vamped by Chick, the town whore, then accidentally kills his own brother in a barroom brawl. Zeke repents and becomes a preacher, but meeting Chick again, he is led once more nearly to destruction. He finally returns to the bosom of his family and marries his childhood sweetheart.[8]

That both *Hearts of Dixie* and *Hallelujah* were set after the Civil War is significant in that both extended through time well-established Old South romance. Just as Page had displayed postwar Negroes clinging to masters and unable to cope with the responsibilities of freedom, these musicals portrayed a gallery of slave types who, in effect, reflected well upon the Peculiar Institution. Thus the chronology is important insofar as it taught audiences (or retaught them) lessons about Page's good ole days.

Hallelujah enveloped also a special fad of the twenties and early thirties, the "exotic Negro." Probably associated with well-publicized white "slumming" in Harlem during the twenties, "exotic" blacks were mysterious, supersensual, and rather lacking in moral discipline. The stereotype was not entirely negative; indeed many whites were envious of blacks' legendary sexual abandon. Yet in *Hallelujah*, Zeke, nearly destroyed by his urgency for the voluptuous and light-skinned Chick (played by Nina Mae McKinney), narrowly escapes to God, family, and the spartan yeoman life—all, significantly, representing "white" moral institutions and discipline, taught by whites during slavery. *Green Pastures*, released as a film in 1936, had a long run on Broadway as an all-black musical. Set in Louisiana, the loose story revolved about a Sunday school teacher's imaginative illustrations of Bible stories. Black characters enact his imaginations, and heaven itself becomes a jolly land of coons, toms, pickaninnies, and jemimas.

Similar themes are found in two best-selling novels of 1929, both written by white South Carolinians: DuBose Heyward's *Mamba's Daughters* (number seven on the list), and Julia Peterkin's *Scarlet Sister Mary* (number nine). Both were good novels and represent considerable advancement and sympathy in white writers' (particularly southerners') handling of black characters. Both treat the war between the superego and the id, as did *Hallelujah*. But in 1929, given the context of white understanding, it would again seem probable that superego—moral discipline—could only represent white values, indeed a discipline imposed with mixed results by whites before the war, by the slavery which Booker T. Washington called the "school of civilization."

Other Hollywood musicals and nonmusical entertainments were simpler, more like *Hearts of Dixie*, and were set in antebellum times or during the war itself. Stepin Fetchit was at his obsequious best as a dumb, dependent coon in *Carolina* (1934) and in John Ford's *Steamboat 'Round the Bend* (1935), which starred Will Rogers. Paramount's *Mississippi* (1935) was adapted from a Booth Tarkington novel. W. C. Fields played a debauched riverboat captain, and Bing Crosby was a yankee crooner who falls in love with a belle (Joan Bennett), whose male kin are cavalier savages, duelists, and brawlers. The Shirley Temple southerns were most popular of all, synthesizing the lighthearted genre with its insidious treatments of blacks in slavery. *The Little Colonel* and *The Littlest Rebel* both appeared in 1935. Temple was the darling of both her white and black "families" on the old plantation. Hattie McDaniel, who later won an Oscar as Mammy in *Gone with the Wind*, was Mammy in *The Little Colonel*. Bill "Bojangles" Robinson, a famous refugee from Richmond, Virginia, appeared in both films as the tom butler and Temple's "guardian." McDaniel's and Robinson's characters were played masterfully, but white audiences could leave with no other impression than that race relations must have been better during slavery than since.

Musicals which evoked "nostalgia" but in which slaves were merely landscape were *Swanee River* (1939), a biography of Stephen Foster (Don Ameche), and *Dixie* (1943), in which Bing Crosby played Daniel Emmett, author of the song. The ultimate expression of plantation harmony after the Temple movies, however, was Walt Disney's version of Uncle Remus tales, *Song of the South* (1946). Between the animated Brer Rabbit sequences, Uncle Remus appears as loving and secure in a retirement provided by white generosity, with white children to whom he tells the stories. The film was still circulating in theaters in the mid-1970s.[9]

There were serious dramas, too. *Secret Service* (1931) and *Operator 13* (1934) were Civil War spy stories with love and sectional reconciliation themes. Both were laden with Dixie stereotypes. In 1935 Stark Young's best-selling novel, *So Red the Rose* (1934) was released as a film. Both novel and film were frankly reactionary, culturally and politically—"a memorial wreath" to the Old South and Confederacy, wrote a literary historian. The novel was well done, but the movie, while popular in the white South, flopped everywhere else. Given the enormous success of *Gone with the Wind* only four years later, as well as the general commercial appeal of the Dixie genre, the failure of *So Red the Rose* must be attributed to poor filmmaking.[10]

Only a year later MGM released a successful film with heavy-handed southern characterizations. *The Gorgeous Hussy* was an unbelievably bad history of the Peggy Eaton affair during the Jackson presidency. Lionel Barrymore played Andrew Jackson, Joan Crawford was Peggy, Robert Taylor portrayed Eaton's first husband. So far, so good. But Franchot Tone played a virile cavalier courtier, John Randolph of Roanoke (who in actuality was impotent, shriveled, and frequently unmannerly); and Sidney Toler, who was already in 1936 known to millions of moviegoers as Charlie Chan, was

BETTMANN/SPRINGER FILM ARCHIVE

Shirley Temple dancing with Bill "Bojangles" Robinson:
The Littlest Rebel, *1935*

cast as Daniel Webster. The scenarist pictured Jackson as a paternal, growling curmudgeon and a patriotic Unionist who, despite his southern identity, puts down John C. Calhoun, Randolph, and other nullifiers. At one point Jackson delivers an ungrammatical speech before Congress which concludes, incredibly, with eloquent phrases that many schoolboys must have recognized as *Webster's* "Second Reply to Hayne." Tone-Randolph, meanwhile, is the tender lover Peggy can never forget; but Jackson finally steps in and discourages her on account of Randolph's extremist politics. It turns out, bafflingly, that Randolph really loved the Union as much as his native Virginia (and Peggy) after all. At a loss for a finale, the screenwriter has noble Randolph assassinated, a martyr to deepening misunderstanding between the sections. On his death night, faithful slaves moan spirituals outside, beneath the live oaks and magnolias.

Bette Davis won a well-deserved Oscar in 1938 for *Jezebel*. Having nearly singlehandedly introduced genus *Dixie bitch* to movie-goers in *Cabin in the Cotton* ("I'd love to kiss you, but I just washed my hair"), Davis now devoted her talents to a film utterly given to narcicism, fickleness, and connivance, characteristics of the Old South stereotype. A lovely queen-spider, her lover-drones perish one after another.[11] In Hollywood's "real life," actress and gossip-entrepreneur Tallulah Bankhead, émegrée belle of a notable Alabama family, played rather the same role.

Margaret Mitchell's Scarlett O'Hara and Jezebel were of course of the same genus, although certainly Scarlett was more complicated and perhaps admirable in some respects. Yet she, macho beau Rhett Butler, frail-noble Melanie, sensitive-romantic-tragic Ashley Wilkes, and Hattie McDaniel's Mammy—were stark as stereotypes. The novel (which won a Pulitzer in 1936) and the acclaimed film (1939) were so good because Mitchell drew her stereotypes so well and set them in such drama. On the screen *Gone with the Wind* was in Technicolor, accompanied by a memorable musical score, and peopled by as many actors and extras as filled the 1,039-page novel itself. Through 1966 the novel had sold nearly seven million copies. David O. Selznick, producer of the film, was originally possessed of a wild hope that the movie would earn as much as $15 millions. As of December, 1971, *GWTW* had made $74,200,000 in United States and Canadian rentals alone. One film student estimates worldwide rental returns at $116 millions.[12]

Gone with the Wind was another generation's *Birth of a Nation*, although apparently a far greater proportion of the population was entertained, educated, reinforced in their southern imagery by *GWTW*. No doubt there were real antebellum white people to substantiate the characters of Scarlett, Rhett, Melanie, and Ashley. Novel readers and moviegoers may, but probably do not, thoughtfully contemplate the use of stereotypes. They are entertained and go on their way, never tidily segregating history from vivid written and/or pictorial

COURTESY ATLANTA *JOURNAL*

Vivien Leigh, Clark Gable, Margaret Mitchell, David O. Selznick, and Olivia de Havilland, the creators of Gone with the Wind, *1939*

imagery. If this is true, Americans (and countless foreign consumers) were reinforced mightily in the Never-Never Land of Dixie, where the social order contained no middle class and the darkies were gay. A notable exception was Scarlett's father, Master O'Hara of Tara, a florid Irishman who has risen, like Andrew Jackson, from frontier penury to respectability. He is not unlike the archetypic "Irishman" W. J. Cash created for *Mind of the South* (five years after Mitchell's novel), who demonstrated for Cash's readers the humble origins and crude manners of planters. Mitchell's and Selznick's field hands march out to the red clay fields like jive soldiers, swinging nearly in step, with hoes on shoulders. House servants are toms, mammies, and pickaninny types. Tara's overseer is a rogue, later a scalawag, implying a direct link from slavery's own sinister side to Reconstruction.

Selznick regarded himself as a liberal, eliminated the Ku Klux Klan, and gave directions to his chief writer "to be awfully careful that the Negroes come out decidedly on the right side of the ledger, which I do not think should be difficult." He was not Griffith, and it was not 1915. Yet Selznick's authority on authenticity was Mitchell; so he hired a coach to teach Kansas-born Hattie McDaniel how to speak the Georgia Negro dialect, and he had actress Butterfly Mc-Queen magnify with her bizarre whine the brainless, fibbing maid who "didn' know nothin' 'bout birthin' babies." [13]

Principal objections to the film by whites, however, did not concern the stereotyping of plantation characters. "Most," reported Selznick, "have come to us from various patriotic organizations [and] are based on an alleged distortion of history by us to the detriment of Northern troops." These probably referred to images of Sherman's phalanx in 1864, one of whom, entering Tara and threatening robbery and rape, Scarlett dispatched with a large, loaded pistol. Selzinck, with no apparent sense of inconsistency, wrote to liberal yankee friends that there was no injustice done nor inaccuracy committed. In all respects, he asserted, "we have followed Miss Mitchell." Such was the power of the quiet little lady from Atlanta. Mitchell herself maintained a low profile and avoided public discussion. However, when she learned that some New York critics complained that she glorified the slaveocracy, she reportedly declared: "I would be upset and mortified if the Left Wingers liked the book." [14] Sad for Mitchell, it seems unlikely that there would have been no leftists among the millions who adored the book and the movie.

National advertising of products and services during the thirties also followed traditional Dixie themes. A survey of *Time* magazine reveals exploitation of the popular genre in ways both logical and absurd. In 1930, for instance, the Tidewater Red Cypress Company sponsored a photograph of "century-old Southern mansions" to promote lumber sales. The next year Virginia's Commission of Conservation and Development advertised for tourists with pictures and blurbs about historical monuments. Another advertisement promoted "Hams from Ole Virginia" "as good as though you went to the plantation and had Mammy cook it." In 1934 the Illinois Central Railroad advertized tours of the Lower Mississippi: "Land O' Lee where the 'white man's burden' can be laid down" in the "Sunny South." [15]

Rather less consistent, the Old Colony Trust Company (of Boston!) published a full-page picture of belles and Confederate soldiers, with no attempt at explanation. In 1931 the brewers, Anheuser-Busch, wished to "Thank the State of Virginia for enriching the American table" with a full page, color picture of black servants assisting lovely belles and dashing white gentlemen. The same year *Fortune* magazine bought space in *Time* to present a large painting entitled *Low Water*, portraying a riverboat passing slave quarters where happy darkies frolicked in the shadow of the big house. Presumably *Fortune*'s ad people wished merely to attract readers' attention. An idyllic Dixie scene was adjudged sure-fire. In 1935 a gasoline firm published a picture of an old colonel inquiring of a young modern, "What kind of oats do you feed your car, son?" The reply: "Ethyl, Colonel!" [16]

The most persistent employment of Old South/Confederate themes, however, is to be found in liquor advertisements. The name of Dixie Belle gin (Richmond) spoke for itself. Four Roses whiskey was limned "soft as Southern moonlight" in 1934, with a color picture of rebel colonels with juleps. "Yes, suh, Colonel, I'se comin'!" captioned another Four Roses ad (1935), showing an eager black servant rushing with his tray of juleps. Paul Jones whiskey strummed the reconciliation theme yet again in 1934, showing two aged veterans, one Confederate, the other Union, sitting beneath a tree with their glasses, reminiscing: "It was back in '65." Another Paul Jones message depicted a Dixie patriarch giving orders to his black servant: "Toby, fetch me the key to the springhouse." Good booze deserves appropriate vessels, so Libby Glassware Company suggested in 1935: "Even a Kentucky Colonel's best mint julep would suffer if served in a glass with a chipped . . . edge."[17] Of course, aficionados understand that juleps are served in silver cups, not glasses. But no mind, never matter.

To those who would read, watch, and listen, there were alternatives to Pagesque sentimentality and neo-Confederate romance. In fiction, at least three novels took up planter lubricity, slave rebellion, or both. Edward Larocque Tinker's *Toucoutou* (1928) was a miscegenation drama set in 1850s New Orleans. It had nearly all the elements characteristic of sensationalist, prurient novels in the sixties: a Creole planter, his octoroon mistress, voodoo, the Mardi Gras, and of course the servile insurrection. In 1936 black author Arna Bontemps created a powerful fictional account of the 1800 Gabriel Conspiracy in Virginia, *Black Thunder*. Frances Gaither's *The Red Cock Crows* (1944) centered upon a Mississippi slave uprising and whites' awful retribution.

Historical scholarship, too, began in the mid-1930s to move ahead of popular culture. At the turn of the century the historians had followed, validating the popular media. Now the process was turned on its head, and academicians slowly began to initiate revisionism. In the case of southern and Afro-American History, white professors were finally accepting what black scholars such as Du-Bois and Alrutheus A. Taylor had already propounded. This was not insignificant, nonetheless; and during the Depression, when few old verities escaped inquisition, it was exciting to be alive and a graduate student.

Reconstruction historiography, always with implications for the Old South, was most active. In 1935 DuBois' massive treatment, *Black Reconstruction in America, 1860–1880*, appeared. DuBois' Marxist framework and some important specifics—especially his slave "general strike" during the war—were almost universally rejected by the white establishment. But whereas DuBois' progressive-era work had been ignored, in the thirties and forties white scholars took him seriously and began to look anew at old assumptions. DuBois' magnificent last chapter, "The Propaganda of History," was a scathing indictment of the Dunning-Bowers tradition, to which

C. Vann Woodward

COURTESY YALE UNIVERSITY

many young scholars responded very constructively. Before the end of World War II several new, revisionist state studies had already appeared which virtually reversed Dunning, Fleming, and Bowers. Young white southern scholars Francis Butler Simkins and Robert Woody rewrote South Carolina's experience. Black scholar Horace Mann Bond (father of Julian) stunningly disassembled Fleming's version of Reconstruction in Alabama in 1938. In these and subsequent works, Radical Republicans (including carpetbaggers and scalawags) became more complex. Among them were men and women of good will and high purpose. Conservatives and Klansmen became more complex, too; some were plain villains, burning schoolhouses and beating yankee schoolmarms. Blacks, perhaps most importantly, were now observed as often competent as voters and cautious and conscientious as officeholders. Corruption was properly placed in context: it was a national phenomenon, not just southern and Republican; and whites committed practically all the grand larceny. The last act of this historiographical drama was played in 1951, when two books by C. Vann Woodward (another white southern revisionist trained in the thirties) indicted the Redeemers (the Bourbons who overthrew the Radicals) as heartless and corrupt.[18] Along with Owsley's and his students' work on the yeomanry during these same years, these new histories formed a composite of southern experience which represented a more accurate portrait than had ever before existed.

Alas, the popular media (including textbook publishers) were glacial in their movement to incorporate revisionism. The public image of slavery and Old South civilization hardly changed until the early 1960s. Kenneth Stampp's masterful revision of U. B. Phillips' *The Peculiar Institution* (1956) was avidly consumed in cloth and paperback versions by college students and their teachers, but Virginia's official high school history, *Cavalier Commonwealth* (1957, 1963) still described slavery as a "sort of comprehensive social security system," disparaged Reconstructionists, and explained the 1902 disfranchisement of black and poor white voters as "improving the electorate."[19] As recently as 1965 high school history teachers in Ohio were aware of "northern" and "southern" editions of their U.S. history text. The latter downplayed inhumanity in slavery and enlightenment in Reconstruction. As late as 1960, too, when this writer was an undergraduate student at a Virginia college, revisionism seemed new and exciting and intensely personal. In all those intervening years the nonconforming novelists and the younger scholars had little impact. Magnolia blossoms were more potent than sharecroppers' weeds.

Chapter 5

The Visceral South

I'm southern and I know neurotic behavior.
Actress Fay Dunaway, 1974[1]

It is a little disconcerting to find, in a book called *The Mind of the South*, so little brain and so much bottom.
David Hackett Fischer[2]

For God's sake let's have a little more freakish behavior— not less.
Tennessee Williams, 1945[3]

According to the historian of southern "laziness," as early as the seventeenth century it was believed that the salubriousness of the Chesapeake climate induced lassitude. Nature gave men virtually all; little effort was needed. The "allurement" of Dixie spread beyond physical aspects to produce inevitably a mental lassitude as well. Thus southern laziness has long implied more than veranda-sitting (the gentry) and catfishing (blacks and white trash). It has meant the absence of thinking, too.[4]

Where there is a salubrious clime and scant thought, there should be, logically, happiness and at least that species of peace that lobotomies bring. In a sense this logic and imagery was applied to the grand Old South: it was a sleepy time and place, with blacks as lazy as whites, the two races depending on each other and muddling through until their civilization collapsed before the bourgeois onslaught of 1861–1865.[5] In the postwar generations, however— consistent wth the Manichean Old/New Souths of the thirties— brutal passion and neuroses came to rule where paternal compassion and gentility once dwelt. Faulkner and Caldwell introduced and mastered this genre in novels and stories. In the forties and early fifties the tribal, passionate, and neurotic New South achieved a currency and validity which have persisted in the media to this day.

To scholars, the literati of all regions, and to thousands upon thousands of college students, the magnum opus to the visceral, mindless South was and remains Wilbur Joseph (Jack) Cash's *The Mind of the South*. First published early in 1941, only months before Cash's pathetic suicide, the book achieved "a mild *succès d'estime*" (in the words of Cash's biographer), then "was swallowed up" by the author's death and World War II. After the war, as racial tensions worsened and the human rights movement focused on southern violence and segregation, the broody, inspired work achieved the stature of a "classic," an eloquent explanation of the past which led to the unhappy present. After Knopf, Cash's publisher, released a Vintage paperbound edition early in 1960, a second printing was made in August of the same year. Never a national best seller, *The Mind of the South* has nonetheless made an enormous impact upon probably millions of people, both directly and indirectly. As late as 1965 eminent professional historians of the South lauded the book in an important historiographical work, *Writing Southern History*. Two Vanderbilt Agrarians who originally reviewed *Mind* were outraged by Cash's irreverence for the Old South and for southern religion, but virtually all the other reviewers—historians, journalists, literary critics—were favorable-to-enthusiastic. *Mind* became the one book to read on the subject of the American South.[6]

Cash was a "middle" southern white, born in Gaffney, South Carolina, in 1900. His ancestors were Scots and Germans who settled in the Carolina Piedmont, farmed, and remained when the Piedmont became the scene of the South's textile revolution after the Civil War. Cash's father and uncle served as mill mechanics, supervisor, and company store clerk. A town boy surrounded by "linthead" mill hands just in from Appalachia, Cash's own ties to the land and humble folk were strong. Like Herman C. Nixon of Vanderbilt and Auburn, whose documentary, *40 Acres and Steel Mules*, appeared almost the same time as *The Mind of the South*, Cash was a self-proclaimed hillbilly out to propound a hillbilly view.

Cash's family were pious Baptists who labored hard but whose work ethic did not prevent their falling backward during the late thirties and forties. Cash rejected both formal religion and the work ethic while still a boy in Boiling Springs, North Carolina, where the Cashes moved from nearby Gaffney when Wilbur was twelve. Bookish and disinclined to physical labor, he was bound for higher education and literature. At Wake Forest College (near Raleigh) he wrote stories and news for campus papers and took devilish delight in agnostic attacks on remaining conventions at the Baptist school. He relished H. L. Mencken's sallies at the preacher-ridden South, too, and joined the struggle against Ku Kluxery and fundamentalism which raged in North Carolina through the twenties. Following a disastrous year teaching at a small Kentucky college, he gained a reporter's job with the Charlotte *News*. There he remained (with a couple of breaks) until near the end of his short life. In Charlotte Cash became obsessed with his region, wrote several clever, iconoclastic essays for Mencken's *American Mercury* (one was entitled "The Mind of the South"), and for a dozen years he fitfully, agonizingly worked on his opus.[7]

The Mind of the South is 440 pages long. Barely a quarter of it is devoted to the Old South. Cash lavished 335 pages on the seventy-five years between the war and 1940. Nonetheless in his Book One on the Old South he introduced two major concepts which he developed in continuity to his own time: the "Man at the Center" and the "Proto-Dorian bond." The first epitomized Cash's southern sociology. His middle southern white ("at the center") was the yeoman, the common man. More so than Owsley (in that Cash exaggerated), the yeomanry *was* the South. Cash's aristocrats (save a tiny handful of "Virginians," a breed he loathed) were yeomen in disguise. In a brilliant literary device employing a hypothetical "Irishman," he described the booming cotton frontier of the 1830s as the historical kiln that produced the glossy gentry of 1860. Cash's Proto-Dorian bond referred to what recent scholars call the *herrenvolk* democracy of the

South: all white men, regardless of class, were brothers bound by their determination to protect white supremacy. Back in 1928 U. B. Phillips had in different words identified racism as the "central theme" of southern history. Cash's Proto-Dorian theme carried further, though, particularly as an explanatory model for the apparent lack of class consciousness in the industrialized South of the early twentieth century. Poor whites and blacks in both industry and agriculture may well have shared economic woes, but they could never combine because of the whites' racist bond across class boundaries. Thus the backwardness and failures of protest in the region, from the rural rebellions of the 1880s and 1890s to the textile wars of the 1920s and 1930s.[8]

Cash's third concept was the "savage ideal." Herein lies the visceral theme. In the desolate postwar South—"the frontier and Yankee made"—whites were thrown backwards not only politically and economically, but culturally, too. Yeomen became sharecroppers. Sons of college graduates were unable to proceed past bare literacy. The remaining intelligentsia lost ground. Everyone became mean. Economic depressions in the 1870s and 1890s brought on despair no other white Americans have known. In such straits southerners clung the more tenaciously to their sense of folk and to their god, the latter becoming more and more tribal, more and more a grim Calvinized Jehovah who tested His Chosen People beyond the trials of any ancient folk. "In the end," Cash wrote (by now meaning his own day), "almost the only pleasures which might be practiced openly and without moral obloquy were those of orgiastic religion and those of violence." Thus was "established what I have called the savage ideal as it had not been established in any Western people since the decay of medieval feudalism, and almost as truly as it is established today in Fascist Italy, in Nazi Germany, and in Soviet Russia—and so paralyzed Southern culture at the root."[9]

The theme of the savage ideal in effect synthesized the other two —the Man at the Center and the Proto-Dorian bond; and it summed up Cash's South. The savage ideal included a few occasionally endearing southern traits: hedonism ("hoggishness in enjoyment"), extravagance (particularly in language), good-ole-boyism, physical bravery, loyalty, patience in suffering. But mostly the "ideal" encompassed the "darker phases" (to borrow Tannenbaum's 1924 title): militant ignorance and anti-intellectualism; brutal, violent racism; xenophobia; self-righteousness and blind defensiveness. Thus the low state of high art, the Negro-lynching and Ku Kluxery, the suspicion of anything foreign, the incredible claims to superiority by the most impoverished of Americans. Cash's was a South acting upon distorted folk memory and visceral response alone. And to a generation witnessing the Dixiecrat movement of 1948, the *Brown* school desegregation decision's aftermath, the Montgomery bus boycott, and the ensuing "Negro revolt" in the South, Cash's South was more than adequate as an explanatory model. It was brilliant.

Only toward the end of the sixties, as the "Second Reconstruction" waned, did significant criticism of *The Mind of the South* come forth. C. Vann Woodward, the premier academic historian of the region, who had himself expressed but a few "reservations" back in 1941, led the way.[10] Woodward first attacked what should have been obvious to all, that Cash entitled a book *Mind* whose thesis was "no mind." Woodward suggested "The Temperament of the South," "The Feelings of the South," and "The Mindlessness of the South" as more descriptive of the book's contents. More telling of Cash's apparent predisposition was his omission of legitimate intellectual history in favor of the visceral. Jefferson, Madison, and Calhoun are barely mentioned. William Byrd II, John Taylor of Caroline, John Randolph of Roanoke, John Marshall, George Fitzhugh, Edmund Ruffin, Hugh Swinton Legare, and Alexander H. Stephens are not mentioned at all. Cash endorsed and quoted Henry Adams' disdainful barb, "Strictly, the Southerner had no mind"; and in *Mind* he foreclosed even a southern *need* for thought. There is no late eighteenth-century Enlightenment led by Jefferson, no Calhounian political theory worth explication, no "Reactionary Enlightenment" (Louis Hartz' term) in the 1850s, exemplified by Fitzhugh's writings.[11]

Cash's sociology and his "South" were both seriously distorted. His "mind" is really the guts of the Carolina Piedmonters and Appalachian hillbillies. He, like his contemporary Thomas Wolfe, knew no other South and could write of no other. Unlike Wolfe, Cash magnified his home alley into vast proportions. Cash's limited experience was compounded by his Carolinian's hostility toward "Virginians," a symbol of haughtiness no less perjorative in *Mind* than in Joseph G. Baldwin's witty *Flush Times of Alabama and Mississippi*, published a century earlier. Back at Wake Forest Jack Cash was most often aroused from classroom lethargy by Professor C. C. Pearson, a Virginia-born historian who baited Tar Heel students by invidious comparisons between "the mind of the Virginian" with "the mind of a North Carolinian."[12] Cash had the last word by relegating "Virginians" (aristocrats) to an inconsequential pocket of Dixie society.

In 1970 David Hackett Fischer, relentless exposer of historians' fallacies, employed Cash's book as a "classic" example of "the fallacy of composition," consisting "in reasoning improperly from a property of a member of a group to a property of the group itself." As Woodward had already observed, "Cash knew nothing first-hand of the Tidewater, the Delta, the Gulf, the Blue-Grass, or the Trans-Mississippi South." He did know that the nabobs had had their say; now "it was time to . . . have an unbiased history of the South from the hillbilly point of view." Fischer (like Woodward) conceded that with all its flaws, *The Mind of the South* remained "the indispensable guide" to the hill South—"a veritable Baedecker to the boondocks."[13]

Woodward, however, was equally disturbed about two other features: the absence of concern for southern blacks (one-third of the population) except for the injustice and violence whites did to them; and Cash's exaggeration of white consensus in describing the Proto-Dorian bond. In the first instance Cash was perhaps inadvertently evoking the helplessness of the segregated-but-sympathetic heart in even making contact with the Negro "mind." In the second, his exaggeration of the bond's hold caused him to ignore or minimize actual class conflict among whites. In *Mind* southern dissenters—abolitionists, Unionists, Republicans, Readjusters, Populists, progressives, liberals—get little if any shrift. Despite Democratic hege-

*Wilbur J. Cash,
photographed by
Alfred A. Knopf,
1939*

mony from the 1870s through Cash's life, the South was seldom solid.
Woodward, a liberal born and educated in the region, was heavily
influenced by Charles Beard's writing in the economic-conflict
school. Out of Woodward's own work—especially *Reunion and Reaction* and *Origins of the New South* (both 1951), and *The Strange
Career of Jim Crow* (1955)—emerged a drastically different South
from Cash's. In Woodward's South the bond of white supremacy ultimately foiled radical Populists and often simply precluded poor
people's cooperation, but there was class conflict aplenty. Woodward was indebted to Cash for a concept that explained the *illusion*
of white consensus, hiding the turmoil beneath. But to troubled Jack

Jimmie Rodgers, the first country music "super star," ca. 1931

Cash, illusions—of the Lost Cause's grip on southerners' imagination, of the bond's extent of power despite economics, of his hillbilly's pervasiveness—became compelling realities. And despite the
scholarly recognition accorded Woodward's work in the 1950s, it
would seem apparent that for a long time, until Woodward himself
delineated the inconsistencies, his work and Cash's coexisted peace-
fully and Cash remained the preeminent interpreter of the region in
print.[14]

In Cash's own mature decades there were emerging other significant communicators of southern heritage and culture—whom Cash
himself probably loathed—but who reached millions more than the
writer: the hillbilly musicians.[15] As Cash labored unsuccessfully to
teach language to Kentuckians in 1923, missionary record agents
from New York entered darkest Appalachia and north Georgia to re-
produce the wailing, mournful sounds of the Carter Family, "Fiddlin'
John" Carson, and others. Soon Okeh Records' artists were being
aired by pioneer radio stations all over the South and Middle West.
By the early thirties a true "country star" with national recognition
emerged in the person of a light-hearted but frail tubercular from Mississippi named Jimmie Rodgers. Rodgers was from a lower middle-
class family and worked for railroads in his home state until disease
forced his retirement at twenty-eight (1925). On the railroads he had
picked up guitar, yodeling, and much of the Negro country blues
style from black gandy dancers. Rodgers synthesized these with traditional white styles, and with his easy-going tenor became popular
not only with fellow southern whites, but with "pop" fans as well.

After Rodgers' death in 1933 country music expanded, became
yet more commercial, and encompassed the style and gaudy garb of
"western." Rodgers himself had incorporated some "western swing"
into his music. It came from Mexico via Texas and was distinguished
by its inclusion of percussion for a more distinct beat, and occasionally the piano. Rodgers, however, wore a straw boater and suit—
never the elaborate trimmed and spangled cowboy outfits affected
by Ernest Tubb and Gene Autry (both Texas-born), who imitated
Rodgers and became famous just before World War II. For all the am-

bivalence regarding southern identification that seems implicit in the "western" emphasis of the forties, however, few people could have doubted that the C & W stars were down-home boys and girls, Cash's own folks "at the center." During the war the nostalgia, homeyness, and moaning forlornness of their music infected many thousands and reinforced old fans. This despite the growth of instrument electrification and Nashville's noticeable flight from them hills to uptown.

No one better exemplified country music and all the tension in southern white values and styles after 1945 than Hank Williams. Farm-born near remote Georgianna, Alabama, in 1923, Williams grew up in the poverty southern farmers had known for several generations, and which got far worse when Hank was still a prodigy guitar-picker, composer, and singer on local radio stations. From the depths of the Depression, the war brought unprecedented population movement and economic prosperty, a dizzying turnabout in fortunes which transformed much of the region. The hold of the farm was finally broken. Urban migration, compounded by war separations, played havoc with traditional extended-family life and with marriages. The now-trite formula of hayseed-goes-to-city, findstrouble, was stark reality then—and more intensely so for southerners because proportionately more of them had been poor farmers and because the changes were so sudden. Hank Williams' life was a glittering, surreal monument to the times.

At fourteen (1936) he, along with his string band, the Drifting Cowboys, became regulars with station WSFA in Montgomery. They continued for a dozen years, in the meantime making appearances at Nashville's Grand Ole Opry which were broadcast nationally over WSM. In 1947 he began a lucrative arrangement with MGM records, at age twenty-three. His name became synonymous with white man's blues, and at least a dozen of his compositions were also recorded by popular singers such as Joni James, Frankie Lane, and Tony Bennett. Williams was twice married. On New Year's Day, 1953, he died in the backseat of his Cadillac, still "movin' on," but burned out by work, drugs, and booze at twenty-nine.[16]

Williams wrote and performed some notable light-hearted numbers which had the southern rural brand, such as "Jambalaya" and
"Settin' the Woods on Fire." But his genre was the sad song. More so
than Tubb and other honky-tonk singers, Williams was the trouba-
dour of sin and repentence, heartbreak and survival, alienation and
redemption through return to roots. The word *blues* predominates in
his titles: "Low Down Blues," "Weary Blues," "Lovesick Blues,"
"Long Gone Lonesome Blues," "The Blues Come Around." Syn-
onyms for *blues* were not uncommon, either ("Alone and Forsaken").
Even Williams' wit, understated in his nasal moan, conveyed a re-
signed sadness:

> I'm gonna do some ridin' on that midnight train
> Takin' everything except my ball and chain
> I'm leavin' now (repeat)
> I'm a long gone daddy
> I don't need you anyhow.

His down-home advice for losing "those jumpin' honky tonk blues"
was invariably something like "scat right back to my pappy's farm."
Perhaps, following his own remedy might have saved Williams.
"This city life has really got me down," he sang.[17]

In Williams' time a few country musicians composed political
and "social" songs. Bill Cox, a West Virginia partisan of the New
Deal, recorded the "NRA Blues" and "Franklin Roosevelt's Back
Again." Uncle Dave Macon did "All in Down and Out Blues," put-
ting down Wall Street. Roy Acuff poked fun at the New Deal. The
Martin Brothers sang ballads about the North Carolina textile strikes;
and Dave McCarn, who left his native hills for the mills, wrote sar-
donically in "Serves 'Em Fine" about the foolishness of giving up
green mountains in quest of green bills in the dirty Piedmont towns.
Outside the South the best-known protest singer was Oklahoma-
born Woody Guthrie, who migrated to California and wrote "Dust
Bowl Refugee," "I Ain't Got No Home in This World Anymore," and
many others. Guthrie became celebrated in New York leftist circles
as a proletarian artist and lost contact and popularity in the South.

He became a main link between southern country and the "urban folk" music of the future.[18] Performers who remained in the region probably did so at least partly because they were uninterested in "intellectual" pursuits, if indeed they were not actively anti-intellectual.

Yet it would be tendentious to brand country music as base and anti-intellectual, even though it has sometimes been both. The same could justly be said of the Tin Pan Alley ("pop") product. Most of the music is simply and properly nonintellectual. In terms of American perception of the South, the significance of country music's commercialization is that it pressed out to national boundaries a pervasive image of the visceral white southerner. He was languid, innocent of caprice and wisdom in handling money, moonstruck, and often drunk. Cash's word was "extravagant."

On the American theatrical stage of the late forties and fifties, more complicated southerners appeared, although the neurotic and glandular dominated, to be sure. New Orleans-born, Alabama-raised Truman Capote made noteworthy grostesque contributions, but the bizarre, engrossing characters created by Tennessee Williams veritably populated Broadway and its satellites from 1945; then they moved on to the movies. Meanwhile Williams became the best-known, most commercially successful, and probably the most critically controversial playwright in American history.

"Tennessee" is really Thomas Lanier, and he was actually born in Mississippi (in 1914), son of a rather footloose salesman. He chose the pen name to honor the Tennessee heritage of the Laniers (his mother's line), and because of a very brief happy time spent as a youth in Memphis with his maternal grandparents, who were strong and gentle. Several critical biographers have perceived Williams' father's influence—unreliable, mobile, materialistic—as symbolic of Williams' dramatic New South (or modern world); the mother's family's influence—security, books, religion—as symbolic of a doomed Old South. Williams was uprooted, insecure, and sexually ambivalent (until becoming exclusively homosexual in his early twenties). He finally finished college at the University of Iowa, tried unsuccessfully to secure government (WPA) support for his dramatic ambi-

tion (he was insufficiently social-minded); so like a legion of the
Depression young, he went "on the road"—to New Orleans, where
he became a happy Bohemian, and to California. His apprenticeship
was as onerous as Erskine Caldwell's. His entire experience and his
continuing strong southern identity confirmed Williams in the Gothic
School. Like his contemporary French existentialists, Williams was
overcome by an "underlying dreadfulness in modern experience,"
by inexplicable mystery and terror. He became, then, in his own
words, an "anti-realist," and with but a few exceptions the stage of
Williams' anti-realism was the South.[19]

Tennessee Williams was no more a student of southern history
than Hank Williams. Yet his chosen name, his nasal drawl, foppish
eccentricity, his residence in New Orleans' Garden District, and his
drama all convey a profoundly historic imagery. Taken very generally, many of the plays juxtapose Old and New South modes and
"values" which seem evocative of the playwright's parents. The Old
South was gentle, high-minded, but "Puritanical" and sexually re-
pressed. The New South (modern life, nemesis of the Agrarians) was
barbaric and anti-intellectual, but sexually liberating. Sexual fulfillment was the equivalent of liberation. Old South was prison and
death. Yet in that the doomed South embodied also gentility and art
as well as death, the struggle with liberation was hardly a simple
and righteous one without attendant tragedies.[20] The agony of Williams' characters exemplifies such "underlying dreadfulness."

In *The Glass Menagerie* (1945), the first of his long series of successful productions, Williams introduced two of his great females:
Amanda and Laura Wingfield. Utterly different, both are Old South
types. Amanda, who fancies herself still a belle, is middle aged,
abandoned by her husband, and stranded in a St. Louis slum. Her
poverty, pathetic tenement, and the brassy dancehall across the alley
are not her reality, however. Amanda is a dissociated personality
who only rages intermittently at her environment; most of the time
she dwells in her past (which may or perhaps may not have existed).
Daughter Laura is pretty but shy, wan, and victim of a crippled leg.
She cannot meet people, has never matured, and has dropped out of

business school because of persisting nausea. Indisposed to even occasional railings, she merely withdraws to her own dreams and her collection of delicate glass animals, the "menagerie."

Tom, the male protagonist and Laura's brother, is virtually a prototype for Williams' southern white men in future plays. He is a Hamlet—ambivalent, unforceful, torn between the sensibilities of the past and the competitive drive and materialism of the new world. Poor Tom has other burdens, too—his mother and sister, who repel and appeal to him in ways complex and poignant which help make the play a great one. But in the end he runs, just as his father had before him.

The romantic interest in *Glass Menagerie* for Laura is the Gentleman Caller, an acquaintance of Tom's from work. He is dynamic and attractive, but as it becomes plain, an artless, simple-minded stereotype of babbitry. He charms Laura, then breaks her glass unicorn and her heart. He is, of course, Williams' model modern-world man. He will probably "succeed." And it is significant that the Gentleman Caller is not a southerner.

In *Streetcar Named Desire* (1947) the magnificent female part is that of Blanche Du Bois, even more a dissociated personality than Amanda Wingfield, Blanche has arrived in a New Orleans slum to stay with her sister, Stella, who has married a virile ruffian named Stanley Kowalski. Blanche and Stella were to the family manor born, but now the old place has disintegrated and slipped away. Blanche herself has been obliged to leave her teaching position under sordid circumstances. So she arrives a pathetic mendicant. Yet like Amanda she pretends to gentility, condescension, culture. All the pretense is obliterated by Blanche's besotted bawdiness and exhibitionism, however. Finally she invites rape by her brother-in-law and goes mad, her ultimate dissociation with unpleasant reality, the surreal modern city. In madness she returns to her Old South.

There is no counterpart to Tom in *Streetcar*, but here the Gentleman Caller, Mitch, is southern; and in his ambivalent ineffectualness he suits Williams' typology. Stanley Kowalski, the simple-man/id, is not southern. His sexual power "liberates" wife Stella, but in her happy liberation-subjugation she has lost higher sensibilities. Poor sister Blanche, hardly immune to miscibility, loses her mind partly at least in order to retain her dignity and culture.

Streetcar was released as a film in 1951 and earned both commercial and critical success under Elia Kazan's direction. Marlon Brando played Kowalski; and Vivian Leigh (formerly Scarlett O'Hara, now Blanche), Carl Malden (Mitch), and Kim Hunter (Stella) won Oscars.

After Streetcar on Broadway came Summer and Smoke (1948), which introduced yet another memorable Williams female, Alma Winemiller. Alma is a prudish spinster, daughter of a minister in a small Mississippi town. She conducts prim, boring musicales and gives piano lessons to proper children, but secretly lusts for John Buchanan, a wild and handsome young physician who lives next door. Buchanan is a rare virile young southern male in Williams' plays. But there is a twist involving Buchanan which in the end renders Alma's reality the more pathetic and dreadful. Hungering for him, Alma ambivalently campaigns to convert John to righteousness. Following his father's tragic death, John is indeed reformed, but it is to someone else that he turns for married love. Alma ends up courting a vulgar casual lover in a public park.

In The Rose Tattoo (1951) Williams once more made his virile male nonsouthern. Alvaro Eats-A Horse (literal translation) is the magnificent, bellowing lover of the Italian widow. They all live on the Gulf Coast. Williams used the Dixie setting at least partly to introduce ugly southern neighborhood women who express Victorian (i.e. Old South) outrage at the sensual goings-on at the Latin household. In Twenty-Seven Wagon Loads of Cotton (published 1946), made into a Williams-authored film called Baby Doll in 1956, Williams once more employed a liberated-Latin versus ineffectual southern male scheme. Baby Doll (Carrol Baker in the movie) is a brainless but affectionate sexual object married to Archie Lee (Carl Malden), a bumbling incompetent as both lover and farmer. Enter Vicarro (Eli Wallach), an Italian (Williams' favorite nationality) somehow stranded in the rural Lower South. Vicarro cuckolds Archie Lee, Archie burns down Vicarro's property, but the Latin and the liber-

ated southern woman triumph in their own way. *Baby Doll* provoked a national uproar during the winter of 1956–1957, as Cardinal
Spellman and the Roman Catholic Legion of Decency condemned
the movie's "raw" sexuality. The South was becoming scandalously
voluptuary.[21]

Williams' own favorite play is *Cat on a Hot Tin Roof* (1955). It
takes place on the Lower South estate of an extravagant, lusty, self-
made planter-businessman, Big Daddy, one of Williams' best characters and certainly the most memorable and complex male. Other engrossing characters are Big Mamma, the long-suffering, subservient
wife; Gooper, the greedy, unimaginative son; his wife, Sister Woman,
with her brood of kids; and especially Big Daddy's favorite son,
Brick, and his wife, Maggie the Cat. Brick is a former football hero,
incipient alcoholic, a failure since college, and sexually ambivalent.
He is married to nubile Maggie, but still loves his dead friend and
sports buddy, Skipper. There are many important themes in the
play, but aside from Big Daddy's and Brick's roaring and painful
confrontation, the most memorable lesson in *Cat* is Big Mamma's
preachment to Maggie: "When a marriage goes on the rocks," she
exclaims to her daughter-in-law, pounding on Maggie's and Brick's
bed, "the rocks are right here!" Once more southern manhood (except dying Big Daddy's, anyway) is not up to snuff, and the thesis of
modern Dixie is ambivalence and impotence. Mind—culture and
sensibility—must give way to gonads.

Literal loss of his testicles by a weak young southerner climaxed
Williams' *Sweet Bird of Youth* (1959). Character Chance Wayne (one
of Williams' silliest puns) is a luckless gigolo who decides to go
straight, but ends up attacked and castrated by a mob for his trouble.
Suddenly, Last Summer (1958) was sheer Gothic horror, à la New Orleans. Violet Venable, the principal woman character, is no Amanda,
Blanche, or Alma, but a domineering, villainous grande dame of the
Garden District. She has abetted the perversion of her weird, homosexual son, Sebastian, who does little save dabble at writing one
poem per year. Sebastian marries Catherine Holly, however, and
Violet sets out to destroy her rival with psychological warfare. In the

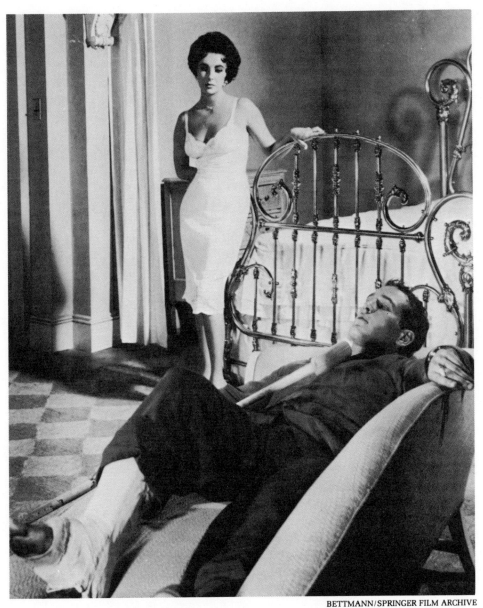

*Elizabeth Taylor as Maggie the Cat, Paul Newman as Brick in the
film version of Tennessee Williams' Cat on a Hot Tin Roof, 1958*

meantime Sebastian himself is destroyed during one of the family's bizarre vacations. He is eaten alive by hungry boy-waifs.

Tennessee Williams' modern South was more abnormal than Erskine Caldwell's. Females are mere creatures who have surrendered mind for physical liberation, or they are neurotics tortured by the Manichean forces focused upon the South. Or like Violet and the WASP ladies of *Rose Tattoo* they are simply vicious. Southern men are pusillanimous and doomed, or utter converts to modernity who have lost their southernness along with their ambivalence. Big Daddy of *Cat* is the great exception, but he is an anachronistic frontier builder, and he is dying, too, soon to be anachronistic no more. Brick may properly take Big Daddy's place, or he may not, leaving the "twenty-eight thousand acres of the richest land this side of the valley Nile" to just another machinelike modern man.

Hank Williams' mindless South was soulful and occasionally wry. Jack Cash's mindless South was violent but endearingly extravagant. Tennessee Williams' mindless South was pathological, doomed unless it put mind aside, then doomed to lose its distinctive identity. The media were set for a deeper plunge.

Chapter 6

Dixie Mellow

A man don't want to get above his raisin's, you know.
Stockcar driver Richard Petty

Before 1935 militant white supremacy pervaded much of both the popular and academic history of the South. After that, negrophobia waned in academia but moved toward the subterranean and insidious elsewhere. Faulkner's and Caldwell's blacks are few in number, usually only part of the landscape, and are treated rather sympathetically. Southern movies and a few best-selling novels perpetuated the coon, tom, and mammy.[1] Meanwhile academicians and a few members of government officialdom attacked racist history and stereotypes, and the Depression's impersonal forces lent urgency to an environmentalist social interpretation which stressed "conditions," "adjustment," and the need for harmony. After World War II traditional racist formulae were gradually turned upon their heads and employed by novelists and filmmakers for antiracist purposes. The results of this long-term movement upon the imagery of Afro-Americans would become revolutionary by the 1960s. But during the fifties the effect of scholarly revisionism upon southern and black public status was complex and ambivalent. The decade was a mellow hiatus.[2]

The black stereotypes created on film by Griffith and his contemporaries faded fast in the forties. Wartime anti-Fascist films such as *Casablanca* and *Sahara* attacked bigotry and portrayed Negroes with sympathy (albeit with superficiality, too). Then at the end of the decade came a remarkable series of racial message pictures: Ar-

97

Jeanne Craine and Ethel Waters in Pinky, 1949

thur Laurents' *Lost Boundaries*, Stanley Kramer's *Home of the Brave*, Darryl Zanuck's *Pinky* (directed by Elia Kazan), and a fine version of Faulkner's *Intruder in the Dust*. *Lost Boundaries* dealt frankly with the confused identity and fate of a middle-class New England family passing as white. Kramer's *Home of the Brave* was a war movie shot in secret to protect the production from hostile Hollywood bankers and bookers. It told the story of a black soldier irregularly assigned to a white reconnaissance team in the Pacific. A striking feature of this film about racism is that the South and southerners play no role. It would have been easy for Kramer to have exploited Dixie's savage ideal, but the black soldier and his chief white antagonist are both from the North. *Pinky*, on the other hand, was set in the South. The white actress Jeanne Crain played the title role of a mulatto nurse who migrates to Boston, passes as white, and becomes engaged to marry a white doctor. Returning home to be with her grandmother (played by dark Ethel Waters), Pinky confronts her own two-ness, rejects finally her fiancé, and decides to be a Negro. (Only in the United States could such a choice be available to one so light!) At the end she opens a nursery and hospital for blacks in a plantation house inherited from a benevolent white. The conclusion was "Faulknerian" in that southern blacks and whites worked out a settlement among themselves without yankee courts or bayonets. It is a magnificent film in every respect—even though the plot seems unreal now. Yet in 1949–1950 *Pinky* created a public furor, and like *Lost Boundaries* and *Home of the Brave*, it was banned over nearly all the South.

Intruder *in the Dust* was shown in the region, won critical acclaim, but strangely was not the financial success the other three films were. Thirty percent of American movie houses were located in the South, and Hollywood business people had believed the "southern market" could make or break a movie. *Intruder's* box office flop exploded the "southern market" myth, and courageous Laurents, Zanuck, and Kramer banked profits which inspired more cautious filmmakers to make more "Negro" movies in the fifties. These included *The Joe Louis Story* and *Go, Man, Go* (about the Harlem Globetrotters), and the weirdly 1929ish *Carmen Jones* (1954), Otto Preminger's all-black movie set in a New South factory town. Dorothy Dandridge played an animalistic vamp who seduces nice guy Harry Belafonte into deserting the army and fleeing with her to Chicago. But *Blackboard Jungle* (1955), set in New York City, and *Island in the Sun* (1957), set in the Caribbean, cast Belafonte and Sidney Poitier in struggles against oppression.[3]

Another concern of Americans in the late forties and fifties was the subversion of democratic institutions by wicked demagogues. It was the age of Senator Joseph McCarthy and the Red Scare, and Louisiana's Huey Long was still a living memory. The former Agrarian Robert Penn Warren's famous 1946 novel on demagoguery, *All the King's Men*, became a document for the times. Although only loosely based upon Long's career, Warren's novel reeks of the bayous and red-neck mobs. On the very first page an automobile speeds down a mirage-hot concrete highway past fields where "niggers" chop cotton in disinterested slow motion. Robert Rossen's film version, rather like Kramer's *Home of the Brave*, dramatically nationalized a phenomenon usually associated with Dixie alone. New York *Times* critic Bosley Crowther thought the movie was set in "an unspecified southern state," but viewers not so conditioned by the novel and Long's memory could (and can) see that *All the King's Men* on the screen could be anywhere in the United States, except possibly the Northeast. There are no southern accents. Actor Broderick Crawford, who won an Oscar for his portrayal of Willie Stark, spoke as he always does, in nonspecific, monosyllabic northern. Stark taunts his followers as "You hicks," not "You rednecks." In one long shot there is a palm (the movie was made in California); and Burden's Landing is rather bayou-like. But in practically all other respects Rossen flushed the southern association from his important statement about demagoguery.[4]

There were at least two other fifties films about demagogues. The first was definitely southern. *There Is a Lion in the Streets* (1953) starred James Cagney as the florid rooster of red-necks who campaigned against local cotton-gin barons. *A Face in the Crowd* (1957) was a more sophisticated feature which explored image manipulation and the psychology of megalomania. North Carolinian Andy Griffith, known until then primarily as a country humorist and as the comic hick in *No Time for Sergeants*, played an Arkansas hillbilly who becomes a media monster. Griffith promotes himself as well as products in radio and television commercials, then moves into politics. Finally, at a point where he threatens to become a dictator, he destroys himself through egotistical overexposure on TV. Writer Budd Schulberg and director Elia Kazan told a story with national significance, as Robert Penn Warren and Robert Rossen had. That they chose a southerner as subject is important only in that they

wished to demonstrate how an unknown—a face in the crowd—
might achieve power through the electronic media.[5]

In stark contrast to prewar fiction, the southern setting in Margaret Long's 1950 best seller, *Louisville Saturday*, was only incidental, too. It was a "woman's" book comparable to the "woman's"
movies of the forties. In the novel Long followed eleven female characters through an October, 1942, weekend in the Kentucky city near
Fort Knox. The women included an old woman grieving for her son,
an often-pregnant moron, flirtatious playgirls, a fortyish librarian;
there is even a four-year-old whose daddy is being shipped out.
Southern characterization does not control the novel. There is an absent cuckold—a pompous, cast-iron aristocrat from Charleston, as
well as poor whites from the rural South who work in war plants.
But the Charlestonian might have been a Bostonian, and plant
workers might have easily been one-time farmers from Anywhere,
U.S.A. The war, the army camp's proximity, and women's experiences dominate and direct the imagery created by this southern author. She was not obsessed with the past and locale.[6]

In contrast, bizarre twists of past and locale do dominate *Copper
Canyon*, a "B" western with stellar actors released also in 1950. Here
Confederate veterans and their families have gone west to start life
anew, mining copper. They cannot get their copper to market, however, because of a yankee syndicate which employs a smart agent-
saloon keeper (Hedy Lamarr) and a crooked, mean deputy (Mac-
Donald Carey!). Enter Ray Milland, a former rebel cavalry hero who
poses as an itinerant trick-shot showman. At night he becomes a sort
of Confederate Zorro, fighting the syndicate incognito to preserve
the American Way—which happens to coincide with the interests of
former comrades-in-arms. Neo-Confederate movies were possible in
1950 when the setting was moved away from the Reconstruction
South and the black population. In all other respects *Copper Canyon*
was in fact a Griffith-Dunning-Bowers sort of Reconstruction movie.
It was "progressive," too, in that here the underdogs, the Confederate immigrants, struggle against "the interests" and triumph. Milland is a one-man Ku Klux Klan. In addition to the elimination of the

racial element, the movie was softened by the old device of sectional reconciliation through romantic love. Lamar repents, deserts the syndicate, and falls for Milland; and a nice young yankee lieutenant falls for the belle of the southern encampment.

Comparable adjustments were made in *The Iron Mistress* (1952), an Old Southern-Texas frontier saga based upon a fictional biography of Jim Bowie. The "mistress" is his famous knife. Alan Ladd played Bowie, a Louisiana country boy who goes to New Orleans and falls in love with belle Virginia Mayo and her kind of life. Too poor to live his ideal, Bowie and his brothers decide to get rich. The film's director tried to convey this procedure in Louisiana during the 1820s by setting fast-paced, industrious music to shots of fields, white men sweating, and flashing newspaper advertisements for "Men Wanted"! The institution of slavery is virtually eliminated, except for the appearance of incidental tavern waiters and some house servants. The film thus avoided a "statement" about Negroes and slavery. By 1952, apparently, such circumnavigation was becoming necessary in order for more traditional motifs—the duel, adventure, belle-beau romance—to thrive.

Professional historians who wrote college textbooks could not avoid slavery and its cruelty altogether, like moviemakers. But Samuel Eliot Morison and Henry Steele Commager, two Pulitzer-winning yankee historians and coauthors of the influential *The Growth of the American Republic*, made an eloquent effort to defuse resurgent neoabolitionism. On black slaves they wrote in 1930: "As for Sambo, whose wrongs moved the abolitionists to wrath and tears, there is some reason to believe he suffered less than any other class in the South from its 'peculiar institution.' The majority of slaves were adequately fed, well cared for, and apparently happy. Competent observers reported that they performed less labor than the hired man of the Northern States." Not one word was changed in either the 1942 or 1950 editions.[7] As late as 1960 Dumas Malone and Basil Rauch (southerner and northerner, respectively) made a neat attempt at synthesizing Thomas Nelson Page and revisionism in their popular text, *Empire for Liberty*: "The typical slaveholding planter of Tidewater Virginia and Maryland was kind and patriarchal towards his human chattels, particularly towards those who served him personally, but he was greatly interested in 'getting a crop,' and he generally left the field hands to the mercies of overseers, who were notoriously brutal as a class."[8] Thus masters escaped the moral hook, just as in *Uncle Tom's Cabin*. What would sentimentalists have done without overseers?

In the most popular of fifties fiction about the Old South, race was meticulously avoided, while belle-beau romance and sabre-clashing adventure reigned supreme. One ingenious author dominated this genre, the extraordinary Frank Yerby. He is another of the great communicators about the South in this century. Between 1946, when *The Foxes of Harrow* appeared, and 1970, he published more than twenty novels. More than half concern the South, five were annual best sellers, and three are all-time best sellers: *The Vixens* (1947; 3,170,056 copies through 1966), *The Foxes of Harrow* (2,702,597), and *Floodtide* (1950; 1,801,097). Yerby is one of but a handful of humans to earn wealth at writing; at last report he works but half of each year. Since 1952 he has lived in Spain and on the French Riviera. He skiis in the Alps, races his own Jaguar in Nice, and relaxes at considerable lengths on the beach. Perhaps equally remarkable, Frank Yerby is a southern black man.[9]

Yerby was born in Augusta, Georgia, in 1916 and grew up segregated in the high age of Jim Crow. He attended all-black Paine College in Augusta, then earned a Master's Degree in English at Fisk. Following more graduate work at the University of Chicago he began teaching at black southern schools in the late thirties (Florida A & M and Southern University). In 1942 he quit teaching to take a Detroit war plant job which paid much better. He married a blond, very light-skinned octoroon, fathered four children, and settled in New York to write fiction to sell. Dial Press bought *The Foxes of Harrow* and *The Vixens*; then there was trouble with white neighbors; the Yerby's moved to Spain; then they were divorced—all within half a dozen years after the first book. Yerby ultimately remarried (to a Spaniard ironically named "Blanquita"), bought a Madrid apartment, and hardly missed a step in his rhythmic production of novels. If John Fox's name had been "synonymous with best seller" before World War I, Yerby's became an even better synonym after World War II.

Yerby's South was Margaret Mitchell's without Mammy. There are baronial estates supporting fabulous wealth, decadent aristocrats and frontier swashbucklers on the make, palid indoor belles and flushed hellions à la Scarlett or Jezebel. There are many duels among gentlemen over honor, horses, and women; and there is outright warfare where boys can nurture machismo. Principal characters in Yerby's books must be, he once wrote, "picaresque" and "romantic." Males must be "dominant" because United States men are emasculated, and middle-class women, the vast majority of his readership, want fantasy men to supply the needs their husbands do not provide. Sex there must be, but discreet. Plots revolve about "exterior conflict"—action; so characters need not be particularly ordinary, normal, or approachable. Blacks figure as characters hardly at all. That Yerby himself is dark was downplayed for years, and thousands of readers assumed he was white.

In 1959, at the height of his success, Yerby published a disarmingly frank essay in *Harper's* entitled "How and Why I Write the Costume Novel." Here he explained his fiction with an apparent cynicism as bold as Caldwell's, but Yerby made a strong case for his work. Few authors of popular literature (or of academic history for that matter) have been so clear and honest in revealing their *raison d'ecrir*. The "costume novel" was not history or historical fiction, he declared, but rather "a certain genre of light, pleasant fiction." Yerby reads extensively and conducts research for his novels, but after such efforts have driven him to write "history," those segments inevitably end up "on the Dial Press cutting room floor. Which is not a complaint," he insisted. "That is exactly where it belongs. For, at bottom, the novelist's job is to entertain. If he aspires to instruct, or to preach, he has chosen his profession unwisely." This rationale related closely to Yerby's position in the face of growing criticism that

Frank Yerby, 1969

COURTESY THE DIAL PRESS PUBLICITY DEPARTMENT

his works did not serve the human rights cause. He was concerned, but it was not his profession.

"Entertainments" set in the southern past were not to be seriously regarded, then. (One wonders how many Yerby enthusiasts read the *Harper's* article.) To literary critics who waved aside his novels as slight and therefore unworthy of their consideration, either, Yerby reminded readers that yesterday's popular culture often becomes today's high culture: "the classics of today are the best sellers of the past"; and, "a writer is unread only because he fails to communicate." Alexandre Dumas, a dark-skinned nineteenth-century popularist with whom Yerby liked to compare himself, wrote amusing and escapist novels that became classics.

Yerby disdained "realism," too. He wrote for average people, and the average person's real life was "a crashing bore." Life is shapeless, he philosophized, and "many, if not most of life's problems cannot be solved at all." The role of fiction then is to amuse, provide a shape of sorts, and happiness, escape.

Ironically, within a few short years Yerby disobeyed his own dicta and took up racial themes. *The Old Gods Laugh* (1964) was set in Haiti and sympathetically portrayed an Afro-Franco-American culture. Yerby set *An Odor of Sanctity* (1965) in Moorish Spain, where he had an African princess marry a white saint. *The Dahomian* (1971) reached at least metaphorically toward "black power," dwelling upon old West African kings and their dominative culture. All three sold relatively poorly—and were well received by major critics, verifying the errant author's 1959 thesis.

By the late fifties the typical southern film was a Hollywood version of stories or plays by Faulkner, Caldwell, or Tennessee Williams. Most of these movies were very good box office and critical successes. Blacks again had few roles, either as individuals or as preoccupations of whites. Whites appear as bigger-than-life characters preoccupied with each other. They are frequently perverse, but usually in ways somehow to be envied by moviegoers. The South was so *interesting*; it became chic. Except for the Irish and the Jews, perhaps, other white American minorities were hopelessly bland in comparison with these silver-screen rustics, parvenues, decadent gentry, nymphomaniacs, neurotics, and psychopaths. Passion flourishes in the same steamy earth as tobacco and cotton.

In 1958 alone Hollywood released *Cat on a Hot Tin Roof, God's Little Acre, The Sound and the Fury, Hot Spell* (an adaptation of Lonnie Coleman's play, *Next of Kin*, starring Anthony Quinn as a New Orleans husband unfaithful to Shirley Booth), and *Long Hot Summer*. *Long Hot Summer* was loosely based upon several Faulkner stories and starred Orson Welles in the role of Will Varner, the Big Daddy-style magnate of Jefferson; Paul Newman as Ben Quick, a charming Snopes type; and Joanne Woodward as Varner's prudish daughter whose resistance Quick overcomes to the satisfaction of her father. Anthony Franciosa played Varner's weak, gullible son, who is bested by Quick. The National Board of Review's Committee on Exceptional Films chose *Cat* and *Long Hot Summer* among its "ten best" films of the year (numbers six and four, respectively), and audiences loved both. Writing, scenery, and southern accents (except Franciosa's) were excellent.

God's Little Acre, finally filmed a quarter century after publication of the novel, apparently did well at the box office even though critics justifiably panned it. The novel's incest was excised, and casting was incredibly bad: Robert Ryan as Ty Ty, Aldo Ray as Bill Thompson. *The Sound and the Fury* was poorly adapted, too. Yul Brynner, utterly unbelievable as a southerner (even with hair) was cast as Jason Compson. Ethel Waters was a very credible Dilsey, however.[10]

Tennessee Williams' play, *Orpheus Descending*, about a young southerner's corruption, failed on Broadway, but as *The Fugitive Kind* (1959) it was a box office success. This may have been largely the result of casting. The producers chose three actors vastly experienced in Williams plays and southern movies: Marlon Brando, Anna Magnani (who had starred in *Rose Tattoo*), and the gifted Georgian, Joanne Woodward.[11]

Williams' *Suddenly, Last Summer* and *Sweet Bird of Youth* became movies in 1960 and 1962. Both were commercially successful, especially *Suddenly*. Gore Vidal wrote the screenplay, and Katharine Hepburn was cast as Violet Venable, Elizabeth Taylor as Catherine Holly. Williams was disappointed that Vidal (no doubt under pressure) provided a happy ending, with Catherine walking away arm in arm with her psychiatrist (Montgomery Clift). Veteran "southerner" Paul Newman played Chance Wayne in *Sweet Bird*; but Williams was embittered that Hollywood eliminated the venereal disease and the castration from his play.[12]

One of the National Board of Review's "ten best" films of 1960, however, departed drastically from this familiar, mellowing South, and may be said to have begun the wave of devilish southern movies of the sixties. That year Stanley Kramer made the popular play *Inherit the Wind* into celluloid.[13] It was an enormous success both critically and at box offices. The scene was the 1925 Scopes trial, in which Tennessee's antievolution law was tested in the hamlet of Dayton. Fredrick March, magnificently made up to look like William Jennings Bryan, portrayed the grand prosecutor and statesman of southern fundamentalism. Spencer Tracy played the Clarence Darrow character, the clever liberal from enlightened Chicago. The young John T. Scopes character represented a promise of future enlightenment from within the South. But of course in history and in the play-film, Scopes lost and darkness triumphed. Kramer abetted this Menckenesque portraiture by having his young schoolteacher appear the victim of local bigots and a larger savage ideal. In fact Scopes volunteered to provoke a test of the law for the American Civil Liberties Union; he was not set upon while innocently plying his profession. A small quibble, though. Kramer made not only great drama, but a perfect rehearsal for a grand new unveiling of Jack Cash's South at its worst. In the decade following *Inherit the Wind* southern whites made the Civil War Centennial an ugly, racist charade, murdered civil rights workers and black children, stood in schoolhouse doorways to bar Negroes—indeed fulfilled every explication and intimation of narrow-mindedness and cruelty displayed in 1925.

Harper Lee's best-selling novel (number three in 1961) *To Kill a Mockingbird* represented a sort of half-way between the homey, idyllic South and the devilish South. A mild-mannered Deep South lawyer has a wonderful relationship with his motherless children, who are growing up happily, but suddenly lose Eden because of fellow whites' Proto-Dorian bond. A hysterical white woman accuses a black man of rape. The lawyer takes the case, exposes the woman's injustice, but the black man dies anyway. Here Faulkner's "southern solution" to the racial problem fails dramatically. And in 1961, with black southerners on the march and Robert Kennedy as United States Attorney General, logic dictated "outside" intervention. But the portraiture was still softened by Lee's gentle and courageous lawyer and by her engrossing world of small town Dixie children.

In 1962, also, Dixie remained mellow on the best seller lists.

Faulkner's comedy of turn-of-the-century northwest Mississippi and Memphis, *The Reivers*, ranked tenth on the annual list. And Virginia Cary Hudson's *O Ye Jigs & Juleps* placed number four. (It placed fifth in 1963, also; and ultimately sold more than one and a half million copies.) At the age of ten in 1904, precocious, mischievous Miss Cary of Versailles, Kentucky penned a number of essays on school, going to church, her family, and neighbors. The essays were discovered, collected, and published, finally, to the delight of probably every reader. Southerness is not obtrusive, but rather an environmental feature which enriches the little book. Matrons are addressed as "Miss" so-and-so; there are black servants, holy rollers, Confederate veterans. "Mr. Lincoln said my grandfather's money was no good," Virginia wrote, "and he had to burn it all up." And there was this exercise in reasoning, à la Dixie youth: "China has millions of people. The tall ones live up North and the short ones live down South. My grandmother says my legs are too long. I would have to live up North and that would be awful. But maybe China does not have Yankees." [14]

A near-omnipresent southern image before the public during the fifties and after was the stockcar racer. Foreigners and yankees might dominate the chic grand prix and Indianapolis 500, but in the rough world of the souped-up family sedan, romantic fellows from the South were elemental. Stockcars apparently evolved from bootleggers' getaway machines, and they seemed a natural solution for speed lovers in a poor country: "formula" racers cost too much. In 1958 actor Robert Mitchum's bootlegger thriller *Thunder Road* aroused considerable interest in fast jalopies. Other publicity and the relative low expense of racing stockcars combined to launch a national craze. Of all drivers, however, Richard Petty was most famous, enduring, and southern. A native of Level Cross, North Carolina (near Greensboro), Petty is the son of a great driver and brother of a great mechanic. Well before his fortieth birthday he was a wealthy "superstar," yet Petty remained modest, folksy, and beyond corrupting glitter and materialism. In 1975 he still dwelt on the simple, extended-family compound in rural Carolina, explaining to a New

York *Times* reporter: "A man don't want to get above his raisin's, you know."[15]

The mellowest of public southerners, however, was easily Jay Hanna ("Dizzy") Dean. Born in 1911 the son of an itinerant share-cropper in Lucas, Arkansas, Dean grew up in a dozen rural cross-roads between Alabama and Texas. Left motherless at three, Dean quit school in the second grade to pick cotton with his father and brother. He grew tough and strong and pitched baseballs faster than anyone. His professional ball-playing career spanned 1929–1940, with the full seasons of 1932–1939 in the National League with the St. Louis Cardinals and Chicago Cubs. There his speed earned him the nickname "Dizzy." He was also wild, gregarious, and garrulous, having frequent brushes with the police and baseball management. His brother Paul played with the Cardinals, too, and was called "Daffy" because he vied with his brother in zaniness. Dizzy was a braggart, wit, and a rustic raconteur. A broken toe upset his pitching rhythm toward the end of the thirties, and his active playing career came to an end when he was only twenty-nine.

Dean moved then into broadcasting baseball (later football, too). Insofar as he was the most notoriously ungrammatical, malaprop-dropping man in public, this was a rather remarkable new career. A player might "lift up them feet," then "slud into thud base" in the Dean vernacular. He could never pronounce the word *statistics*—one of the most important in the sport; so he said "statics," and American fans relished a good ole boy whose wisdom in the game, unlimited supply of stories, and infectious enthusiasm made him seem one of us. In 1946 Missouri schoolteachers protested his gram-mar, syntax, and pronunciation to the Federal Communications Commission. Dean was, the teachers averred, a nefarious influence on youth, undermining formal education. A national debate fol-lowed in which *Saturday Review* publisher Norman Cousins (de-fender of many unusual causes) championed Dean. Network exec-utives apparently had periodic misgivings, but Dean remained popular. To sophisticates and other haters of country wit and music, nonetheless, "the Diz" remained a burden. During dull moments of televised games (there are many) throughout the fifties and sixties exuberant Dean could not resist breaking into his loud rendition of Roy Acuff's classic, "Wabash Canonball."

Dean represented to millions the best side of Cash's middle southerner. He was all fun and extravagance.[16]

Chapter 7

The Devilish South

I wonder if we'll ever see . . . the Southerner get any acceptance at all. I mean, it's the fault of the motion pictures, that have made the Southerner "a shitkickuh, a dumb fuckhead." He can't be sensitive, he can't be liked, and he sounds disgusting. . . . But it's just his sound. That's why Lyndon Johnson is a fluke—because we've never had a president with a sound like that. Cause we know in our culture that "people who tawk lahk thyat"—they may be bright, articulate, wonderful people—but "people who tawk lahk thyat are shitkickuhs." As bright as any Southerner could be, if Albert Einstein "tawked lahk thayat, theah wouldn't be no bomb."

"Folks, ah wanna tell ya bout new-clear fishin—"

"Get outta here, schmuck!"

Lenny Bruce, ca. 1964[1]

The new revisionist scholarship on the South, black history, and race relations flourished after World War II and came to dominate academic writing by the late fifties. A direct link exists between liberal scholarship and the momentous *Brown* decision of 1954 which declared unconstitutional school segregation. The NAACP legal team led by the future justice, Thurgood Marshall, argued against racial discrimination from an authoritative fourteen-hundred-page 1942 report compiled by the Swedish social scientist Gunnar Myrdal and entitled *An American Dilemma*. Myrdal's foreign citizenship lent the study an aura of objectivity, but the seventy-odd researchers and writers whom Myrdal's team comprised were overwhelmingly neo-

112

abolitionist Americans, including none other than W. E. B. Dubois. The result was an overwhelming report that deemed black Americans "inferior" only in terms of opportunity and environmental conditioning. Segregation was a critical instrument of this imposed inferiority. In 1954 the Supreme Court agreed unanimously.

A few months following the decision C. Vann Woodward read three lectures at the University of Virginia which were published the following year as *The Strange Career of Jim Crow*. His main thesis was that back in the 1890s and 1900s, southern whites had imposed segregation by law and that the law of Jim Crow had in turn imposed different behavior upon the South—a rather uniform practice of apartness which came to replace a haphazard nonsystem that had combined segregation and integration. *The Strange Career of Jim Crow* was a devastating attack on the social Darwinist assumption that segregation was a "folkway," and upon the irresolute Eisenhower policy of drift and procrastination, awaiting a gradual change in folkways before executing the Court's "stateway."

The same year Woodward's book appeared Alfred Knopf released a large revisionist history of slavery, Kenneth Stampp's *The Peculiar Institution*. Stampp, a white liberal professor in the University of California at Berkeley, spent years at research which went deeper into the subject than U. B. Phillips had during the progressive era. But Stampp forthrightly announced his personal intention of turning Phillips' open racism upside down, too. In his now-famous preface Stampp declared that to him Negroes were only "white men with dark skins" and that in studying the question of slave treatment, he assumed that the institution was unconscionable tyranny. His slaves were not Sambos, either, but runaways, rebels, malingerers, arsonists, and clever psychologists who "put on ole massa."

Already (in 1947) Knopf had published the first edition of what has become the standard reference on Afro-American history, *From Slavery to Freedom*, written by the University of Chicago's Professor John Hope Franklin. Franklin is an Oklahoma-born black man, but the thoroughness of his research and the all-business modesty of his writing lent his history a winning credibility even among southern white college students. In 1960 Franklin became the first to publish a short, revisionist synthesis of Reconstruction, too. His *Reconstruction: After the Civil War* was published in paperbound edition by the press of his own institution and won wide circulation. Kenneth Stampp's competing synthesis, *The Era of Reconstruction*, appeared in 1965 and remained a steady seller a decade later, when many others had entered the market, too.

Meanwhile, as Woodward's *Strange Career of Jim Crow* gained wide notice and provoked heated debate among academicians, the Reverends Ralph David Abernathy and Martin Luther King, Jr., launched their Montgomery bus boycott and founded the Southern Christian Leadership Conference. As Franklin's *Reconstruction* appeared five years later, the Baptist preachers were joined by more militant black college students, beginning in Greensboro, North Carolina, their famous sit-ins against segregation. The civil rights movement was approaching its take-off stage. Black and many white historians, political scientists, sociologists, and psychologists were in touch and in step.

Among popular culture communicators Lenny Bruce, the iconoclast-comedian, had been developing a brutally Menckenesque treatment of the fundamentalist white South for some years. About 1960 he included this material on a record album which reached a wide audience of aficionados, particularly college students. After suggesting that no one would take seriously a nuclear physicist with a southern accent, Bruce launched into a mumbo-jumbo "religious" harangue which concluded with a clear shout, "Have a snake!" [2]

In July 1962, madcap writer Terry Southern visited Oxford, Mississippi, arriving the day following William Faulkner's funeral there. His mission was to observe southern "culture" at the Dixie National Baton Twirling Institute, being conducted on the Ole Miss campus. Searching for the institute, Southern approached some local men sitting on town-square benches. He reported:

"Howdy," I say . . . "Whar the school?" The nearest regard me in narrow surmise: they are quick to spot the stranger here, but a bit slow to cotton. One turns to another. "What's that he say, Ed?" Big Ed shifts his wad, sluices a long spurt of juice into the dust, gazes at it reflectively before fixing me again with gun-blue cold eyes. "Reckon you mean, 'Whar the school *at?*' don't you, stranger?"[3]

Hollywood, in the meantime, moved very slowly toward the development of the neoabolitionist genre. The break with the Old South sentimentalist tradition which had sold so many movie tickets was difficult. Ambivalence over the break as late as the late fifties is best exemplified in the film version of Robert Penn Warren's 1955 novel, *Band of Angels* (1957). Hollywood took little of the book except its opening device and its title. Yvonne DeCarlo played Amantha Starr, a raven-haired plantation beauty of the Kentucky Blue Grass. Visiting Ohio, she rushes home following news of her father's death—to discover that *she* is among the "property" to be sold as part of his estate. Daddy had been a miscegenator; mother was really Mammy. So far a far cry from Margaret Mitchell or Thomas Nelson Page. Amantha is thus sold down the river to New Orleans; but she is purchased by none other than Clark Gable, playing Rhett Butler again. He takes her to his riverside estate, where they are greeted by respectful, singing darkies. But Gable also owns a different sort of slave portrayed by Sidney Poitier. Poitier is bright, proud, and profoundly unhappy as a slave, even though Gable treats him well and he has something approaching executive secretary status. During the Civil War Poitier deserts his master straight away, dons Union blue, and fights to free fellow blacks.

Practically all the film's genre breakthroughs were compromised at the conclusion, however. Poitier and other Federals track down Gable, a wanted Confederate, in his bayou hideout. Poitier would personally lynch ole massa for slave trading and owning. But Gable unloads a sentimental revelation which stuns even the bitter Poitier: In Africa Gable saved boy Poitier from a burning village being plundered by black slave traders. Poitier will fight on for equality in Reconstruction Louisiana, but he allows Gable to escape—with De-Carlo, thus tying a romantic bow on the package. In the end it is only Poitier's image and the prospective miscegenation of Gable and the alabaster complexioned Ms. DeCarlo which represent a new treatment of the Old South. Gable was still a gentle and wise master, and practically all the slaves except Poitier and DeCarlo seem contented.

The same historiographical ambivalence, incongruity, and exploitation of sex characterized the two remarkable, best-selling novels of Kyle Onstott: *Mandingo* (1957) and *Drum* (1962). The novels are remarkable, among other reasons, for their origin. In 1957 Onstott, a white man, was a seventy-year-old bachelor living in California. He had been raised in Illinois, and although an experienced writer, his work up until *Mandingo* had been entirely on the subject of dog breeding. He allowed later that since childhood he had "always been horrified and strangely drawn to slavery," and that "I've always felt that the human race could be regenerated by selective breeding." His Falconhurst novels, however, were not quite "the sort of thing I mean." Onstott worked at his twin obsessions, slavery and breeding, and finally his adopted son informed William Denlinger, new owner of the animal-breeding publishing house in Richmond, Virginia, that his father had thirteen-hundred handwritten pages which might interest Denlinger. "The book doesn't have any significance," said the son, "but it's like eating peanuts." William Denlinger decided to diversify, bought the manuscript, and put on a herculean one-man drive to promote *Mandingo*, personally visiting bookstores over much of the country and boosting the novel onto several national weekly best-seller lists. *Mandingo* did not immediately rank in an annual tally, but in a decade had sold 2,635,250 copies in cloth and paperbound editions. In the all-time best-seller listings of 1967 *Mandingo* ranked thirteenth among thirty-two selected southern books—ahead of John Steinbeck's *Grapes of Wrath*, Faulkner's *Sanctuary*, and several of Caldwell's and Yerby's novels.[4]

Mandingo takes place in the early 1830s at Falconhurst, the Alabama plantation of the Maxwells. Master is a sadistic miscegenator who has personally sired a large brood of mulatto children by his stable of sable wenches. Meanwhile he acquires a magnificent male specimen from the West African Mandingo tribe, whom he begins to breed selectively with slave women. The progeny are so attractive in the local and New Orleans markets that Maxwell abandons cotton and devotes his property exclusively to human reproduction. Onstott not only portrayed his planters as materialistic lustpots, but his white women are anything but pedestalized belles. Hammond Maxwell's blond wife, rejected by her sickly, neurotic husband in favor of his dusky beauties, seeks out none other than the Mandingo stud. Maxwell finds them out, and although he loves the stud better than his hound dogs, he has the Mandingo boiled alive for his transgression. Maxwell plunges a pitchfork into the Mandingo's chest toward the end as an act of mercy.

In 1961 Jack Kirkland (who earlier had dramatized *Tobacco Road* for Broadway and the screen) wrote a stage version of *Mandingo* which omitted the boiling conclusion. Dennis Hopper played Hammond, Franchot Tone his father, and Rockne Tarkington the Mandingo. The play folded early. In 1975 the novel was finally released as a film, infused with "black power" symbolism and advertised as a portrait of the "real Old South." Playing mainly along the "B" theater circuit, it drew a huge audience of blacks and made a great deal of money, even though Onstott's genre had more or less passed with the sixties.

Historian Kenneth Stampp, the principal authority on slavery at the time of *Mandingo*'s great popularity, affirmed the existence of perhaps two or three such "plantations" as Falconhurst. In addition, breeding probably took place in slave-trading centers such as Richmond and Washington, D.C. However, Stampp submitted that most slave breeding probably occurred as an "unconscious" policy of individual masters who lived in a country without access to resupply from Africa (after 1807), and which needed to increase the black laboring population to serve an expanded cotton kingdom. Falconhurst was a remote and bizarre historical possibility and hardly adequate reading for those seeking the "real" Old South. Yet young readers of my acquaintance saw Stampp's *Peculiar Institution* and Onstott's *Mandingo* as complementary. Stampp exposed breeding and renewed the abolitionist indictment of the masters for the humiliation of black families; Onstott wrote the novel: *Q.E.D.*

Drum, published by Yerby's Dial Press in 1962, is a pointless, 502-page rambler which had sold 1,148,260 copies by 1967. Here Onstott traced the lives—principally sexual—of three generations of African males, beginning with Tamboura, heir to the Hausa throne, who, as a boy about the year 1800, is betrayed by jealous relatives to slave traders. He ends up in Cuba, where after but a little field work he becomes valet to his master and chief stud to the wenches. Tamboura runs afoul of the system by becoming the secret paramour to master's French mistress, Alix. Tamboura is killed, naturally, but he has left the royal seed in Alix. She flees to New Orleans and gives birth to Drum, who is thereafter called the son of her black maid. Alix sets up a fancy bordello, and young Drum is a favored servant who inevitably must display his inherited sexual prowess. Alix stages live pornographic "dramas" for her customers' edification and delight. Drum's physique also equips him well for boxing, and he is champion of the city for some years before his violent death (not at the hands of whites for a change). Drum's black wife had just borne him a son, however, perpetuating the line as Drumson. Drumson grows up in the bordello, too, but Grandmother Alix decides to sell him at eighteen to an Alabama planter who was a regular visitor to the city—none other than Hammond Maxwell! At Falconhurst Drumson becomes a stud, naturally, and endeared to Hammond. Finally, in the midst of a bloody slave rebellion, Drumson lays down his life for the Maxwells. There may well be royal Hausa seed in some womb or another, but at book's end it appears that the line has been sacrificed to save the slavemongers from the slaves! This is but the most obvious evidence of Onstott's inconsistency as a revisionist communicator.

Onstott's peculiar institution existed not so much as a labor system to produce corn, tobacco, sugar, and cotton, as a system to impart prestige to slaveowners and a means for white men and women to gratify forbidden sexual urges. Masters, though sometimes ingeniously cruel, are generally fair and generous to slaves, because of economic considerations. Slaves were valuable; but Onstott also had a peculiar respect for the code of paternalism. Still, characterizations are "Freudian," one-dimensional stereotypes. The books are filled with lurid all-night couplings (never, curiously, described in detail) of fierce females trying to "dry out the sap" of "hot blooded stallions." Men are evaluated according to the number of times they can copulate within an hour. Between black and white Onstott indulged in vulgar, racist typing. Blacks are by definition more lusty; they have no minds, only glands. Whites generally are lacking sexual energy, but have more vigorous imaginations which lead to a wide variety of perversities, including homosexual attacks upon blacks.

In the end Onstott must be judged only a prurient abolitionist, and his betrayal of poor Drumson in the final sacrifice for the Maxwells practically disqualifies him from the new genre altogether. Yet his portraiture was still a death blow to the essentially Victorian cast of the Old South. He liberated prurient fascination long in the closet, and styled southern whites rather like those appearing on ugly television news reports on the civil rights movement.

Back in Hollywood the moviemakers gradually moved toward ugly portraiture of the white South, too. Stanley Kramer once more led the way. His *The Defiant Ones* (1958) was a formula chain-gang drama with a liberal twist. Tony Curtis (an unlikely southerner) and Sidney Poitier are two prisoners who, chained together, escape devilish Deep South lawmen. Hateful and distrustful of each other, their enforced "integration" leads finally to mutual respect which lasts long after the chain is sawed away. Then a white woman directs Poitier off into a swamp. Curtis, discovering her treachery, plunges into the morass to save Poitier even though this means certain recapture for them both. After a long chase during which Poitier chooses to help wounded Curtis rather than hop a freight, the lawmen find the pair, Poitier tenderly nursing his erstwhile racial enemy.

In 1960 Columbia Pictures released a Korean War drama called *All the Young Men*, with Poitier as a sergeant who prevents a southerner from raping a Korean woman. By this date such a portrayal was inevitable. (In 1949 Kramer, in *Home of the Brave*, resisted the temptation to make his bigoted soldier a white southerner.) Three years later Otto Preminger offered the southerner-as-beast genre in a sequence of his film, *The Cardinal*. Black Georgia priest Ossie Davis goes to Rome for aid in desegregating a school. Finding no support, he and a future white cardinal, Tom Tryon, initiate their own protest movement and for their trouble are mercilessly beaten by Ku Kluxers. In 1967 Preminger exploited virtually every Gothic stereotype of modern white southerners in *Hurry Sundown*, a ramshackle portrait of post-World War II Georgia. There are snobbish United Daughters of the Confederacy types; a spoiled belle (Jane Fonda); a dumb sheriff in sweaty khakis; a mammy; racist red-necks; an amoral, alcoholic New South business promoter; and a demented white child who screams through much of the movie. There are also violence, adultery, and a strong hint of interracial sex. The only thread of plot connecting it all is an integrationist morality play taking place in the nearby boondocks. On small adjoining farms young black and white soldiers return from the war to take up their simple agrarian existences again. They distrust each other (like the literally chained men in Kramer's picture nine years before), but a voracious land development company which would gobble up their bucolic bases drives them together. Brotherhood triumphs.

Preminger's formulaic juxtaposition of small white and black farmers in an otherwise rigidly segregated twentieth-century South is in theory at least historically valid. While urban residencies were separated by law early in the century, a movement to segregate racially rural "neighborhoods" failed. Considerable *de facto* segregation in rural areas is evident in census records, but no doubt many instances of such "integration" remained. Little else in the film rings true.[5]

Meanwhile, as Dr. King delivered his "I Have A Dream" speech at the 1963 civil rights march on Washington, as television revealed "live" the brutality of southern police and red-neck "segs," and as Congress moved toward enactment of the civil rights bill of 1964 and the voting rights bill of 1965, the black struggle and the cause of integration triumphed at last in Hollywood. In 1963 the Broadway show *Purlie Victorious* was adapted for film as *Gone Are the Days*.

Ossie Davis portrayed the loquacious black preacher who tricks a dumb planter into turning his barn into an integrated church. The same year Roger and Gene Corman released a cheap integrationist movie, *The Intruder*. A mysterious white provocateur comes to a little town and causes riots, bombings, and KKK rides. His final undoing proved that black and white folks could get along without troublemakers. The *Intruder* also proved that the integrationist genre had become acceptable to "B" filmmakers, the last echelon of Hollywood. *Black Like Me*, a 1964 version of the famous 1961 book, was perhaps the American film world's high statement on the subject. James Whitmore played the white investigator who had his skin dyed dark and set out for darkest Dixie, to "feel" racial hate.

Sidney Poitier and Tony Curtis flee Dixie justice in
The Defiant Ones, *1958.*

BETTMANN/SPRINGER FILM ARCHIVE

Some blacks expressed scorn, but whites following Whitmore's odyssey took the film seriously. The heavies were of course white southerners.[6]

One of the genre's best was an "art" film with little circulation. *Nothing But a Man* (1964), a low-budget production acclaimed by critics, was the story of a young black man (Ivan Dixon) in Alabama who does not accept segregation or his elders' accommodation to the system. Insisting upon his dignity, Dixon is constantly in jeopardy. Finally he quits his job, leaves his wife (Abbey Lincoln) and begins wandering through the South. The trip takes him through urban slums and depressing illuminations of unemployment, alcoholism, illegitimacy, and man's identity problems.[7]

In the late sixties the civil rights movement began to falter at the height of its success. Militant Stokely Carmichael of the Student Non-Violent Coordinating Committee (SNCC) raised the cry of "Black Power" on a Mississippi highway in 1966. White members of SNCC and the Congress of Racial Equality were expelled, along with black integrationists such as John Lewis of Georgia, who had been a movement pioneer. Malcolm X, the American black Muslim assassinated in New York the year before, was virtually canonized as a prophet of the doctrine of separation-for-survival. White liberalism was scorned as an insidious form of paternalism; many blacks, especially the young, thought separation from the whites the only road to justice and dignity. Young white activists were drawn off by the Vietnam War protest wave, and, increasingly radicalized by confrontation with police and troops, many agreed with black separatists on the usefulness of counterviolence. Integration was no longer chic; the white South became a brutal paradigm for a racist and imperialist nation, and there was no room left for sentiment and older notions of southern community. Meanwhile Dr. King and his preacher-led SCLC, successful in the South, carried their integrationist cause to the North, marching in the Chicago suburb of Cicero for open housing. King and his cohorts were targets for throwers of eggs and bricks, and Congress defeated an open housing bill. Early in 1968 King was murdered in Memphis; then for the second warm season in a row, black ghettoes across the country were the scenes of riot, fire, and death. Capitol Hill itself was shrouded in the smoke of a conflagration in the nearby black section. They were mean times.

The racial and ideological crisis raged in popular culture, too. In *Finian's Rainbow* (1968), the southern aristocrat was lampooned on film. A black graduate student (Al Freeman) gains temporary employment at the mansion of Senator Rawlins (Keenan Wynn), who requires servants to shuffle. Rawlins, gasping and strangling, desperately calls for a glass of Bromo-Seltzer. His servant assumes a Stepin Fetchit pose, shuffling in place, interminably, while the senator suffers. In *The Heart Is a Lonely Hunter* (also 1968), based upon Carson McCullers' novel, an accommodationist black physician in the South disapproves of his daughter's militancy and also her marriage to a surly laborer. The young husband is hurt by whites; the doctor tries to win redress in the old respectful way and is rebuked; so the old tom is reconciled to his daughter and to the new day of protest.

In 1969 Ossie Davis produced and starred in a revisionist drama called *Slaves*. Black novelist John O. Killens coauthored the script and Davis filmed in Shreveport, Louisiana. Popular singer Dionne Warwick played the slave mistress of a swaggering master, and Davis was a tom who turns into a rebel. It was a poor film which apparently sold well only in predominately black theaters. The film exploited interracial sex, and the plot was trite, with Davis sacrificing himself inexplicably in the end to save Warwick. Curiously, too, the writers had their slave rebels as house servants instead of field hands. Yet there is an abundance of white cruelty in *Slaves*, and no viewer could mistake its message about a very savage Old South.

The New South received its blows, too, in a variety of movies. Perhaps the most effective was not a "southern" film at all, but the drug culture/motorcycle sensation, *Easy Rider* (1970), with Peter Fonda and Dennis Hopper. Buying cocaine in Mexico, the pair sell it and take off on their bikes toward New Orleans and Mardi Gras. They meet increasing hostility from red-neck type local folk as they proceed, particularly from the police. An exception is a drunken lawyer played well by Jack Nicholson—but he is done in by the same violent, intolerant forces which finally destroy the motorcyclists. In one of the most shocking scenes in a shocking age, they are shot nearly to smithereens.[8]

The South perhaps more than ever had enormous metaphoric significance to the interpretation of national concerns and dreams. William Styron's best-selling novel, *The Confessions of Nat Turner* (1967) evokes the age. Reactions to this extraordinary novel reveal, more than could a shelf of *Congressional Quarterlies*, the irreconcilable positions of racial liberals and new black militants. The Old South was battleground.

Styron was then a successful white novelist in his forties who had some years before departed his native Hampton, Virginia, for southern Connecticut and the New York literary scene. Among his friends were a host of yankees white and black, fellow transplanted southerners such as C. Vann Woodward (at Yale since 1962) and Willie Morris, the Mississippi prodigy who became editor of *Harper's* at about age thirty, and who at thirty-two published a delightful autobiography called *North Toward Home* (1968). Morris' book was of course largely about regional (as well as personal) identity, a subject obsessive to Woodward and many southerners, particularly after they leave the Old Country. Styron, a liberal calling the North his home, too, shared this southerner's need to resolve identity through exploration of roots—or reexploration of home from a new perspective. *The Confessions of Nat Turner* was to a considerable extent just such an exploration for Styron.

In 1965 he revealed (in a little book edited by Morris) that he had been searching for a fellow Virginian who had long intrigued him, the Southampton County slave revolutionary of 1831, Nat Turner. Styron had read and reread Turner's dictated "Confessions," taken down by a hostile white lawyer as Nat awaited his trial and execution. And Styron had combed Southampton for scenes and artifacts of those bloody late-August days. He did find a ramshackle house— then used as a corncrib for hogs—which the rebels had visited and where Nat had personally slain a teenage white girl, Margaret Whitehead. Otherwise the "quiet dust" of that old Southside county did not speak to him. The exploration thus became a "literary" one for Styron. The historical record would never reveal answers to all his questions, so the novelist chose to employ his imagination, within the context of historical foundations, and compose a "meditation upon history." [9]

Styron labored under the mistaken impression that Turner's was the only nineteenth-century slave revolt in the United States. [10] Allowing for this error, Styron still legitimately wondered why there were fewer U.S. rebellions than elsewhere in the Western Hemisphere. He also wondered why a slave who said his first master was kind would murder "good" whites; and why did a gentle, deeply religious preacher become a rebel leader? Nat's own "Confessions" raised more questions: especially, why did Turner himself kill but one of the fifty to sixty white victims?

Styron's literary-historical solution was a portrait of an institution so capricious, and controlled by whites so ambivalent about slavery and slaves, that kaleidoscopic possibilities were more the rule than the exception. Masters were hard-nosed materialists exploiting powerless black laborers, but they were also sincere Christians. Whites were brutal racists who raped slave women (such as Nat's mother), but who also believed the family sacred and insisted upon converting slaves to their puritan concepts. As for the blacks, they understood their misery and knew their enemies, but they also discriminated among whites, who included the bad, good, and indifferent. At best Styron's whites are profoundly mixed up, trapped in an ugly world not entirely of their own making—slavery was a very old system—but guilty of receiving power and reward handed down. At worst his whites are ugly-eloquent specimens of Dixie at its most vicious.

Nat, through whom Styron composed all the portraiture, is a very special man. Pampered as a child by a loving white family who taught him to read the Bible, Nat learned that he was special, and that after further education for life out in the world he would be freed. But the premature death of his owner and the hard economic

The capture of Nat Turner, 1831

times of the family and region played a cruel trick. Nat was sold; thus the framework of his paradoxical behavior toward whites and the system.

Styron wrote in the heyday of neo-Freudian explanations of culture and behavior, and Nat's sexuality played a determining role in the author's solutions to certain explanatory problems. Styron has Nat masturbate weekly and have a homosexual encounter at fourteen. He never marries, but fantasizes about white women, who symbolize a sort of ideal of cleanliness as well as the dominant white esthetic standard, which also logically denigrates darkness. Toward the end, then, Nat's murder of Margaret Whitehead may represent for the fictional revolutionist a personal and cultural statement and resolution of inner conflict as well as a revolutionary act.

Nat as Styron's holy man learned his religion from whites, as well as his cultural standards. Sensitive and dreamy, his idealism is shattered by white models' hypocrisy. Cruel reality, a growing sense of his own magnetic power, and religious dreams of battling black and white angels converge. He foresees a new Kingdom of God forged in righteous carnage. One must conclude that Styron's black man became the extraordinary rebel because of cultural training and conflicts whites set up in him.

On the bloody path to the Southampton town of Jerusalem, Nat's continued ambivalence is evidenced by his inability to kill. His sword was light and dull (we are informed by the real Nat in his confessions); it glanced off the head of Travis, merely wounded another. So slave Will, the bloodthirsty chief executioner of the rebellion, did Nat's work, finally threatening Nat's authority. Thus the necessity of Nat's one killing, carried off awkwardly with a broken fence rail.

That blacks carried word of the insurrection to Jerusalem and that some stood with white troops and defeated Nat's band in battle, was the final cruel irony, the last statement on the insidiousness of slavery. Nat escaped, tried to rally survivors, then took to the woods. At last he gave himself up for jail and the hanging oak. Skin was taken from his dead body, and at least one white claimed later to carry a purse made from it.

White critics praised Styron's "meditation"; historians expressed disapproval of a novel using historical names and altering some facts, but generally approved the portrait of slavery. C. Vann Woodward declared Styron's "the most profound fictional treatment of slavery in our literature." [11] Liberal white readers North and South were deeply moved, and several not-so-liberal middle-class ladies of my acquaintance were converted to warm support of Dr. King's integrationist movement because Styron awakened social conscience. James Baldwin, probably the best-known American black writer then, also applauded Styron's work.

But Baldwin was virtually alone among the black intelligentsia. In 1968 ten distinguished intellectuals delivered a blistering rebuke: *William Styron's Nat Turner: Ten Black Writers Respond*. The contributors included Lerone Bennett, Jr., senior editor of *Ebony* and a much-published popular historian; psychiatrist Alvin F. Poussant, a veteran of the movement in the South; novelist John A. Williams; Professor Charles V. Hamilton, chairman of Roosevelt University's political science department; and John Henrik Clarke (editor of the response), associate editor of *Freedomways Magazine* and editor of two books about Harlem.

A few of the black writers were hysterically illogical, sounding rather like members of the Daughters of the American Revolution defending the Founding Fathers against debunkers. One objected to Styron referring to the rebel as "Nat"—another honkey addressing a grown black man familiarly. Nat's last name was his first owner's, of course; he never subsituted "X" or a name of his own choosing. Nearly all the contributors objected to Styron's character's masturbation, boyhood homosexual experience, and fantasies about sex with white women. Styron demeaned a hero. Here the critics were behaving like early nineteenth-century white romantic nationalists who, among other mythmaking deeds, expunged the "damns" and "hells" and bad grammar and spelling from George Washington's papers before publication. Most Americans were aware of Alfred Kinsey's findings that masturbation is normal and that most boys have pubescent encounters which might be considered "homosexual." As for fantasies of sex with white women, not only did the dominant understanding of racism at the time include the theory of lust for forbidden fruit, but many militant blacks were broadcasting its veracity. In 1963 black sociologist Calvin Hernton published a widely circulated paperback called *Sex and Racism in America*. More renowned was Black Panther Party leader Eldridge Cleaver's *Soul on Ice* (1968). In 1968, too, white Professor Winthrop Jordan of Berkeley published *White Over Black*, a long, carefully researched, National Book Award-winning study of the historical origins of white racism in the English-speaking world. Jordan, a neo-Freudian historian, affirmed what W. J. Cash and countless others had offered *a priori*: that U.S. racism was a white male's ideology designed partly to emasculate black males. It was not Jordan's task to elaborate and extend the logic so, but Hernton and Cleaver were brutally insistent that black men dreamed of retaliation through sexual access to white women.

On other grounds the critics were more justified, although some asserted "truths" without empirical proof. For example, Styron chose to make Nat utterly the creature of white culture. Exactly who taught him to read is uncertain; Styron chose the white Turners. Nat knew his father was a runaway, and he was probably influenced by an African-born grandmother; but Styron chose to minimize early links to protest and a separate black cultural alternative. Nat may have had a wife and a "normal" heterosexual existence; but Styron chose to render him a tortured, celibate priest.

Styron was correct in wondering why Nat did not kill until late. But he chose to ignore another aspect of Turner revealed in the original "Confessions." Leaving the Travis house, Nat was reminded of an infant left behind. Kill it, he ordered a follower: "Nits make lice." There could hardly be imagined a more bone-chilling instance of revolutionary purpose. No ambivalence here.

In truth many, many details of Nat Turner's life will probably never be established in certainty. They are lost or garbled in conflicting, unsubstantiated reports after the rebellion. Some of the black critics grabbed at assertions made by the white abolitionist and

Union army officer Thomas Wentworth Higginson, who wrote about Turner thirty years following the revolt, basing much of his story upon fuzzy memories in Southampton. Historians cannot adjudge such assertions any more valid than Styron's.[12]

The novelist's *Nat Turner* remains a great artifact of the late 1960s, not of the early 1830s. It is a very good novel (in my opinion) which many white people perceived in a positive, soul-searching way, emerging more humble through knowledge of a continuing tragedy in American history. I believe that the black writers were wrong in attacking Styron as a "racist" and polemicist.

On the other hand Styron's Turner appeared at the most inopportune moment in Afro-American experience. Creation of a black rebel without what most Americans consider macho nobility, at a time of complicated and emotional cultural renaissance for blacks, was to stab at least part of Black America at the heart. In justice to Styron, it was an accidental crime. As a historian, however, I still cannot forgive his use of a real, vitally important name in his novel. "The Confessions of Ceasar Jones" would have eased some of the tension, but in the late sixties it was unfortunate for any white to have presumed a black identity. It was a time, once more, for a simple, devilish South, one useful for building a proud black self-concept and for the purging of national sins.

Yet in very short time redeeming blacks would reach their own cul de sac. This is nowhere better illustrated that in John W. Blassingame's excellent *The Slave Community: Plantation Life in the Ante-Bellum South* (1972). Blassingame is a Yale-educated Ph.D., a young colleague of C. Vann Woodward in Yale's history department, and sometime director of the Black Studies program. His *Slave Community* is the best short treatment of slavery and is widely used in college courses.

Blassingame's book is first a comprehensive attack upon Stanley Elkins' remarkable 1959 study, *Slavery: A Problem in American Institutional and Intellectual Life*. Among other important theses, Elkins had declared *a priori* that "Sambo," the docile slave, was the "prevalent" personality type among the Old South's black population. Sambo was not endemic to Africa, however; he was created in America by an insidious closed system which robbed him of any psychological references except those provided by masters. Blassingame, militantly entitling his work *Community*, asserted that a host of black references existed inside slavery: cultural survivals from Africa including music, dance, and folklore; stable families with strong fathers; a nurturing Afro-American religion; and many strong individuals such as conjurers, whom whites as well as blacks respected and feared. Blassingame did not propose Nat or Will as stereotypic replacements for Elkins' Sambo. Rather, he wisely proposed a credible variety of slave personality types that existed in a system that was not closed. Generally, however, his slaves were very troublesome, not docile. They are a prideful resource possessing a comprehensive subculture (community) which represents something approaching an ideal for many black people today.

The problem with *The Slave Community* is Blassingame's parallel emphasis upon the neoabolitionist model. The volume is amply illustrated with pictures of torture devices and scenes of pursuit and family division—most of them drawings from antebellum abolitionist papers which are not specifically identified for readers. Combined with a text which characterizes masters as heartless, the pictures evoke an institution more like Elkins' closed system than one in which a strong black community could exist. On one hand, for example, Blassingame presented Henry O. Tanner's warm painting of a man with boy and banjo in lap (*The Banjo Lesson*, 1918)— which he did not identify by artist, title, or date, but retitled *A Father's Love*, apparently wishing to show strong paternal role models in slavery. On the other hand Blassingame showed parents and children being sold apart. The inconsistency is not reconciled. College students asked to write essays confronting the myths that slaves were docile and without their own culture, and that slavery was a benign institution, almost invariably perceive this paradox and conclude that Blassingame has exaggerated one or the other sides of his story. Having read that the black family was a ruling influence and seen "a father's love" illustrated, students discover late in the volume Blasssingame's assertion (supported by evidence from the Lower Mississippi) that *most* families were broken by whites who were concerned only with profit. Thus the cruel *cul de sac* of "black power" history: if slaves were to be rehabilitated as models for late twentieth-century cultural development, logic seemed to demand that slavery (and the masters) be rehabilitated, at least somewhat, along with them. Such dilemmas signify the end of genres.

Chapter 8

Dixie Redux and Demise

Went to sleep last night in Detroit City.
Dreamed about the cotton fields back home.

from Mel Tillis' "Detroit City," 1970

Country music makes America a better country.

Richard Nixon at Opryland, 1974[1]

Well, the so-called Southern thing is over and done with, I
think.

Walker Percy, 1974[2]

Spanish Moss Business Dying Out

Labadieville, La: The last known person to make a living
by ginning Spanish moss, the tangled symbol of the Deep
South, says it is disappearing and he may have to go out of
business.

"There's something killing the moss," Laurence Duet, 59,
said, ". . . mostly pollution in the air, I believe."

Associated Press Report, September 26, 1975

Readers of Leon F. Litwack's *North of Slavery: The Negro in the Free
States, 1790–1860* (1960) knew very well that the South was not
the exclusive preserve of racial prejudice and segregation. Indeed
Litwack's work, especially in tandem with C. Vann Woodward's
Strange Career of Jim Crow, showed that segregation as a systematic
replacement for slavery's social control function, actually began in
the North during the decades following the Revolution and northeastern emancipation. But Litwack's readers were probably nearly
all fellow professors and college students. The dramatic revelation

133

(to whites at least) of racism's ugly pervasiveness north of the Ohio and Potomac had to wait until toward the end of the sixties, when Dr. King and fellow open-housing marchers were rocked, spat upon, and vilely cursed by northern whites. Television recorded it all. Suddenly the devilish white South, for years evoked on live TV by plump mothers verbally abusing frightened little black children at schoolyards, dissolved in the vision of plump yankees behaving the same way. In the fall of 1969 a federal judge ordered Mississippi school administrators to "desegregate now, litigate later," and the following academic year (1970–1971) southern schools became the most unsegregated in the nation. During the early seventies most bad publicity regarding desegregation came from the North. Boston —the old refuge of abolitionists—disgraced itself during 1973–1975, while news from Charlotte, Little Rock, and scores of smaller southern places was good news. Demoted southern black teachers and principals paid heavily for desegregation, but on the other side of the ledger, students adjusted well. Whites abandoned "Rebels" as school sobriquets to accommodate black schoolmates with somewhat different historical consciousnesses. The Stars and Bars came down.[3] These events and many smaller but telling signs announced a watershed in southern history and imagery. For example:

About 1971 Winston cigarettes finally abandoned its infamous slogan,"Winston tastes good, like [sic] a cigarette should" in favor of "Down Home Taste." One full-page magazine advertisement showed a chic couple (perhaps returned to the rural South from some big city), relaxing at mama's Thanksgiving Day table and preparing to blow smoke on the turkey. The message about the region was clear: the white South represents home, family, good old values.

During the fifties Old South and Confederate advertising imagery had fallen off sharply. In their place the industry hunters came on full steam ("every day is production day in Georgia") with a new roar: Yankees settling in Dixie would find yankee culture. Even small towns possessed theater groups, orchestras, art museums, and concert and lecture series, promoters bragged. There was a resurgence of Civil War exploitation during the Centennial: Old Crow bourbon's makers sought to identify themselves with Nathan Bedford Forrest, and the First National Bank of Chicago dated its founding from a battle in 1863. But not until the early seventies was anything approaching the volume of the thirties and forties resumed. Distillers, as usual, led the pack: "Bourbon drinkers in this fast-paced automated age are hankering for a taste of the easy-going past." Auto-makers tested the imagination. General Motors parked a 1972 Chevrolet before a plantation manse and appealed to Margaret Mitchell: "You can almost see Rhett Butler swooping Scarlett O'Hara into his arms."[4]

In 1971 James Meredith returned to his native Mississippi to set up residence and a law practice. Nine years earlier his admission to the University of Mississippi had provoked a statewide furor and pitched battle on the campus between segregationists and federal marshals. Five years before Meredith had been wounded by a shotgun-wielding white who lurked by a "freedom march" highway. Meredith had moved to New York City, but now decided that Dixie was his home after all.

He was not alone among Afro-Americans. The same year Meredith moved back down home, George Gallup polled black Americans across the country with the query: "All things considered, life in the South is better for blacks." Nationally, a remarkable 49 percent agreed; 30 percent disagreed; 21 percent expressed no opinion. Regionally, western blacks tended most to disagree (36 percent). Tellingly, southern blacks (63 percent) most agreed with the statement. Some time in the 1950s the ongoing outmigration of southern Negroes had finally reduced the southern black population to the point that for the first time in American History, a majority lived outside the old slave states. In the late sixties and seventies the region continued to become whiter, but the rate of black migration slowed, and a much-publicized return to the South began. The August, 1971, number of *Ebony* magazine was devoted entirely to the South and the subject of resettlement in rural and small-town areas.[5]

Simultaneous with this national refocusing upon the black South there emerged in Nashville a *black* Grand Ole Opry singing star,

"Country" Charley Pride. The debt of country music to Negro musical influences has been noted already, but to a public accustomed to associating Nashville with all the ugly implications of "red-neckism," Pride's ascendancy in the close aftermath of the civil rights movement was nothing short of revolutionary. A handsome, drawling Mississippian with a passion for baseball, Pride specializes in older ("hard core") country songs and sounds rather like a husky Hank Williams.

Another item: by 1970 there were 650 AM "all country" radio stations in the United States and Canada. California alone claimed the twenty-four which collectively reached the largest audience. By mid-1975 the number of AM and FM country stations approached a phenomenal 1,150, as hundreds of older stations around the nation hastened to capitalize upon the explosive popularity of a music previously described only pejoratively as hillbilly.[6]

White Americans increasingly identified the South with rustic simplicity. This association became even easier after 1970 with the sudden appearance of an opossum cult, headquartered in Alabama but claiming 40,000 followers nationwide. (For their membership fees, cultists received a bumper sticker stating "Eat More Possum.") The Possum Growers and Breeders Association of America, Incorporated, held its first national conclave and opossum judging in Clanton, Alabama, in 1971. To the victorious creature the association awarded its "Beauregard" designation. The 1972 Beauregard sold for $10,500, and Frank B. Clark of Clanton, president of the association, announced plans to breed "superpossums" weighing fifty pounds which would provide protein for the Third World's starving multitudes.[7]

Before leaving the culinary realm, who could ignore the late sixties and seventies Kentucky Fried Chicken phenomenon? The franchise operation was founded by "Colonel" Harlan Sanders, a robust old Kentuckian with snow-white hair, van dyke, and the white suit of a late nineteenth-century Bourbon. A master of advertising, Harlan had by 1975 extended his image and ubiquitous red and white striped eateries to Alaska, Mexico, Japan, and Abu Dhabi.

In the world of scholarship, early in 1974 two white economists blasted through John Blassingame's slavery *cul de sac* and created a rehabilitory highway for both slaves (they insisted) and masters. Robert Fogel and Stanley Engerman, pioneers in applying computer technology to history ("cliometrics"), published *Time on the Cross* after some years of gathering new data and resorting the old. Among the score of startling theses they offered: (1) slavery was a profitable, viable labor system largely owing (2) to capitalist incentives offered to slaves by wise whites. (3) Black women were seldom sexually exploited by white (or black) men, typically remaining chaste until the ripe statistical age of twenty-two. (4) Only about 2 percent of black families were broken by the slave trade. (5) Within the strong slave family system, husbands and fathers were not only dominant, but this dominance was encouraged and protected by masters for both cultural and moral, and practical economic reasons. Thus in contrast to the image evoked by their title, Fogel and Engerman created a slave system more closely resembling (as some outraged critics put it) a bassinette than a cross. Most historian-specialists were skeptical, and in 1975 a thorough critique appeared in the *Journal of Negro History*, then in book form from a university press. But in the meantime Fogel and Engerman appeared on NBC-TV's "Today" program, and interested educators and other readers seemed to assimilate their theses without regard for the historians' doubts.[8]

In the nation's capital during 1973 and 1974 television cameras trained every day of the Watergate hearings upon a previously obscure North Carolinian, Senator Sam Ervin. Ervin was a character out of fiction. Heavy, gray, in his seventies, he personified the country's amazement and righteous indignation at the crimes of the Nixon administration, quoted the Bible and the law from memory, and charmed millions with his learning and wit. With country musicians and television's Walton family, he embodied the new respectability of the South. Students wore T-shirts bearing his raised-eyebrow image and the legend, "Uncle Sam." Sophisticated Dick Cavett treated Ervin reverentially when the senator appeared on Cavett's ABC-TV program early in 1974. Fellow North Carolinian Tom Wicker of the New York *Times* noted disdainfully this yankee "discovery" of southern wit and character; he remembered hearing far better "hot stove" stories than Ervin's while a cub reporter in the Tar Heel State. Wicker also recalled Ervin's opposition to desegregation in the fifties and support of United States involvement in Vietnam in the sixties. But no mind, never matter.[9]

Yet, as fast as the devilish South genre was fading, few genres so deep-rooted as neoabolitionism disappear suddenly. In fact television viewers in particular were treated to some of its best examples in the early months of 1974: "The Autobiography of Miss Jane Pittman" (CBS-TV, January 31); "The Migrants" (CBS-TV, February 3); and "Wedding Band" (ABC-TV, April 24).

"Miss Jane Pittman" was the best of the dramas and the best example of neoabolitionism (better, in my opinion, then anything in any medium during the sixties). Written by a white, Tracy Keenan Wynn, from Ernest Gaines's novel, the story followed Jane Pittman (Cicely Tyson) from her girlhood in Louisiana slavery to extreme old age in the early 1960s, when after a lifetime of accommodation to whites, she defied the law of segregation by drinking from a courthouse "whites only" fountain. Except for a few insidious paternalists, Wynn's whites, Old South and New, are vicious and depraved. During the Civil War a pathetic white woman recoils when Jane and a boy drink from her cup, and curses them as the cause of her menfolk's deaths in battle. At the turn of the century and again prior to her dramatic walk to the fountain, men close to her are murdered by whites in retribution for their civil rights activism. Wynn's symbolism was most heavy-handed when he had Jane's Texas cowboy husband, Joe, killed by an albino horse. The black characters are stark, from toms and mammies safely ensconced in servitude by benevolent whites, to powerful heroic types such as Joe Pittman and Ned, the Spanish-American War veteran murdered by a Cajun hitman. Ned's mother is an earth-mother heroine who lays low a number of pattyrollers in hand-to-hand combat before meeting her own violent end.

"The Migrants" was a New South drama by Lanford Wilson,

based upon a Tennessee Williams story about migrant farm workers. The Barlow family includes parents (Cloris Leachman is the strong mother), a pregnant daughter, her tubercular husband, two younger daughters, and a teenaged son (Ron Howard). They are cynically exploited by a labor boss who extorts money from police who collaborate in controlling the migrants' work choices and keeping them away from town merchants. The boss sells groceries and whiskey from his truck, on credit, and pads his secret accounts. Leachman and a black woman deliver the daughter's baby in a field when a hospital will not admit her without assurance of $150. Then the son-in-law dies at work after a bloody spasm of coughing. No welfare agency or church will bury him, so his half-covered corpse rides about in the back seat of the Barlow station wagon, beside his wife and new baby. The boss finally produces a $700 burial loan which mortgages the family's labor for the foreseeable future. The ambitious teenage son, meanwhile, despairs of ever working the family clear and flees with a factory girl from a nearby Carolina town. They think they are escaping, but one knows that, in Cincinnati, their destination, there are thousands of southern refugees like them, little better off, and now cut off from loved ones. The remaining Barlows head north into Virginia, more debt, and utter hopelessness.

Wedding Band was a miscegenation drama based upon Alice Childress' 1972 off-Broadway play. Joseph Papp produced and codirected the teleplay, starring J. D. Cannon as Herman and Ruby Dee as Julia. The tragedy is set in Charleston in 1918. Julia, a black seamstress, has had a love relationship with Herman, a white baker, for a decade. Julia is the focus of harassment, white and black, and she changes residences often. They are unable to marry because law and public and family sentiment forbid it. Herman, furthermore, owes his mother $3,000 and is unable to protect Julia financially. But they celebrate their tenth "anniversary"; Herman presents her with a ring. They are shown kissing, caressing, and in bed together. Then the crisis: Herman falls seriously ill at Julia's place. His mother and sister, refusing to recognize the relationship, must fetch him. They humiliate Julia. Herman, feverish and hysterical, launches himself

Charley Pride

into a racist recitation of a famous John C. Calhoun speech on inequality. Julia is alienated. Later Herman wanders away from his mother's home in delerium. The white women again march to Julia's, argue violently, and Julia denounces whites and whiteness with painful intensity. Finally Herman shows up with two tickets for New York in the "colored section" of a steamer. Julia confronts him with his racist values and latent hostility to her. He insists upon his innocence, but gradually sees her truth and they are reconciled. A black has succeeded in educating a white on her own terms. There will be no escape, though, for Herman dies in Julia's arms as his white womenfolk howl for admittance at her locked door. The South is a devilish place, indeed, and while we may know that New York would have been a poor refuge, the playwright made no point of this.

Despite the considerable artistic and historical value of these three television films, they were rather anachronistic in 1974. Their genre had already been undermined. Even during the sixties, for example, the television comedy series, "The Beverly Hillbillies," had been popular. A picaresque Appalachian family strikes oil, resettles in a southern California mansion, but never gives up its quaint ways. The situation established, the writers devised scores of episodes exploiting the Clampitts' obliviousness to conspicuous consumption and modern conveniences. Only slightly beneath the ridiculous surface of the comedy was a portrait of honest, guileless simple folk, not far in fact from the nobility of John Fox's highlanders and the sympathetic sharecroppers of 1920s fiction. "The Andy Griffith Show" was also a link to the South's return. As popular as the Clampitts, Griffith, a native of North Carolina, portrayed a friendly, small-town sheriff. Other characters in the all-white cast included a comic incompetent deputy (Don Knotts); Griffith's Tom Sawyerish son (Ron Howard); Aunt Bee, a sort of white mammy; and an assortment of townspeople who demonstrated that the South possessed as much homey charm as the Middle West. These two programs were exceptions to the prevailing genre and, in effect, maintained a reference while the devilish imagery ran its course. In the meantime media "events" of 1967 and 1971 reveal decisive shifts away from the hostile to a very friendly Dixie.

The first was the release of a movie, *In the Heat of the Night* (1967). In many respects it was a fine example of neoabolitionism. Sidney Poitier plays a Mississippi-born black who has become an ace Philadelphia police detective. During a visit back home he is drawn into a dangerous criminal investigation by the local sheriff, a paradigm of the red-neck constable played by Rod Steiger. Steiger has a chilling resemblance to Sheriff Rainey who had been implicated in the 1964 murders of three civil rights workers near Philadelphia, Mississippi—sweaty khakis over bulging body and all. Steiger calls Poitier "boy," "nigger," and tries to humiliate him as a professional policeman; but of course Poitier wins the day and becomes a credit to his race. More significant, Steiger's sheriff shows genuine reform, finally volunteering to carry Poitier's suitcase to the depot. The devilish Dixie sheriff had begun a remarkable metamorphosis. No direct connection is asserted here, but within three years, by coincidence, the Chrysler Corporation began spending enormous sums advertising Dodge automobiles, employing a jolly southern rural "sheriff," dressed in unsweaty khakis, who stopped attractive young people in sporty cars, then sent them on with a cheery "Y'all be careful, now, heah!"

More bizarre is the history of Earl Hamner, Jr.'s novel, *Spencer's Mountain* (1961). Virginian Hamner set his story of a Depression-era family in his native Blue Ridge country. In 1963—heyday of neoabolitionism—a Hollywood film company set the movie version in Wyoming's Grand Tetons (and starred Henry Fonda and James MacArthur as the father and number one son). Then in 1971 CBS-TV launched a series based on Hamner's work, but reset the story in Virginia and called it "The Waltons." It was an enormous success both critically and in viewer-count: 40 million each week in 1973. By 1975, in its fifth season, nonsoutherners were beginning to think of the program without specific regional identity, so great was its appeal. But Hamner's own drawling voice-overs at the opening and closing of each segment were strong reminders that the South had risen again—even for yankees who did not realize that often-mentioned Charlottesville is in the heart of the Old Dominion. Vir-

Earl Hamner,
creator of
"The Waltons"

COURTESY EARL HAMNER/LORIMAR PRODUCTIONS, INC.

ginians regarded Hamner as a cultural hero, and even in the Tide-water flats his name inspired pride.

In 1973 the Virginia Press Association named Hamner "Virginian of the Year," and the famous novelist, now "executive story consultant," descended from New York to Virginia Beach to accept his award and to explain the charm and power of "The Waltons." His speech was a folksy paean to conservative sociology, a rebuke to the "counterculture" of the late sixties, and a masterful exploitation of the then faddish escapism called the "nostalgia cult." "They say that you should never let a Virginian start talking about his family," he said, "because you're liable never to shut him up," although Hamner demurred, as a self-proclaimed introvert. He was born in Schuyler, Nelson County, in 1923, and grew up during the Depression with his parents, three sisters, and four brothers. They were poor; yet "it seemed to me then, as it does now, that we were blessed with a good life." They climbed hills, flew kites made of brown paper, feasted on "fried chicken on snow white cloths over picnic tables," ate watermelon, and atoned for sins at the Baptist church. At night "we would call goodnight to each other, then sleep in the knowledge that we were secure. We thought we lived in the best of times."

Much later, after Hamner had become a New York writer, he related, "I learned that we had been 'economically deprived': That we lived in a 'depressed area' and that we suffered from a disease called 'familism.'" Familism is "a type of social organization in which the family is considered more important than other social groups or the individual." Unaware of the affliction, "we thought we loved each other. Even today, with a highfaluting sociological name for it, I still prefer to call it love."

On "The Waltons," Hamner said, his primary "aim is to entertain. But certain values keep creeping in": "We are reaffirming such old-fashioned virtues as self-reliance, thrift, independence, freedom, love of God, respect for one's fellow man, an affirmation of values which are typically Virginian and which have sustained our country for nearly 200 years." The show, he declared, preaches "familism," a "disease . . . rampant here in Virginia." [10]

There is an unmistakable conservative militance in Hamner's remarks which seems to go beyond crowing over personal success. Yet other than unnamed "sociologists," there is an absence of designated foes who do not affirm self-reliance, thrift, independence, freedom, love of God, and respect for one's fellow man. Hamner returned to the home sod from New York, which provincials south and west have long designated as the lode of iniquity. Virginians of my blood and acquaintance perceive "The Waltons" as an affirmation of their way of life, a long overdue "true" picture of the South, and a rebuke to something vague, unsettling, urban, impersonal, criminal, alien— perhaps New York. "Waltons" fans in Cincinnati, Dayton, Cleveland, Pittsburgh, and New York (of my acquaintance) do not of course perceive the show quite that way. They are innocent of sec-

Cast of television's "The Waltons"

tionalism, but like southerners they do not like the alienation of person from person, person from place, in modern life; nor are they happy about rising divorce rates, runaway children, crime, soaring welfare rolls, or immorality in private and public life. "The Waltons" presents a small, tractable world where place, people, and extended family ties are real. It is a pleasant escape, but certainly no more an escape than the films of the Depression years themselves.

Nor is "The Waltons" much better history than its Manichean opposite in genre, Caldwell's South of the 1920s and 1930s. This is not to deny the specific accuracy of either Hamner or Caldwell—although I believe Hamner closer to the mark, or "norm." The Hamner-Spencer-Walton family and the Lesters may well have coexisted in reality. No doubt for many Europeans the Hundred Years War was the best of times—for others the worst. The issues are of course typicality and popular perception. Historians must take both extremes into account, but generalize that neither is representative. To the student of popular culture, "The Waltons'" significance is that it reversed dramatically the Caldwell-Faulkner portraiture of the humble white South, and furthermore that it created a *national* reference whose very southernness began to evaporate. No Pittsburgher could personally relate to Ty Ty Walden's cotton patch; it set southerners apart by definition. But "The Waltons," where actors' poor attempts at Virginia accents got worse as the years passed, evoked a set of responses with an appeal far beyond Confederate borders. In the seventies Americans needed a sense of community perhaps more than ever. Southern literature, for all its Gothic quirks, had traditionally offered intense loyalty to locale and family. Finally, on television, the tradition served the middle-class masses everywhere.[11]

Hollywood offered several subgenres of a sympathetic South. *The Flim Flam Man* and a version of Faulkner's *The Reivers* (both 1969) fell into the realm of folksy comedies. George C. Scott portrayed a charming rural con artist (flim flam man) outwitting Harry Morgan's not-so-bright sheriff. Steve McQueen played Faulkner's character Boon Hogganbeck in *The Reivers*, a turn-of-the-century yarn about a wild trip to Memphis in a "borrowed" automobile. Rupert Crosse played Ned McCaslin, a black man rendered somewhat cleverer and brassier than in the novel.

Sounder (1972) may be the best small film ever made about southern black people. Directed by Martin Ritt and based upon William H. Armstrong's prize-winning novel for children, it tells a very simple story very well. In 1933 Louisiana, a young sharecropper is sent to jail for a year for stealing meat for his hungry family. Will the family survive his absence? Make a crop? With the aid and comfort of a lovable dog named Sounder—the answers are yes; a happy ending. In a Negro school a teacher raises black consciousness, invoking the name of W. E. B. DuBois, but *Sounder* is not a "black power" statement, à la 1966. Whites are oppressors, but petty rather than vicious; they are merely part of the system. The film is a bittersweet statement about survival and dignity, light years removed from 1930s films about blacks and the South. There is little to offend the historian.

Tick . . . Tick . . . Tick (1970) was contemporary history. Football hero Jim Brown starred as the new (and black) sheriff of a Lower South county at a time when southern blacks were indeed being elected to such offices (as well as to state legislatures and Congress). Here the whites are suspicious and hostile, but Brown endures and finally proves to their satisfaction that his administration is more loyal to justice and fair play than to racial solidarity. Compared with contemporary movies which celebrated black power and emphasized hostility to whites and separation (e.g. Melvin Van Peebles' *Sweet, Sweetback's Baadasssss Song*, 1971), *Tick . . . Tick . . . Tick* was mild, accommodationist stuff. But the film has the ring of authenticity, too. In black belt Greene County, Alabama, in November, 1970, William Branch and Thomas Gilmore were elected judge and sheriff, respectively, gaining the county's highest elective offices and bringing to an end the age-old domination of the area by the white minority. They had power and the opportunity to throw out virtually every white officeholder and wreak revenge for past wrongs. Instead Branch and Gilmore, both preachers and Martin Luther King disciples, were firm but conciliatory. They "left open the door" to whites, sought ways for them to save face while adjusting to the new order, and took care to leave many in offices while securing control.[12]

The Liberation of Lord Byron Jones (1970) was a sensationalist film based on Tennessee writer Jesse Hill Ford's popular 1965 novel. There is a cruel and corrupt white policeman and a nymphomania-cal black temptress (Lola Falana), but Ford reversed Kyle Onstott's sex-stereotypes. Falana is the policeman's lover, and it is her black husband, a staid, tomish mortician, who is the cuckold. When he pleads with his wife to end her affair, she exclaims, "No, daddy, why he's twice the man!" [13]

Buck and the Preacher (1972) is another post-black-power movie. Harry Belafonte directed and starred with Sidney Poitier and Ruby Dee. Belafonte is the preacher; Poitier is Buck, a former slave and Union soldier; Dee is Buck's eloquent woman. The film is set in the Southwest just after the Civil War. A wagon train carries black pio-neers away from the old Confederacy and white oppression to some all-black settlement-to-be. On the way, Dee declares her bitter disil-lusionment with the American Dream: Racism "has soaked the soil like a poison. There ain't goin' to be no forty acres—an' no mule." Conflict comes in the form of white marauders who stalk the wagon train, hoping to return the former slaves to some new bondage back in the Southeast. Buck and the Preacher defend the pioneers, kill the marauders, and rob a bank to raise money. So far the scenario is pure "black power," with two-dimensional whites and a separatist mes-sage. But the film is post-black power in that with the exception of Dee's dialogue, little of the ideology is treated seriously. Rather, *Buck and the Preacher* is delightful high farce—a parody of the "B" western with some telling jabs at "white" history, as well as some historical nonsense.

There were indeed former-slave pioneers from the South, the "Exodusters," who established all-black settlements in Kansas and Nebraska. There were black cowboys, too, and outlaws who held up banks. When Belafonte had his oppressed pioneers join up with In-dians to defeat the bad white guys, however, creating a sort of Third

World liberation front, he indulged in sheer fantasy. A sizable number of the U.S. troops who policed and subdued the Plains Indians between 1865 and 1890 were blacks (contrary to Hollywood's traditional story), and many of them were southerners and Civil War veterans like Buck. The historical scenario pitted white and black together against red. But the film treatment of this improbable combination is tongue-in-cheek, just like the marathon gunfight at the end, in which the two heroes, apparently perforated with bullets, get up and ride away in triumph.[14]

Conrack (1974) was another southern directed by *Sounder*'s Martin Ritt. He also produced and coauthored the script, based upon Pat Conroy's autobiographical novel, *The Water Is Wide*. Set in the contemporary South Carolina Sea Islands, the novel and film related Conroy's adventures as a teacher on one of the impoverished, marshy islands, populated almost entirely by blacks. Conroy (called "Conrack" by his engaging charges) is a southern white convert from his bigoted upbringing. As portrayed by actor Jon Voight, Conroy is charming, mod, enthusiastic, and ingeniously unorthodox as a teacher and man in a tough situation. His adult antagonists are the old-fashioned superintendent who finally fires him, and the island's other teacher, Mrs. Scott, a delightful but authoritarian personality who despite her dark color believes in "fundamentals" and the maxim that "colored people must be beaten" to learn. Conroy disagrees, romps with the children, earthily broaches sex education, unveils the world of Beethoven and Brahms, and introduces football and swimming. His downfall comes when he defies his boss and takes the children to a white neighborhood in Beaufort for Halloween trick-or-treating.

It is a "white liberal" movie with an unprecedented southern hero. In the abolitionist and neoabolitionist genres, the liberal white must be a yankee; but *Conrack* successfully bolted tradition. During the late sixties black militants such as Stokely Carmichael had rudely exposed the smug, paternalistic motivations of white liberals supporting the civil rights movement: whites would "uplift" their poor degraded black brothers, guiding their progress all the way.

The historical analogue was the bigotry of antebellum white abolitionists exposed by Leon Litwack and other historians in the sixties. The real Conroy and director Ritt appeared sensitive to this situational danger, and they have Voight comfortably escape paternalism in defiance of Mrs. Scott and the superintendent. "The old plantation is gone," Conrack declares to his colleague, "and you're not making an overseer out of me." Voight's egalitarian love of the children and the rest of the black community is convincing, too.

The only problem with *Conrack* is that while the white teacher expands his students' horizons with the learning of Europe and greater South Carolina, there is no awareness that the black Sea Islands may have cultural attributes of their own worthy of study and preservation.[15] Given the recent furor over Styron's *Confessions of Nat Turner* (in which a white author had purportedly denied a black access to his own people), as well as scores of popular and scholarly encomiums for black studies, *Conrack* is remarkable for its lack of consideration for Gullah (the low country slave language) and other aspects of Afro-American culture rich between Charleston and Savannah. Nevertheless it is a fine film which has probably gratified southern white liberals at least as much as "The Waltons" has pleased the nostalgic and conservative.

Far more popular than the folksy South and the liberal South subgenres, however, was a new direct-action, law-and-order South introduced in *Walking Tall* (1972). Made on a modest budget, the film earned a reported $35 millions in two years and inspired a 1975 sequel (. . . *Part II*). *Walking Tall* was based upon the career ("80% real") of Buford Pusser of McNairy County, Tennessee. Joe Don Baker, a near look-alike, portrayed Pusser. After being beaten nearly to death by hoodlums working for rural gambling and liquor racketeers, Pusser is elected sheriff and proceeds to clear out the gang, wielding an enormous club instead of a gun. Raging like a vengeful Yaweh, he smashes bottles, bar furniture, auto windshields, and a few folks. To the delight of viewers who believe the court system coddles crooks and deters the police, Sheriff Pusser also humiliates a local judge who rests too heavily on procedure. *Walking Tall* ex-

ploited the national outrage over crime, the inadequacy of the law
enforcement and penal systems, and impatience with liberal Supreme Court interpretations designed to protect the rights of the accused. It had most of the ugly, majoritarian sentiments of Richard
Nixon's "law and order" reelection campaign that same year.[16]

Yet the right-wing moralism and violence of *Walking Tall* are not
without their counterpoints, and the film is not without positive significance in the historiography of the South. Traditionally, violence-
prone, moralistic white southerners have been arch racists, saddling
up and hooding up to defend white womanhood against Thomas
Dixon's evil buck Gus or a comparable diabolic stereotype. In the
time of Buford Pusser, "law and order" was a vague slogan widely
interpreted as negrophobic: black crime soared in proportion to population; memories of the urban ghetto riots of the late sixties were
vivid; weariness mounted with the disorders attendant upon both
civil rights and anti-Vietnam war demonstrations. An intolerant,
xenophobic mood prevailed, enveloping and lending a sort of dignity to open racism.

But Hollywood's Pusser is no bigot. He has black friends, hires a
black as his deputy, treats the community fairly, and roots out a ring
of bootleggers who had sold bad corn that blinded and killed several
black customers. "Walking tall" meant overcoming fear and evil's
heavy odds and emerging with pride. If the means of rising from the
crawling posture seem frightening and quasifascist, the positive
ends, for once, did not exclude people on the basis of color. Southern violence was redefined, and Cash's savage ideal, thriving still,
was no longer quite so solidly based upon the Proto-Dorian bond of
white supremacy.

Gratuitous violence, usually dealt out from automobiles in cheap
movies with no blacks, issued in a torrent from Hollywood in the
seventies. Arthur Penn's *Bonnie and Clyde* (1967) had established
some of the subgenre's distinguishing traits. Set in Texas and Oklahoma during the Depression, the film offered no pretense of authenticity as to the real story of the tragic bandits; but the cars and sets
were period and locale masterpieces, and the wild pace was accentu-

ated with hard-core country instrumentals, notably Lester Flatt and Earl Scruggs's rendition of an Appalachian classic, "Foggy Mountain Breakdown" (now, sadly, renamed "Theme from *Bonnie and Clyde*"). The lighthearted, lightning fingering of banjo made the shootouts and fast getaways, with all the horror and blood, altogether unserious. Running moonshine in souped-up cars, traceable at least as far back as 1958's *Thunder Road*, and simply running wild in hot cars, were complementary subjects very popular in the seventies. *Macon County Line* (1974), a "B" guns, gasoline, and banjo thriller, was so popular it resulted in a sequel in 1975.

White Lightning (1973) was a vehicle for Burt Reynolds, a charming, athletic actor raised in Florida. It is also good drama which reveals a maturing treatment of several traditional southern themes. Down south a crooked sheriff is in cahoots with a rustic moonshine kingpin who pays off the law to stay in business. The sheriff (named Connors, and perhaps a satire of Birmingham's notorious police chief in the sixties, Eugene "Bull" Connor) is a bigot and xenophobe who cannot tolerate blacks or hippies or "Commie pinkos." The scenarist made such a two-dimensional stereotype of Connors that he is to be taken seriously only as an initiator of plot development. Connors murders a white college student named McCluskey, and the student's big brother, "Gator" (Reynolds), a grinning ex-convict, comes to town to investigate on his own. Gator infiltrates the moonshiner-bootleggers as a "blocker" driver—the man who follows the car carrying the liquor, blocking the state police or revenue agents and then leading them on a wild chase while the carrier escapes. Making a connection between the racketeers, the law, and his brother's murder, Gator plots the sheriff's destruction. It comes at the end of an incredible chase when Gator tricks the sheriff into driving his cruiser off a river bluff into a watery grave. A corrupt representative of a necessary institution is done in, but the parody of sweaty rural lawmen is more important than Gator's hot car and quick reflexes in the devastation of a staple of the sixties. Smiling with tongue in cheek at the same time, Reynolds nonetheless is a very significant rebel hero: not a yankee, not Sidney Poitier, but a barely educated southern white is the interloper who saves a small town from itself. Gator McCluskey is a red-neck Conrack, a source of pride for southern whites who would rather do it themselves.[17]

In 1974 Reynolds again played a southern kamikazi driver in *W. W. and the Dixie Dance Kings*. He lives in and drives a black and gold '55 Oldsmobile, from which he also robs gas stations. W.W. runs from the law into the arms of a country music band, persuades them he is a Nashville agent, and off they go to make their fortune. The process is slower than anticipated, so W.W. again robs gas stations, charming the attendants as usual into misleading the police. Meanwhile the film introduces some of Music City's cynical side, along with Art Carney, who portrays a black-garbed preacher-lawman hired by the oil corporation to find the mysterious bandit. It is delightful farce about the "good old days" of the fifties. If there are any value messages, they are about loyalty to friends, persistence, and the ultimate worthiness of Nashville.

In the actual music world, yankees began liking it the red-neck way. After Hank Williams' death in 1953 the country and western business came upon hard times and nearly disappeared as a set of distinctively southern rural styles. Elvis Presley of Tupelo, Mississippi, appeared in the mid-fifties and rapidly moved past simple country ballads to rock and roll, a new style combining country Negro and white blues with driving percussion and distinctly "popular" signatures. Popular singers continued to raid Williams' and other country writers' repertoires, too, and Nashville businessmen panicked in the direction of "uptown." Chet Atkins, Eddy Arnold, and others abandoned rural simplicity and introduced the "Nashville Sound," featuring saxophones, "pop" pianos, crooning, choral and orchestral backgrounds, and jazz guitar fingering. By 1960, as the popular and academic media were launching their devilish South portraiture, simple country music was less in evidence and less chic than ever before.

Reinvigoration came slowly from within and without Nashville. Even before 1960, singers Johnny Cash, Johnny Horton, and Marty Robbins won acclaim with "saga" songs such as "Two Feet High and

Risin'" (Cash's memory of a flood in his native Arkansas), Horton's "Battle of New Orleans," and Robbins' "El Paso." Later Loretta Lynn, a superstar of the 1970s from Butcher Hollow, Kentucky, specialized in this form, too. Saga songs are deeply rooted in precommercial folk music, and though less often "pure" in the sixties and seventies (they are sometimes presented in "pop" style), their reappearance struck a responsive chord among Americans.

Meanwhile Bluegrass music originated in the South, but its popularity was first established in the North while Nashville wriggled in its slough of despond. Bluegrass is "old timey" instrumental music sometimes accompanied by high, whining voices. The style closely resembles the playing of some of the early commercial musicians from Appalachia such as the Carter Family and the North Carolina Ramblers. It represented the ultimate in "hard core" rural music from which Nashville was fast retreating. The name *Bluegrass* is actually incongruous in that the style is highland, not of the flatter region of middle Kentucky. Modern Bluegrass was invented by Kentucky musician Bill Monroe in the 1940s. Earl Scruggs, the great North Carolina five-string banjoist, joined Monroe's band in 1946 and introduced the three-finger style, moving the banjo into the lead previously occupied by fiddle and guitar. Despite continued refinements by Monroe, Scruggs, and guitarist Lester Flatt, Bluegrass would support very few full-time pickers before 1965. But then northern "urban folk" musicians Woodie Guthrie, Pete Seeger, Mike Seeger, and the New Lost City Ramblers, as well as Bob Dylan discovered "pure" country music on their own and began offering it to big city and college audiences. By the late sixties the popular back-to-nature sentiment so prominent in the hippie counterculture as well as with the middle class, was beginning to attach itself positively to rustic southern imagery. Bob Dylan, leftist yankee intellectual, visited Nashville and cut an album with Johnny Cash, downhome fundamentalist. *Bonnie and Clyde*'s soundtrack provided incalculable momentum. Hippie communards sought cheap wilderness settlements in the South as well as in Colorado. "The Waltons" began on television. The connections were made. Both counterculture and middle America had discovered a different Dixie, not W. J. Cash's or Caldwell's, but Jefferson's and John Fox's land of nature and simplicity.[18]

Country music has never been "pure" or static. Even Hank Williams used amplified instruments. But the booming nationalization of country which began at the end of the sixties placed Nashville, great symbol of southern aural culture, under pressures of prosperity and kaleidoscopic change that endangered its integrity more profoundly than Presley and pop had earlier. The Country Music Association, promotional agency of "Music City," and individual Nashville businessmen themselves have been largely responsible for abetting the industry's deep ambivalence about its cultural mission. Many are *arrivistes* who want middle-class respectability and "jet set" chic while purveying down-home rusticity. Business-social functions often require black tie and are entertained by jazz combos, and music moguls such as Shelby Singleton wheel and deal and rush about like any yankee entrepreneur.

Nashville spokespeople have been perhaps less successful than other businesspeople in clearly articulating mission. Occasionally someone offers a gem of southern rural awareness. Mel Tillis, author of "Detroit City" and other hits, reflected on becoming successful and being invited to perform at the Golden Nugget in Las Vegas: "I just recently played at a spot . . . in Lavonia, Georgia, a town of about 1,500," he mused. "The park's out on the side of a mountain, has a creek running through it. People that run it are country people. They're fine people. And when I left they gave me a dog. And I took that with me. I've been wonderin' what the Nugget will give me when I leave." Probably more typical of Nashville's collective ambivalence was the Country Music Association's invitation to President Richard Nixon, then deeply mired in the Watergate scandals, to appear at the grand opening of the Disneyesque new Opryland early in 1974. Nixon played with a yo-yo on stage and then told the crowd that country music "talks about family. It talks about religion. And it . . . makes America a better country." (He made no reference to, and perhaps was unaware of, "slippin' around" ballads, divorce blues, seductive numbers, honky-tonk blues, or to Merle Haggard's bitter exposition of the current economic recession, "If We Make It Through December.") Earlier Farron Young, an ageless Nashville favorite (deep into his third scotch), told one writer bluntly: "My vision of this country has changed to where I've got more values than I did. And maybe this sounds stupid, but the value to me now is the dollar. . . . you got that dollar, you got America." Symbolically at least, one-time poor boy and girl pickers and singers, conquering the nation, had in turn been conquered by the same yankee "values" the Nashville Agrarians warned about forty years before.[19]

For this reason and simply owing to the vast popularity of country music, Nashville became but one center of production. During the sixties Bakersfield, California, became a serious rival. The Bakersfield, area—like sections of Detroit, Indianapolis, Chicago, and Columbus—amounts to a Dixie irredento, a focus of southern migration since the Depression where southern identification remained strong. There, singers Buck Owens and Merle Haggard flourished. Haggard in particular led a hard-core country revival against Nashville's modernism and identified himself with the "straight" reaction against the counterculture and antiwar movement. "Okie From Muskogee" and "Fightin' Side of Me," along with Johnny Russell's 1974 hit, "Red Necks, White Socks, and Blue Ribbon Beer," evoked proletarian patriotic sentiments and anti-intellectualism.[20] The faraway Californians were walking taller than the Tennesseeans.

Meanwhile, "progressive" country musicians gradually deserted Nashville for Austin, Texas, at the very western edge of the South. Many of the progressives wore long hair and beards and were college educated, liberal, and socially conscious. Among the better known were Kris Kristofferson, singer, writer, movie star, and former Rhodes scholar; former Nashvillians Waylon Jennings and Willie Nelson; and an outrageous crew called Kinky Friedman and the Texas Jewboys. Friedman had been a classics major at the University of Texas and served with the Peace Corps in Borneo before launching a musical career which is part a serious appreciation of old-fashioned music, part put-on. At one point his group included a small-town Arkansan of Chinese ancentry named Willie Fong Young, a "yellow redneck." Progressive country (also called "Redneck Rock" and "underground" country) includes "issue" themes such as Jennings' interracial ballads, but often merges with latter-day "rock" in style. It inspires pride in Texans, but its cosmopolitan practitioners and untraditional themes call into question its southern identity. In late 1975 Willie Fong Young and his partner, Kentuckian Fred Burch, had actually sold a "country rock" version of *King Lear* to a Broadway producer.[21]

The paradox of wealth and recognition built upon a bucolic, nonmaterialistic music grew ever more acute, and Nashville, Incorporated, seemed unable to respond in any coherent way, except to capitalize again, By 1975 only about half the city's recording establishment cut country music; the rest made pop, rock, soul, sacred, and all the bewildering hybrids that made style typing exasperating. It was the best of times for growth and innovation, the worst for ethnic and regional identification. The generations battled, too. Older country star Webb Pierce planned a bus stop/ramp in front of his residence to facilitate tourism and souvenir sales; younger star Ray Stevens (a neighbor) battled him in court and before the press as a mawkish philistine. Pierce wears sequined cowboy outfits and drives Cadillacs. Stevens is quiet, middle class, comes from Atlanta, and amidst the fracas cut a Bluegrass version of the Johnny Mathis pop ballad, "Misty." In this chaos appeared beefy, tattooed, David Allen Coe, decked out in black leather trousers and plunging neck shirt, black mask and hat set in silver studs, turquoise Indian jewelry, and calling himself the Mysterious Rhinestone Cowboy. His music defies easy description, too.

In 1975 self-proclaimed purists in Nashville rebelled and formed a group to rival the Country Music Association, the Association of Country Entertainers (ACE). The last straw had been CMA's election of Olivia Newton-John, a *foreigner*, as "Female Vocalist of the Year" in 1974. "Outside" interests had "watered down" the southern product, ACE announced. Spokeswoman Del Wood, a piano player and twenty-year veteran of the Grand Ole Opry ("Down Yonder"), declared that "We're not against anybody. We just don't want to see country music lose its identity." But there was deep rot in the woodpile. The spokeswoman herself confided to a reporter plans to cut a Bluegrass album. Bluegrass by definition is a consort of dobro (guitar), fiddle, banjo, mandolin, and string bass. Insinuate a piano, and it is not Bluegrass. But Ms. Wood wanted to "boost her career." [22]

Musical confusion, greed, the CMA's ill-advised haste in identifying with Richard Nixon—all had a souring effect which by 1975 threatened to spoil the country mystique once and for all, and with it, a last symbol of southern identity. In January, 1975, Buddy Rich, jazz drummer and orchestra leader, publicly lambasted country music as beneath serious notice. In June prestigious Stan Kenton followed suit, terming the business "a national disgrace" appealing to the "four year old mentality." According to radio reports of the Rich-Kenton blasts, Nashville took little notice of them. But the release (also June of 1975) of Robert Altman's epic film, *Nashville*, was a far more serious matter.

That Director Altman and his yankee scenarist wrote and produced such a film was a testament to country music's national stature in the seventies, and the film was reviewed everywhere, including major *Time* and *Newsweek* features. Reviews and controversy about *Nashville* in the New York *Times* continued the entire summer, while the film promised to be one of the great money-makers of a year in which the phenomenal *Jaws* was part of the competition.

Nashville was occasionally brilliant, eccentric, well-acted; it was also a nigh three-hour-long bore. Its subject is the country music scene and "culture," but these are but the vehicle for a devastating doomsday statement about American values. Thus had the South by 1975 been set up for a kill of national metaphoric proportions. Among the two dozen characters in the film are sincere, naïve kids such as have always come to Nashville to pick, sing, and win stardom. But the dominant types are hucksters, hypocrites, cynics, and the dull-eyed disillusioned. Haven Hamilton (Henry Gibson) is the residing senior star, a cherubic monster who manipulates feelings without feeling ("Welcome to my lovely home") and confers or denies not only theatrical opportunity but political grace. A young country rock star played by Keith Carradine is amoral. An ill woman star (Barbara Jean, played by Ronee Blakley) is propped up and driven onward for the profits she generates. Swirling around these are sybaritic conventioneers and gullible, wide-eyed hicks and middle Americans. The portraiture is bone-chilling, for not only are so many of the stars jaded, but much of the music itself is sheer fraud, Nashville's plastic and sequined rusticity for suburbanites who cannot find identity anywhere else.

In fairness to country music it must be said that the music in *Nashville*, composed and performed by the actors and film company, is awful—worse in terms of lyrics and performing musicianship than the sloppiest of the real Nashville's products. Southern accents in the film are poor, too. Nevertheless the film's impact was to expose Nashville as a country and western Disneyland, or a Tennessee Hollywood, where reality is seldom more than the reflection of a spangle and the decibels of amplified fiddles. In the end senselessness is climaxed with the public murder of gentle Barbara Jean by a clean-cut boy from Ohio. There is no apparent motive, although the young man has carried his battered violin case with the pistol inside throughout the film As bloody Barbara Jean is carried off Nashville's absurd replica of the Parthenon, the remaining entertainers lead the crowd in singing Carradine's banal ode to nihilism: "Oh you may say that I'm not free/But that don't bother me." Altman was best at the last.

Willie Fong Young "loved" the movie, but more typical was Webb Pierce's reaction: it was "a nightmare." Record entrepreneur Billy Sherill complained: "When you show the anatomy of a man, you should try to show something besides his rear end." Loretta Lynn, regarded as model for Barbara Jean, refused to see *Nashville*. "I'd rather see *Bambi*," she said.[23]

Beneath the communications "reality" of *Nashville* and other sudden attacks upon the just-returned South lay more disquieting changes that proceeded heedless to the ups and downs of cultural genres. Since World War II, most noticeably, the region became urbanized, standardized, neonized. Visually, there is little difference between the superhighways and streetscapes of Ohio and Alabama. The cars, gasoline stations, subdivision architecture, glass-faced office towers, and gaudy fast-food stands are the same. Prosperity has virtually eliminated the Lesters and Waltons, and transformed Snopeses, Varners, and Colonel Cornpones into bland babbitts and (as Georgia writer Marshall Frady put it) "styrofoam politicos." "Below Atlanta," wrote Frady, "in the aboriginal landscapes of 'Gone With The Wind,' one drives through a Santa Barbara gallery of pizza cottages and fish 'n chip parlors, with a 'Tara shopping Center' abruptly glaring out of fields of broom sage and jack pine." The South had become dull.[24]

Community and simplicity, those opposites of alienation and American pace the South had always embodied in history, literature, music—and in fact—seemed to have gone with the wind. Country music was past the age of innocence and credibility; Faulkner was dead. *Nashville* was popular, and Faulkner's successor as the most significant novelist from the Lower South was Walker Percy. Nephew of William Alexander Percy, the Bourbon gentleman who wrote *Lanterns on the Levee*, an intensely reactionary, place-loving memoir of 1941, Walker Percy is—of all things—a southern existentialist. The words hardly seem to belong together. But his characters in *The Moviegoer* (1961), *The Last Gentleman* (1966), and *Love in the Ruins* (1971) are alienated from the past and have no particular feelings for place. Percy's latest novel, *Lancelot* (1977), is set in the South, yet still scorns the "southern thing." Percy has Binx Bolling bluntly declare: "I have inherited no more from my father than a good nose for *merde*, for every species of shit that flies." And in 1974 he confronted an interviewer with a Louisiana version of Frady's Georgia panorama. For writers as well as sociologists, "odd country characters are not the scene anymore; the scene is what to do with a big urban sprawl like Baton Rouge. How're you gonna write that? How're you gonna write about New Orleans—not the French Quarter, but Gentilly?"[25] How, indeed.

James Dickey, the South Carolina poet, in effect addressed himself to this dilemma in his first novel, *Deliverance*, a 1970 best seller made into an excellent (and commercially successful) movie in 1972. Dickey's story is set in north Georgia in contemporary times, and his plot concerns a Hemingwayan test of men's survival against a hostile wilderness. The savage mountain men who sodomize one of the protagonists, probably kill another, and threaten the survivors, render the southern setting of the adventure particular; but in other respects the novel-film might have been located in the West or in Canada. Dickey's Gentilly is suburban Atlanta. His subjects are four middle-aged, middle-class white husband-fathers who, under the goading of Lewis (Burt Reynolds), an avid canoeist, archer, and general sportsman-competitor, set out to canoe down the wild Cahulawassee before a park-development dam ends the river's natural life. There could have been a metaphor here about regional death: an Appalachian river is sacrificed to serve urban weekend recreation; Fox's South dies. But this is either avoided or subordinated to Lewis's existential physical challenge. Jon Voight played the lead, Dickey's narrator/alter ego who must take charge when Lewis is injured in rapids, and finally must kill a diabolical hillbilly with his bow and arrow in order to live. In the end the survivors have only a secret horror story and a brutal creed of survival to accompany their quietly comfortable beer-drinking. Anonymous, alienated suburban existence goes on. *Deliverance* is a gripping story in both media, but in terms of values, perhaps only more merde. The southerner is merely modern Everyman, without special attachments or insights from his soil and past.

So ended, then, about the mid-seventies, one of the weirdest decades in the nation's tumultuous affair with the South. From the devilish depths of Selma and the Wallace campaigns to the warm glow of "The Waltons" and Sam Ervin's homilies, the region's ascent line on the graph of public sentiment seemed to falter, then stop. Yankee viewers' identification with "The Waltons," as I have suggested, tended to obliterate the show's southern setting and folks. This is the no-win Dixie Catch 22 in the national marketplace of images and social types. The obvious saleability of down-home rusticity in the commercial world suggests something far more widespread than the curious fate of Earl Hamner's show. As the South and ever-so-recently nasty white southerners became positive staples, the region came near to disappearing. *Nashville's* national metaphor seems apropos, too, as does the absence of "southern" best sellers in the book market for a long time after Styron's *Confessions of Nat Turner.*

By this I do not mean that the South ceased to exist save as a compass direction with a peculiar past. Most southerners continued not only to perceive themselves as distinctive, but actually to behave in a number of distinctly southern ways. John Shelton Reed, the Chapel Hill sociologist, has demonstrated these objective truths quite convincingly.[26] Rather, I mean that in large measure the South has always been a media colony, an elsewhere for the American majority's amusement or negative example. Some southerners have capitalized upon the imagery, reifying at times the most outrageous stereotypes. Yet colonials they remained, along with those of us who chafed and snarled at imperial manipulations. So by the mid-seventies, when the yankee majority so wholeheartedly accepted the South as its own, the South—that mighty, imaginary one—nearly died. But *nearly* is a potent adverb. Another provoking, fascinating decade was underway.

Chapter 9

Re-Redux and Reconciliation

Now I beseech you, brethren, by the name of our Lord Jesus Christ, that ye all speak the same thing, and that there be no divisions among you; but that ye be perfectly joined together in the same mind, and in the same judgment.

I Corinthians 1:10

Nineteen seventy-seven was "The Waltons" last season among the Nielsen company's top twenty television shows. The program's course was majestic, but it ran out. CBS-TV executives perceived a negative trend and withdrew other "rural" shows as well—"Green Acres," for example. Replacing them on the tube was another run of low, distinctively Dixie action-comedies, "The Misadventures of Sheriff Lobo" and the enormously popular and enduring "Dukes of Hazzard." Both combined elements of *Tobacco Road* and *Thunder Road* to exploit redefined staple types: ineffectual villains (Sheriff Lobo and "Boss" Hogg), voluptuous Daisy Maes, and kamikazi-driving good ole boys. Two other shows of the late seventies were set on the territorial fringes of the South: "Dallas" and "Flamingo Road." No red-neck rousers were these. Indeed both productions focused on the opposite end of the social structure—elite families afloat in Texas oil and Florida development lucre. There were sympathetic characters in these shows, to be sure; but I think both are notable for the reintroduction of an antebellum ogre, that object of abolitionist fury, the "lord of the lash." The Old South model whipped weeping slaves across cotton fields in his drive to wealth. The New South version relishes corporate and human relations manipulations. Neither has scruples or compassion. On "Dallas" actor Larry Hagman played his J. R. Ewing character with such brio that the nation (and many foreigners, too) learned to "love to hate" him. J.R. finally became more sympathetic and less a lord of the lash. He was shot and he suffered certain other disappointments.[1] Other lords seemed irredeemable, however, and in the wake of "The Waltons," nearly all the television signals seemed forboding.

In 1985 the heartless manipulator was resurrected on the stage of real life. This time the putative lord was a live white man from near the heart of Dixie, Ted Turner. Turner had already won celebrity as a handsome, daring sportsman, as well as the founder of Turner Broadcasting in Atlanta. He was a champion yachtsman and owner of professional sports teams. An urbane racial liberal, too, Turner adroitly synthesized the pinstriped corporate image with that of the good ole boy. (Journalists and others described him chewing tobacco while pacing his top floor office, spitting into a styrofoam cup.) But in 1985 Turner attempted to buy that most venerable (and "liberal") of New York City-based television networks, CBS; and his maneuvers seemed to be coordinated with a political right-wing attack upon CBS led by United States Senator Jesse Helms of North Carolina. The delicious prospect of Atlanta seizing imperial dominion over New York was spoiled by the association, and CBS executives leaped to exploit historical imagery as they moved to render their corporation takeover-proof. The *Wall Street Journal* quoted the CBS chairman declaring that Turner was not "moral enough" to guide CBS.[2] William Lloyd Garrison said much more of the original lords of the lash, but the theme remained the same. Turner's bid, meanwhile, failed of course; Jonah could not ingest the leviathan. This was owing much more to CBS's draconian countermeasures than to vocalizing. Yet the incident demonstrated the remarkable durability of historical tags. So, along with J. R. Ewing, "Boss" Hogg, and Luke Duke, Ted Turner in-the-news helped revive Dixie demonology and nincompoopdom in a sorry aftermath to the ambivalent progress of the mid-seventies.

Yet all the while a great countercurrent surged. Two events of late

1976 and early 1977, in particular, bore heavy portent for a South reconciled, not only with the nation, but within itself. They were the election of Jimmy Carter as president, and the appearance of Alex Haley's *Roots* in print and on television. One event affected the recent and contemporary South, the other our memory of the Old.

The Old South, abiding usually in isolation from the New, always threatened nonetheless to impinge upon it, especially in the hands of neo-Confederates. Neoabolitionist professional and popular history during the 1960s probably tarnished the sentimentalist image of the plantation and slavery beyond recovery. Yet *Gone with the Wind* played on television in 1976 to record audiences. Within seven months, however, this venerable relic of racism and romance had been turned inside out, and probably vanquished at last in both Margaret Mitchell's printed medium and on television.

Late in 1976 Doubleday published *Roots: The Saga of an American Family*, by Alex Haley. Haley, a black native of Henning, Tennessee, may be the fomenter of a revolution in the mass perception of slavery and the Old South. An unprecedented advance printing of 200,000 copies of *Roots* sold out almost immediately. A million copies were in print by February, 1977. ABC-TV hoped for a viewing audience of 50 million prior to the airing of David L. Wolper Productions' version, which ran eight consecutive nights in late January. Afterwards, A. C. Nielsen reported that 130 million Americans (85 percent of the possible audience) watched at least part of the series, 80 million watched the last episode alone.[3] These staggering figures exceeded both the 1977 Super Bowl football game and—significantly—the *Gone with the Wind* TV audience. And *Roots* had only begun. Television reruns followed in a year. The book remained at the top of best-seller lists and was adopted for instructional purposes in secondary schools and colleges. Doubleday combined with Random House and Films, Inc., to produce and distribute an "educational materials" package, and even before January, 1977, many schools and colleges owned thirty-seven-minute tape cassettes of Haley recounting his research experiences. Haley himself was constantly on the lecture and television-interview circuit.

Haley's novel consists of a skeleton of factual genealogy (his own), imaginatively fleshed out (to nearly seven hundred pages) with a saga that is largely governed by his knowledge of sound historical context.[4] It is "enriched history" in the tradition of Catherine Drinker Bowen and Edna Forbes. Haley invented feelings, thoughts, conversations, and incidents that no empiricist could discover. But in twelve years of research and writing, this freelance writer learned his southern history rather well. Only a few matters offend the professional historian.

Haley was assisted in his project by an old friend from Henning, "master researcher" George Sims. The advice of a historian-specialist—or merely consultation of recent histories—might have saved them from errors that would not have affected substantively the narrative. For example, Haley dates the African empire of "Old Mali" before Ghana. He has his character, Fiddler, describe the apportionment of slaves among the white classes as they were in the 1850s—except Fiddler speaks in 1770. Haley wrongly establishes cotton culture in northern Virginia, then a cotton kingdom in the Gulf area decades before Alabama, Mississippi, and Louisiana were settled or admitted as states. A character mentions pellagra a century before either the word or the medical condition were known. Haley also exploits the dubious tradition that Thomas Jefferson was a miscegenator. "Massa Abe Lincoln" speaks of freeing slaves before the Civil War. Then the siege of Fort Sumter yields fifteen dead on each side. Haley finally produces a young red-neck couple, "Old George" and Martha Johnson, improbably free of racism because they hail from western South Carolina.

The television version, adapted by writer William Blinn (with James Lee and M. Charles Cohen) alters the novel substantially while committing more errors. The $6 million production enlarged the roles of several white characters and invented a host of others. The slave ship captain (merely named in the book) is an unlikely Christian smitten with guilt. There is a brutal first mate, too (ironically, played by Ralph Waite, who was the kindly father in "The Waltons"). Kunta Kinte, Haley's ancestor victimized by the slave trade, may have seen a few whites in the West African interior, near the mouth of the Gambia, but white traders hardly ever ventured out of their coastal forts. Black and Arab traders delivered the black coffles to the forts. In Annapolis, where Kinte was first sold in America, Blinn has white men jest openly about their sexual exploitation of slave women, in the presence of white women. This is most improbable. Slave women have been abused throughout history; this fact should be laid bare. But the teleplay (not the novel) is downright salacious, necessitating a "viewer discretion" warning to the television audience before each airing. The teleplay also shows mountains in Piedmont Spotsylvania County, Virginia, and has Kinte's daughter, Kizzy, drive there by carriage from Caswell County, North Carolina, in four hours. (Piedmont Airlines might accomplish the trip in that time today.) Curiously, most slave quarters pictured are too well appointed.

Apparently to spice his version for white viewers, Blinn contrived a romantic affair between a planter and his sister-in-law that has practically no relevance to the plot. Blinn outdid himself, however, in an exciting if fanciful climax that is not in the novel. After the Civil War, a white senator (Burl Ives) invents the sharecropping system as a diabolical means to regain control over the freedmen. (Lack of capital for all southerners would be a better explanation.) But the magnificent Chicken George (Kinte's grandson) and his sons trick the whites and head west for Henning, Tennessee. It is a thrilling reenactment of Br'er Rabbit's briar patch adventure.

Haley's saga is black history. Whites are but a shadowy parade who, as in *The Autobiography of Miss Jane Pittman*, are more widgets in a cruel system than special devils. Only Dr. Waller (Dr. Reynolds on television) and Tom Lea (Moore on television) are three-dimensional. Lea, the owner-rapist of Kizzy and father of Chicken George, emerges from the book a callous but human creature. In the teleplay the added complement of white characters creates only a longer parade of two-dimensional beasts. Blacks, by contrast, are vivid and memorable as personalities.

From this situation derives much of *Roots*'s power as popular history, especially on television. Depersonalized white stereotypes, limned at predominantly white audiences, helped argue uncompromising theses: slavery was unspeakably hard on body and spirit; brave slaves both endured and rebelled; black families survived despite all odds.[5] In *Gone with the Wind* slaves are two-dimensional (except for Mammy, perhaps). In *Roots* (especially the teleplay, again) the neo-Confederate version is turned inside out, with ironic justice.

Roots's weaknesses are outweighted by its objective historical value, too. Haley's portrait of life among the Mandinkas of the Gambia region is learned and sensitive (and not quite the nature idyll presented on television). He cleverly wove into his narrative many scrupulously accurate details, such as the nature of the salt-gold trade across the western Sudan. There were shipboard slave rebellions (such as in the teleplay), and Haley both unobtrusively and correctly related the history of slave conspiracy and insurrection in the United States.

The novel/teleplay are in an obvious sense hostile and provocative. They shout at white Americans the sorriest theme in their history. But Haley's mission is conservative and healing most of all. His book climaxes the work of neoabolitionists, yet he asserts that all Americans may find solace and inspiring identity in family roots. He was quickly besieged with queries from whites and blacks concerning his research methodology. Haley is most obviously conciliatory, however, in the person of the white character "Old George" Johnson, the improbable red-neck egalitarian. "Old George" and Tom (Chicken George's son) are salt and pepper partners, despite all the forces that would have made them enemies. On television Blinn went even further, magnifying the relationship into an integrationist hymn.

So Haley administered the *coup de grace* to Margaret Mitchell's ghost, yet like a wise conqueror, held forth the olive branch to her survivors. Anyone inclined towards resuscitation shall have considerable difficulty reviving the Grand Old South. The appearance in 1985 and 1986 of a televised version of John Jakes' *North and South* does not contradict this thesis, I believe. A sprawling costume melodrama (*"Gone with the Mind,"* some dubbed it), *North and South* resembled pre-World War I novels of white division and reconciliation, but its treatment of slavery was rank neoabolitionism.

Jimmy Carter, Georgia yankee as president

The historical quotient of Jimmy Carter's brief but brilliant political success relates to the "New" South—the redemption of the white masses from pity and from racism. Carter is a pleasant, pink-complexioned Baptist from southwest Georgia whom journalist Marshall Frady lumped with the "styrofoam politicos" of the postsegregation era. Elected governor in 1970, he renounced racial demagoguery in favor of a program of governmental efficiency and economic growth. Early in 1975 he announced his candidacy for the presidency, to scant notice. By midspring, 1976, Carter's determination and anti-Washington appeal had produced a political juggernaut that swept him to the Democratic nomination on the first ballot. Despite a frightening slippage of support in the autumn, he won, the first Dixie president since 1869 (not counting Texan Lyndon Johnson and Virginia-born, New Jersey-based Woodrow Wilson). It seemed a cultural as well as a political miracle.

Southern accents, for example, have long been considered liabilities in business and politics above the Mason and Dixon Line. But Mr. Carter's soft flatland drawl remained unsullied. Yankee politicians and professors rushed to his standard, but white and black southerners—who sounded as such—predominated. His sister was a famous faith-healer; his younger brother, Billy, a beer-drinking good ole boy; his mother, "Miss Lillian," a gracious democratic dame of the back country. Carter and his crowd were outsiders, colonials. His nomination in Madison Square Garden, in the heart of imperial New York, then his decisive electoral victory in New York state, were sweet justification to the South. Washington newspeople joked that Dixie pronunciation was now "standard English."

Nor did Carter conceal his southern identity in his campaign autobiography, *Why Not the Best?* He was raised in a clapboard house heated by fireplaces and a wood-burning kitchen stove. There was an outdoor privy during his earliest years, and no electricity until he was thirteen. Young Jimmy mopped and chopped cotton, boiled peanuts, stacked wood, and slopped hogs. His father cut his hair with mule shears. If, following the aphorism, one becomes what one eats,

Carter is sweet potatoes, corn, bacon, and grits.[6] Not only did he proclaim his origins, Carter celebrated the down-home mystique and sought to synthesize his unpretentious, conservationist life-style with what was called in Jefferson's day "republican simplicity." He spoke humbly, carried his own baggage, wore jeans and open-necked shirts, and appeared on television from the White House in a sweater rather than a dark suit.

In such ways Jimmy Carter personified the resurgence of the white South that began about 1971. The memory and burden of *Tobacco Road* were purged by his work ethic and clean living. He was John-Boy Walton grown up. Or better—considering his political partnership with blacks—Carter was a magisterial "Conrack." Lyndon Johnson's advocacy of civil rights might be explained away by his origins in a Texas county virtually without black people.[7] But Carter's sincerity and commitment, arising from dark Sumter County, Georgia, rendered him and his region free at last of the ancient Dixie curse. For many of us, it was too good to be true. A week after the inauguration, James Dickey smiled and drawled on CBS-TV News that southern ambience would redeem the nation from both hypocrisy and the hectic rush. The "southernization of America," he predicted, would spread simplicity, personability, caring.

If only the poet were prophetic! Then the best qualities long associated with the South might help all Americans live at a slower pace, take time to know neighbors, demand fewer material goods, and conserve resources. But these "southern" qualities flaunt obvious realities. Southerners had already become "Americanized" to a pace nearly as fast as yankees', to conspicuous consumption, and to the expansion of employment opportunities in industries both clean and dirty.

So conversely, if the return of the South symbolized by the Carter administration did represent the extension of southern cultural themes across the nation (and it did, in some ways), then the very national acceptance of the South amounted to something like "The Waltons" Catch 22—cooption. For when New York and Minnesota have good ole boys, guitar-pickers, and stockcar drivers who affect drawls, the South at its moment of victory might expire. There is another dimension to this paradox of regional imagery, too.

Certainly Jimmy Carter himself is hardly an exemplar of mellow Dixie. He did not even represent a "southern" political triumph in the usual sense, for a clear majority of white southerners voted for his opponent. "Ethnic" southerners were not loyal to their soul brother; what remained of the "solid South" mystique dissolved in 1976. What gave the appearance of southern solidarity was the *black* vote, 90 percent of which went to Carter. Like "Conrack," Carter was a scalawag, it would seem, to most of his kind. Brother Billy may have personified the good ole boy, a southern standard; but Jimmy was anything but: he neither drinks nor smokes; he does not seem gregarious; he is not lazy; he is incisive and tireless.

Indeed Carter was not merely a farmer, but an engineer and businessman of accomplishment. This combined with his strong sense of community reminds me most of Herbert Hoover—our last farmboy *cum* millionaire businessman-engineer-president. In such a broader (and truer) perspective, Jimmy Carter might have been the ultimate American regional synthesizer. His administration proceeded in step with the vast popularity of *Roots*, and gradually the Georgia accents seeped past amazement into the everyday. Dixie's interment in the national imagination thus *might* have occurred almost unnoticed. But Jimmy Carter ran afoul of international events beyond his mastery and having nothing to do with his southernness; then he puzzled and deeply offended many Americans as perhaps only a southern Baptist might. So the Georgia yankee was to have but a brief time in the limelight, and the repute of the South may have suffered, too, when Ronald Reagan crushed Carter at the polls in 1980.

Carter had inherited as president an inflationary spiral that threatened Americans' standard of living. Yet as good Democrats neither he nor the majority in Congress could attack federal spending programs, nor were they able to develop other strategies to stop the spiral. It grew worse. Then in 1979 came another international oil crisis, creating long lines of irate citizens waiting for scarce, high-priced gasoline. Worst of all, at the end of 1979 revolutionary Shiite Muslims in Iran stormed the United States embassy in Teheran and took Americans hostage. They were not to be released until shortly after Reagan's inauguration at the beginning of 1981. Carter was doomed. His successes as president—notably the Camp David agreement between Egypt and Israel—were largely forgotten, along with his patient humanity and unpretentiousness.

The presidency (as Theodore Roosevelt proclaimed) is a pulpit as well as an executive office. Every holder of the position has used it thus, but Jimmy Carter preached from the White House, over television, in a peculiarly southern way that may have helped do him in, politically. During the inflation/oil crises he had the audacity to suggest to the American masses of the "Me" decade, that they were spoiled and self-indulgent. Restraint, some self-denial, and awareness of the needs of others might, he said, mobilize national resolve and solutions to malaises spiritual as well as economic. (Ronald Reagan told Americans they should have fewer taxes, less discipline, and *more* conspicuous consumption.) All of us who had been subjected to Baptist sermonizing before understood President Carter perfectly: humanity is hopelessly sinful and may be redeemed by Grace alone; in the meantime we must be repentant and mend our ways. Logically, millions of adherents of the new Fundamentalist right (as well as mainline members of the Southern Baptist Convention) should have welcomed Carter's thoughtful preaching. But Reagan had already coopted these masses with his own pious sermonizing about traditional values. Most Americans seemed puzzled, put off, or flatly offended by Jimmy Carter's analysis of spiritual ills. Whichever, the Georgians were swept away, and Californians (some of them former Nixon men and women) returned to Washington in triumph.

The early eighties offered few southern media events or national personalities—save the Reverend Jerry Falwell and other television evangelists. Lynchburg, Virginia-based Falwell, Virginia Beach's Pat Robertson, and Baton Rouge's Jimmy Swaggart built enormous followings as they "went political," identified with Reagan, and at-

tempted to influence elections from coast to coast.[8] Secular human-
ist critics of the political preachers might tar them with W. J. Cash's
Savage Ideal and dwell upon the deep southern roots of Fundamentalism. But the preachers' national base of supporters, and the existence of similar evangelists in non-southern parts certainly blunts
the impact of such reasoning. The South's repute seemed to regress,
nonetheless. The times were confusing, disappointing.

Rapid technological change in television during the late seventies
and eighties presented some of the most perplexing questions about
perceptions of the South. Independent TV stations that specialize in
broadcasting old movies and rerunning lapsed network programs,
for example, have been around since the fifties. So Shirley Temple
and the Marx Brothers, "Gomer Pyle, U.S.M.C.," and "The Beverly
Hillbillies"—artifacts of the thirties through the sixties—live with us
still. One may only wonder how they are understood, or what the
extent of their impact is. Such independent station fare figures little
in Nielsen ratings. Are these movies and shows now merely quaint
nostalgia for insignificant pockets of the mass audience? Now the
problem is magnified many times over by the emergence of satellite
cable transmissions and by the appearance of video cassette record-
ers (VCRs).

Ted Turner's TBS "Superstation" pioneered the former. By the
late seventies his Channel 17 not only beamed reruns of "The Beverly Hillbillies" but made fans of the Atlanta Braves across the nation. In turn, cable transmission of Chicago's WGN and New York's
WOR reached Georgia. My correspondent in Valdosta sets his alarm
clock to ungodly hours in order to awaken and watch antique
"southern" movies on WGN. The VCR, meanwhile, has arisen to
challenge the very existence of conventional broadcast television,
cable, and even theatrical film. Owners of VCRs may not only record
programs for convenient viewing—and the "zipping" past or
"zapping" out of commercials—but they may rent or purchase cassettes of movies old and nearly new, as well as a variety of "how to"
cassettes. By the end of 1985 there was a VCR in one of every four TV

households. Industry analysts expected 1986 VCR sales to be "flat," a mere twelve-to-thirteen million more. This modest prediction would place one in every third TV household. By 1990 the "ultimate impact" of 98 percent of the entire national market—the equal of television's—should be attained.[9]

Another communications revolution seems at hand, but neither its effects on businesses nor on Dixie imagery may yet be gauged. Like recorded music or talk on old-fashioned discs, cheap recorded movies (and soon, too, old TV programs) defy history and generational change. Sharing Fats Domino, Hank Williams, and the Beatles (not to mention Mozart) with children is a joy. John Ford's *Tobacco Road* may be something else. But old "southerns" will hardly dominate the VCR owners' attention. At the beginning of 1986 there were operating in Valdosta and surrounding Lowndes County, Georgia, no fewer than fourteen cassette rental stores. A survey of managers revealed that local customers were most interested in "old classics" starring John Wayne and Humphrey Bogart, horror movies, releases of recent films such as *Beverly Hills Cop*, and of course "X"-rated movies.[10] Analysis of perceptions of the South (and many other subjects) surviving from movies past must await survey and other research tools that as yet do not exist.

Lacking social science, then, one falls back (with trepidation) upon impressions. My only claims to respectability in this dubious enterprise are experience with several historical contexts and maybe the special advantage of being a self-conscious southerner who lives in the North, reads, watches television (with a VCR), and goes religiously to the movies. This caveat filed, I believe that the past decade has witnessed a subtle, then powerful, continuation of the themes of reconciliation begun by the men from Henning, Tennessee, and Plains, Georgia. Following is evidence from several media and from real life.

In 1982, for example, there was a minor movie called *Tank* that fared so poorly in theaters it was broadcast on television less than two years later. I do not suggest that *Tank* was a great event that changed hearts, but rather that it exemplifies some updated southern types and themes that demonstrate something approaching maturity in southern imagery. "B" films may be significant in this fashion. In *Tank* veteran actor James Garner portrays an aging sergeant major at an army camp in north Georgia. He does not seem to be a southern man, and the Georgia setting is unimportant until Garner offends the local sheriff. Here enters a stock devilish-Dixie type from the sixties—a lawman above the law, cruel and bound for revenge against the sergeant major. The sheriff frames Garner's teenaged son on a drug charge and carts the boy off to a rustic work camp to labor among hardened criminals. Garner fails at every legal means to free his son, then turns to direct action. It seems that the good sergeant was a young tanker in World War II, and out of nostalgia has purchased and renewed a vintage Sherman tank. So out of his big garage comes Garner's heavy hobby. (Freudian innuendo is not uncommon in "B" movies.) The armored ex-sergeant—he conscientiously resigns before this mission—blasts and bulldozes the police station and all the sheriff's cruisers within reach, then in company with a sweet young hooker he has liberated, heads for the prison camp. Rescuing his son, Garner finds himself pursued on the ground and from the air by half the constabulary of Georgia. He must strike out overland for the Tennessee border, hoping for understanding and mercy in the Volunteer State. *Tank* has a long and fascinating climax, as national media attention focuses on the chase, and as enthusiastic crowds gather at the border. The Georgia sheriff and his allies are clearly the bad guys, but hosts of other white and black southerners aid and abet the daring refugees. Finally the governor of Tennessee is shamed into helping them, and the Sherman (in a playful historical joke?) makes a successful run north. The good guys win; a bad public official is defeated. More significant, I think, are scenes of southerners dividing among themselves, without respect for race or class, and confounding outsiders who might pin the Savage Ideal on red-necks, indiscriminantly. *Tank* is hardly a great film. But it is a good, satisfying one, and miles beyond the imagery of *I Am a Fugitive from a Chain Gang*.

A political vignette from 1983 also seems revealing. That year there raged in Chicago a mayoralty race nasty even by Windy City standards. A black candidate's emergence polarized the metropolis, and angry racial epithets flew openly. Down in Charlotte, North Carolina, another mayor's contest began, this one, too, with a black candidate, Harvey Gantt. In the South, however, news reporters seemed more fearful of trouble than the candidates and voters. Asked by a reporter if Charlotte would descend to Chicago's polarization, Gantt replied, "We are not going to have that kind of down-in-the-gutter fight." Charlotte did not, and Gantt won.[11]

Gantt is at least equally notable as the first prominent southern black man to use the pronoun "we" to mean "southerners," all of them, regardless of color. By the mid-eighties Gantt's usage probably represented an overdue and hard-won understanding in the South: that the region would not be so rich and interesting had it not been home to blacks as well as white folks. This represents popular *historical* learning, acceptance, and of course, reconciliation. By coincidence in 1984, the year following Harvey Gantt's ascent, John B. Boles, a white Texan and editor of the *Journal of Southern History*, entitled his new book *Black Southerners, 1619–1869*. Intended primarily for college students, this crisply written synthesis of recent scholarship (including Boles' own original research) is widely adopted. The book's title carries much of Boles' argument, and justifies further Gantt's usage.[12]

The political year 1984 included another vignette emblematic—yet weirdly so—of reconciliation within the South. Ronald Reagan was bound for a landslide reelection and Democrats were in despondent disarray. Jesse Jackson, the South Carolina-born black leader (now long a resident of Chicago), provided nearly all the excitement during the primaries, but at the Democratic convention he bowed finally to Walter F. Mondale, an earnest, liberal, rather phlegmatic Minnesotan who had been Jimmy Carter's vice president. Mondale certainly lacked Jackson's mesmerizing charisma—Norwegian middle westerners may be innately inferior to Afro-southerners on this count—but his record and pledges held most blacks in the Democratic fold. Mondale's staff, however, which included few southerners of any shade, coped poorly in the South. The candidate's advance men descended upon Atlanta and undiplomatically trampled the turf of Mayor Andrew Young—the first southern big city black chief executive, Jimmy Carter's ambassador to the United Nations, former congressman, former aide to Martin Luther King, Jr., and a Baptist minister. Young was piqued by the Mondale men's deficiencies of due regard and was quoted castigating them as "smart-assed white boys." The comment provoked a sensation—not an angry one, but a sensation of hilarity. Almost overnight there appeared thousands of smiling white men sporting round white buttons bearing the black letters, "s.a.w.b." Conceivably some humorless white Georgians were offended. Certainly a generation earlier the Reverend Young's remark would have been divisive and dangerous. But in 1984— according to all my Georgia correspondents—the "smart-assed white boys" affair was tension-relieving and more evidence of advancing interracial understanding.[13]

Films, to be successful commercially, must resonate beyond the South. In 1985 Americans of every region continued to worry about the fate of the family farmer, and three movies addressed this issue: *Country*, *The River*, and *Places in the Heart*. The first two were contemporary docudramas. *Country* told the story of Plains wheat growers, focusing on one family desperately attempting to save their heritage for their children. Viewers who did not already know about the agricultural price collapse following Jimmy Carter's grain embargo against the Russians, about the twin crises of shrinking land values and crushing debt both to private banks and to federal lending agencies, about farm families' psychological stresses, and about farm women's great strength—were so informed in heartbreaking detail.

The River, directed by Mark Rydell from a story by Robert Dillon, is a sort of Tennessee corn growers' counterpart to *Country*. But *The River* (it seems to me) is a far more interesting and effective movie. Here the Australian actor Mel Gibson (speaking with a passable southern accent) is a beleaguered third-generation farmer in the hills of East Tennessee towards Kingsport. Sissy Spacek (whose southern accent is native) plays his heroic wife who must later run the farm herself. Past their fields snakes a river that nurtures, then periodically floods and ruins crops. (One is reminded of Jean Renoir's treatment of riparian nature in *The Southerner.*) Early on a conspiracy forms against farmers in the valley. A local agribusinessman (who supplies seed and chemicals and buys corn on contract), a banker, and a politician plot to have the federal and state governments build a dam to hold the river at the end of the valley. The dam will produce hydroelectric power, industrial development, and "jobs for the whole county," but dozens of small farms will go underwater. The plot is all the more dramatic because the agribusinessman lusts for Sissy Spacek all the while he pressures the banker to call in overdue loans and pressures Gibson and others to sell off pieces of farming equipment.

In a remarkable twist of scenes Gibson's character leaves home for industrial work. He must earn cash while wife and children hold the farm front. There, Spacek's arm is nearly mangled in a machinery accident, but she spunkily coaxes a bull to butt the machinery so it will release her. Gibson, meanwhile, learns his industrial job is in fact scabbing on striking workers. Deeply ashamed, he works anyway. The plant itself is surreal—loud, foul, dangerous, and ruthlessly bossed. One day a young deer, its habitat ruined by the plant, wanders in. Everything but the deer is black with grime and otherworldly. All the workers and their machines stop in wonder. Nature has presented itself in beauty and rebuke—à la Renoir once more. The men encircle the deer, at first in a way that may be threatening, for they have been brutalized themselves. But instead the workers gently guide the animal to safety (they hope) at the edge of the plant. Suddenly the boss announces everyone is fired; the strike is over. Now the scabs must walk, in something close to a protective circle, through angry crowds of union men and their families. A woman curses and spits on Gibson, but like the fawn, the scabs, too, may escape, although in deeper shame than before.

The grimy industrial episode within *The River* is the element that renders Rydell's film so much more interesting and important than *Country*. The Renoiresque moment with the deer, then the almost parallel plight of Gibson and fellow scabs, reminds me very much of thirties movies, especially those leftist, social consciousness-raising ones of the Hoover era. For here is postulated in gripping fashion a class struggle in America—in Reagan's neoconservative America, no less! Depression movies dealt separately with farm and industrial matters, however. *The River* brings them together in Gibson's odyssey, then again very dramatically near the climax of the film.

Here Gibson, Spacek, and neighboring farmers battle the river at floodtime once more. The agribusiness conspirator arrives to break their jerry-built levee and ruin the yeomen once and for all. He will accomplish this mischief with the aid of truckloads of down-and-out ex-farmers and out-of-work laborers, all as desperate for cash as had been Gibson-the-scab so recently. There is a tense face-off, a crevasse is blown in the levee; then come pleas for class solidarity. One of the agribusinessman's drones breaks, then others follow. Joining the embattled farmers, they push the conspirator's corporate Jeep into the crevasse and stop the flood. The film ends as the Gibson-Spacek family ride an old corn combine together, making the harvest against all odds.

So what is the significance of *The River* to southern imagery? This is not simple. In the first place the southern setting and characters are not central to the plot nor particularly distinctive. Scene setting and other "southern" signatures are hastily accomplished and almost understated. Early in the movie a brief shot of roadsigns establishes locale. Then we see the Confederate flag license tag on the agribusinessman's Jeep. So aside from actors' accents, the scene might have been Illinois or Iowa. There is no cotton in sight, just corn. Blacks are few, too, except in the industrial episode. But here there is no peculiarly southern racial problem, either. Black and white are together in trouble, and one black character, another scab, is a proletarian hero of a paradoxical sort. So *The River* is a paean to the family farm, a reminder that under concrete and blacktop is God's earth, a well-done updating of early Depression movies, and at last a contemporary docudrama, too. For after the farmers and their allies have beaten the agribusinessman at the crevasse, he reminds Gibson that farmers' struggles are hardly over: "Sooner or later there's gonna be too much rain, or too much drought. Or too much corn. I can wait." Sadly, this was prophetic. Months after the film's release, experts were calling 1986 "the year of the foreclosure."[14] So the agribusinessman's words ruin the following happy harvest scene and, unlike so many Hoover era social movies (consider *Cabin in the Cotton*), deny viewers a neat resolution. *The River* is a document of reconciliation, then, only in the sense that it integrates small farmers, southerners and all. This is progress of a sort.

Places in the Heart, the third "farm" movie of 1985, is hardly a docudrama in any sense and bears practically no resemblance to *The River*. *Places* did better both critically and commercially than either of the other two. Perhaps it was better made. Perhaps writers and mass audiences alike do not care so much for docudramas. But *Places in the Heart*'s success is astounding to me, nonetheless, because it is not only an intensely, self-consciously "southern" movie, but a southern *Baptist* one!

The auteur approach to *Places* is appropriate, for it is the creation of a distinctive filmmaker, Robert Benton, a native of Waxahatchie, Texas. Benton was one of the developers of *Bonnie and Clyde* (1967), a film which, among other virtues, recreated in minute detail the look of Texas and Oklahoma during the thirties. In *Places* Benton had almost complete control—he co-wrote the script and directed— and he accomplished much more. This film, too, is set in Texas, during the mid-thirties, but in Waxahatchie and on a small farm nearby. Benton built his story around the experiences of a heroic grandmother who held a rural family together (before the Depression), from some local events he had learned, and from his and his co-writer's imaginations.

Sally Fields plays the central character, a young wife and mother of two whose husband, the sheriff, is shot to death at the start of the film. His killer is a drunken black boy who did not mean to do the deed, but lynchers take his life, anyway. Now Fields discovers the real world of finance—little insurance, many expenses, and a substantial mortgage held by a banker almost as callous as the one in *The River*. Providence finally brings to her back door a solution, a black dispossessed farmer now hoboing in hard times. This character, brilliantly played by Danny Glover, suggests they make cotton on Fields' fallow land. He knows cotton and will help, and indeed Glover does: at every point he saves the novice Fields from error and from the chicanery of bankers, seed salesmen, and ginners. All this Glover does in the humble, indirect manner demanded of blacks in that time and place. The cotton picking scenes on the big screen are most effective—oppressive heat, stinging insects, torn fingers and hands, aching backs and knees. All those who drive machines over cotton today, glassed in with air conditioning and stereo, should see *Places* for a glimpse of how the harvest used to be.

Glover and Fields make the crop and save the home, of course. This was predictable. What is not are several human tragedies that proceed with the main plot. For example, Fields reluctantly takes in a blind boarder (foisted upon her by the banker) who cannot get along with her and the children—at least for a time. Fields' brother-in-law conducts an affair with another woman who is married, and both marriages are nearly destroyed. And worst of all, the gin man, a Ku Kluxer, sees through Glover's pose of humility and comes with his brethren to beat and humiliate the best hero in the story. Glover is obliged to hobo on, despite his great personal gifts, in an awful scene of injustice.

Some of these tragedies of human relations are resolved on the screen in satisfying if conventional ways. The blind boarder is reconciled to his condition and with his new friends because he finds ways to help the children, then contributes his special talents as messenger and listener to the cotton harvest. The threatened marriages are saved ultimately by forgiveness, and one couple leaves Waxahatchie. But seemingly insoluble problems and irreparable losses remain—the deaths of the sheriff and the black boy, and the injustice to Glover. These Benton resolves in a daringly Baptist final scene.

Places in the Heart begins and ends at a white Baptist church in Waxahatchie. Both times we hear hymns, notably "In the Garden," a sweet, sensual piece of intimacy with Jesus. At the end of the film one finally enters the church. In front sit Fields' sister and her errant spouse. The other couple has just driven off, but the sister's heart is yet filled with distrust. As the music plays, however, they are reconciled and touch hands. On a pew farther back sit Fields, her children, and the boarder, as well as other familiar folks. All are in the communion of spirits. A crisis is past, more will come without doubt, but the community will survive. Then suddenly others magically appear in the pews—the sheriff, and sitting next to him the black boy; and among them too is Glover's character. All glow with happiness, for here we actually *see* Christian doctrine dear especially to Baptists— the acceptance of Providential will, and what is called the "reconciliation of the spirits." In two dimensions we perceive, in other words, a theological fourth dimension. "Be ye reconciled," commanded Paul to the Corinthians, and it came to pass in Waxahatchie in 1935, and in movie houses half a century later.

That such down-home theologizing could succeed with a national audience in 1985 may be shocking. A learned colleague of mine resented Benton's magical ending as "cynical" and "manipulative." But the colleague, an utterly secular Californian, simply did not understand. Most Americans who saw the film apparently did. Perhaps this is owing to the growth of Fundamentalism during the past two decades. Or perhaps acceptance of the visual reconciliation of spirits signifies, simply, acceptance itself, in terms both theatrical and theological. Whichever, *Places in the Heart* seems a profoundly important event in the South's odyssey through media history.

Alice Walker's novel, *The Color Purple* (1982), and Steven Spielberg's movie version (released at Christmastime, 1985) may be even more significant. This is so first because of popularity. Walker's novel not only won the Pulitzer Prize for fiction, but became a best seller in clothbound and paperback printings. Second, Spielberg's film was an immediate hit and appears (at this writing) bound for box office records, at least among "southerns." And third, both the novel and the film are controversial and divisive, especially among blacks. Controversy heightens interest and sales, and sometimes promotes reasoned discussion and reconciliation. Reconciliation among black women and men, and between black and white people generally, *should* be another gift of these poignant works. For Walker, in ways more complex than Alex Haley, does aim for peace as well as justice.

The novel is as stunning in format as in substance. Walker is Georgia-born (but much traveled and long a West Coast resident) and a much-published poet. Her skill with free verse as well as her southern upbringing may have assisted Walker's ingenious approach to the life of Celie, an abused semiliterate who endures the first four decades of this century in rural Georgia. Celie tells her own story—beginning with rapes by a man she thought her father, and childbirth at age fourteen—in the form of letters to God, composed in black English. This same "father" gives her to a brutal widower—a man she calls simply "Mister"—who not only exploits her labor and body but separates her from the only person who loves her, her sister Nettie. Mister later brings into the house his old flame, Shug Avery, a beautiful, flamboyant blues singer. Celie has more work and, in the eyes of the community, more humiliation. Yet Celie idolizes the tough Shug, who in turn gradually effects Celie's liberation. Here liberation means developing a positive self concept, resisting men's abuses, and finally, sexual fulfillment; for Shug is bisexual and Celie becomes her adoring lover. Shug also discovers that sister Nettie has written many letters to Celie over the years, from Africa, where she has gone with a missionary couple and their two children. Mister has withheld and hidden the mail. Much of the second half of *The Color Purple* consists of Nettie's messages, and in these readers learn about native cultures, the tragic consequences of imperial "development" (especially roadbuilding) among natives—and finally, that the missionaries' adopted children are Celie's. Meanwhile Celie and Shug desert Mister for Shug's big house in Memphis. Shug takes one gigolo after another, yet remains Celie's lover, too. Celie becomes an entrepreneur. Her skill as a seamstress leads to a pants-making business. Then following her inheritance of the old home place, she takes herself and her business back to Georgia. It is here that Celie is at last reunited with Nettie and her long-lost children.

Whites in *The Color Purple* are less in evidence, more two-dimensional landscape pieces, than in *Roots*. There is one small family of exceptions, however: the town mayor and especially his spoiled, batty wife and self-centered daughter. Celie's stepdaughter-in-law (about Celie's own age)—the Amazonian Sophia—runs afoul of these whites, goes to a cruel imprisonment, and is released only to serve interminably as the lady's maid, a job Sophia had indignantly refused when she first encountered these whites. The white woman becomes utterly dependent upon Sophia, mindless that the black woman has her own siblings and brood of offspring who miss and need her. As the white daughter grows up, she, too, dotes possessively on Sophia, expecting her finally to rear her own baby. Walker brutally exposes the "Mammy" myth long so dear to whites. By this time, however, Sophia is at last free, and she rudely awakens the white girl to a world outside her own. The white girl is hurt—but by the end of the novel (this story is absent from the film), she demonstrates a certain redemption, a respectful humility and caring for Sophia that is not racist. Sophia responds with dignity and forgiveness, and one of the novel's several great reconciliations is accomplished.

There are others, too, between women and men. But these were not so readily accepted at first. *The Color Purple* is a stridently feminist work. In the novel are a few marvelous men, but all minor characters—Sophia's prizefighter boyfriend, for example. Most men are cruel-to-beastly: Celie's rapist stepfather; the battering, philandering Mister; his weak son, Harpo (Sophia's husband); Mister's arrogant father; and an assortment of juke joint bums. Such low characterizations aroused furious protest from some blacks, especially early in 1986, when the movie opened nationwide. They argued that with so few films portraying blacks, a vastly popular one populated by so many violent bastards harmed the race. Hardly twenty years ago black males were widely perceived as virtually emasculated; women ruled, usually alone, in the home. Lack of jobs and power finished the sadistic operation. The human rights movement and the opening of economic and political opportunities during the seventies had marked the reemergence of black men. Now Walker had done them in once more!

The complaint has at least one merit, that being the rarity of black movies and their impact on mass perception and mood. But the larger argument against *The Color Purple* fails on two fronts. First, Walker is no unmovable man-hater. She insists that men treat women as equals, no more or less, and in the end she brings Mister and Harpo, her worst cases, to accept this premise. After many years of estrangement, Harpo is reunited with Sophia. Mister and Celie never live together again, but now sit quietly on the porch, rocking and talking. In the film version the latter reconciliation is not made so emphatic, but it is clear enough. The second argument for Walker's case against men is objective historical experience. Walker is old enough herself to know some sad truths about relations between the sexes as well as between the races. And my own research on the home lives of thousands of southern rural folks, black *and white*, during the first half of the twentieth century, bears her out. Women were enslaved by family and drudgery in homes and fields. Men, even sharecroppers, were relatively free to go about, to hunt and socialize, to carouse, to leave. Some men were kind, loyal, loving. Most were not, but over the generations showed more consideration to mules and dogs than to their women.[15] So Walker had an important if disagreeable point. Yet she is as conciliatory towards men at the conclusion of her story as Alex Haley was towards white people.

There is another story of reconciliation in the *The Color Purple*, too. This one is theological. The novel's Celie writes to the Christian god, her only friend after her separation from the beloved Nettie. By the time Shug has become her surrogate sister, however, Celie's faith has cracked. She and Shug talk religion and life, and gradually Shug—in perhaps the novel's most fascinating passages—directs Celie towards a new god. This divinity reflects the wonderful Shug's own polymorphous perversity: it is neither a man nor a woman, but a powerful, mysterious force, something not unlike certain traditional African deities, that love and trick, delight and provoke. This god, to show off, made the color purple, and if one walks past, say, a field of purple flowers without stopping to admire them, why the god will become "pissed off." In this fashion Walker reconciles both her feminism and her pan-Africanism with recognition of divine presence. It is a lovely and satisfying element that ties otherwise disparate parts of the novel together.

Spielberg's movie (written by Menno Meyjes) betrays this real meaning of the work's title. Celie is never really alienated from the god of her old-time religion. It is Shug who has troubles, for she is the wild daughter of a stern preacher. During one of her Georgia visits she approaches the old man, but he turns his back. Later, towards the film's end, she is wailing the blues at Harpo's rustic club, on a Sunday morning and within earshot of her father's church. The service is disturbed, the preacher calls for a mighty hymn, and the revelers are outshouted. Shug is, in effect, born again, and like a sequinned piper, leads the sinners in a repentant march through the woods to the church, joining the congregation in the hymn. Striding up the aisle, she is accepted once more by her tearful father. The scene is joyous stuff and reminds me of Benton's reconciliation of the spirits in *Places in the Heart*: no spiritual materializations here, but uplifting live-folks' peacemaking. Purple is reduced to a symbol of Celie's liberation, from gray despondency to bright self-esteem, and into the glorious company of Shug.

Yet the movie has many virtues and deserves, I think, its large, admiring audience. Much as I disapprove of the cliched reconciliation of Shug with conventional religion and her father, I concede certain difficulties in conveying Walker's own meaning of "the color purple"—particularly in a two-and-one-half-hour long film which does deliver well so much else from the novel. The treatment of Nettie's African adventures is nearly a textbook demonstration of the film medium's capacity for telling much briefly and memorably. The film is striking visually, too. Spielberg is as able at southern verisimilitude as he is at surreal special effects. Some critics—notably

Vincent Canby of the New York *Times*—thought the movie's visual beauty incompatible with a largely grim story and with his memory of the South during the thirties.[16] I think the film might indeed have been shot in black and white. This seems appropriate not only to Walker's imagery, but to the well-remembered "women's movies" of the forties, to which *The Color Purple* bears a sort of resemblance. The same argument, however, could be made for John Huston's *Prizzi's Honor*, another fine movie of 1985. Yet both films' vivid color dramatizes physical and psychological horror and pathos, as well as joy. Aesthetics is not an exact science.

Gifted actors interpreting unforgettable roles ultimately make Spielberg's version so important. Whoopi Goldberg—a stage monologist with huge eyes, mouth, and imagination—becomes the tangible Celie. And Danny Glover, the deferential farmer-hobo in *Places in the Heart*, becomes the embodiment of Walker's brutal, libidinous, and finally tamed Mister in *The Color Purple*. I might have cast Diana Ross as Shug, but Margaret Avery inhabited this transcendent character as well as any mortal might have. And Oprah Winfrey, a huge, charismatic Chicagoan, is Sophia's flesh and spirit. Together they become legendary, at last rendering their South as "real" as the white one. Celie, Mister, Shug, and Sophia had so many leftover scores to settle, coming into being at this late date. What is so remarkable about them, in print and on film, is that the settlement leaps beyond victory to peace.

This is, I believe, the emerging message about the South in the eighties: reconciliation within and without, between regions, races, sexes. Reconciliation does not mean bland homogeneity, amalgamization, or passionless androgeny. It is merely a sure step towards every sane person's goal on this earth. Heaven, it has been said, can wait.

Notes

PREFACE

1 Giles Lytton Strachey, *Eminent Victorians* (New York: G. P. Putnam's Sons, 1918), preface.
2 See, for example, Arthur S. Link and Rembert Patrick (eds.), *Writing Southern History: Essays in Historiography in Honor of Fletcher M. Green* (Baton Rouge: Louisiana State University Press, 1965); and C. Vann Woodward, *The Burden of Southern History* (Baton Rouge: Louisiana State University Press, 1960), Chap. 1, "The Irony of Southern History."
3 See Gene Wise, *American Historical Explanations: A Strategy for Grounded Inquiry* (Homewood, Ill.: Dorsey, 1973); Social Science Research Council, Committee on Historiography, *Theory and Practice in Historical Study*, Bulletin 54 (New York: Social Science Research Council, 1946).
4 Frank Luther Mott, historian of best sellers, estimated in the mid-1940s that about 70 percent of American best sellers were also "good literature." *Golden Multitudes: A Study of Best Sellers in the United States* (New York: Macmillan, 1947), 1–5.
5 Fred Colby Hobson, Jr., "The Menckenites and the South, 1920–1930" (M.A. thesis, Duke University, 1967), 157.
6 Gene Wise, cited above, applies Kuhn's model to academic historiography.
7 Andrew Tudor, *Image and Influence: Studies in the Sociology of Film* (London: George Allen, 1974), esp. 184, 224.
8 Donald Bogle, *Toms, Coons, Mulattoes, Mammies, and Bucks: An Interpretive History of Blacks in American Films* (New York: Viking, 1973); Edward Mapp, *Blacks in American Films: Today and Yesterday* (Metucken, N.J.: Scarecrow Press, 1972).

CHAPTER I

1 See Paul H. Buck, *The Road to Reunion, 1865–1900* (New York: Alfred A Knopf, 1937); Paul M. Gaston, *The New South Creed: A Study in Southern Mythmaking* (New York: Alfred A Knopf, 1970).
2 Fritz Maclup, *The Production and Distribution of Knowledge in the United States* (Princeton: Princeton University Press, 1962), 208–10.
3 Sergei Eisentein, *The Film Sense*, trans. and ed. Jay Layda (New York: Harcourt, Brace, 1942), 5; Terry Ramsaye, *A Million and One Nights: A History of the Motion Picture* (New York: Simon and Schuster, 1926), 19.
4 Robert M. Henderson, *D. W. Griffith; His Life and Work* (New York: Farrar, Straus & Giroux, 1972), 3–55; Billy Bitzer, *Billy Bitzer: His Story* (New York: Farrar, Straus & Giroux, 1973), 72–73.
5 Robert M. Henderson, *D. W. Griffith: The Years at Biograph* (New York: Farrar, Straus, & Giroux, 1970), 125–26; *Biograph Bulletins, 1908–1912*, (hereinafter cited as *BB*) intro. by Eileen Bowser (New York: Octagon Books, 1973), 349.
6 Bitzer, *Billy Bitzer*, 106–107, 109; Iris Barry, *D. W. Griffith: American Film Master* (New York: Museum of Modern Art, 1940; 1965 ed.), 19.
7 Thomas R. Cripps, "The Negro Reaction to the Motion Picture *Birth of a Nation*," *Historian*, XXV (May, 1963), 344–62; Raymond A. Cook, "The Man Behind *The Birth of a Nation*," *North Carolina Historical Review*, XXXIX (October, 1962), 519–41.
8 The best essays on Reconstruction historiography are: Bernard A. Weisberger, "The Dark and Bloody Ground of Reconstruction Historiography," *Journal of Southern History*, XXV (November, 1959), 427–47; and Vernon L. Wharton, "Reconstruction," in Link and Patrick (eds.), *Writing Southern History*, 265–315.
9 Jack Temple Kirby, *Darkness at the Dawning: Race and Reform in the Progressive South* (Philadelphia: J. B. Lippincott, 1972), Chap. 6.
10 The contributors were Woodrow Wilson, Hilary Herbert, W. E. B. DuBois, Daniel H. Chamberlain, William Garrott Brown, S. M. McCall, Albert Phelps, Thomas Nelson Page, and William A. Dunning: *Atlantic Monthly*, LXXXVII (January–June, 1901) and LXXXVIII (July–October, 1901).
11 In addition to Fleming's book, see Wendell Holmes Stephenson, *The South Lives in History: Southern Historians and Their Legacy* (Baton Rouge: Louisiana State University Press, 1955), 95–120. Horace Mann Bond brilliantly revised Fleming in "Social and Economic Forces in Alabama Reconstruction," *Journal of Negro History*, XXIII (July, 1938), 290–348.
12 Alice Payne Hackett (comp.), *70 Years of Best Sellers, 1895–1965* (New York: R. R. Bowker, 1967), 105. On *Birth of a Nation* as a technical and artistic monument see Theodore Huff, *A Shot Analysis of D. W. Griffith's* The Birth of a Nation (New York: Museum of Modern Art, 1961). On the poor sales of Dunning histories see for example the complaint of J. G. deRoulhac Hamilton and a North Carolina editor regarding Hamilton's *Reconstruction in North Carolina* (1914), which in a decade sold fewer than five hundred copies in North Carolina (with a population of more than 2.5 millions); unidentified press clipping, 1923, Scrapbook #1, Hamilton Papers, Southern Historical Collection, University of North Carolina Library. Re: Henabery, see Henabery to New York *Times*, February 23, 1975, Sec. D., p. 19.
13 Dwight Macdonald, *Dwight Macdonald on Movies* (New York: Simon and Schuster, 1958), 70–73, 78; James Agee, *Agee on Film* (2 vols.; New York: McDowell Obolensky, 1958), I, 315–16, 396; Sergei Eisenstein, *Film Sense, passim*.

14 Biograph Company film-making is exhaustively described by Henderson, *Griffith, The Years at Biograph*. An appendix lists all Griffith's known films, with the names of scenarists when known; see 238–39 for listings of Hennessy and Hall. Hennessy is also listed in U. S. Library of Congress, *Catalogue of Copyright Entries, Cumulative Series: Motion Pictures, 1912–1939* (Washington: Government Printing Office, 1951), 408. See also *BB*, viii–ix.

15 See Buck, *Road to Reunion*, 203–44; Gaston, *New South Creed*, 151–86; and Rayford W. Logan, *The Betrayal of the Negro, from Rutherford B. Hayes to Woodrow Wilson* (New York: Macmillan, 1965), 242–75, 371–92.

16 *BB*, 36.

17 *BB*, 126; also Henderson, *Griffith, Years at Biograph*, 82–83.

18 *BB*, 203.

19 *BB*, 245.

20 On *Abraham Lincoln* see Henderson, *Griffith, His Life and Work*, 274–75. *The Girl Who Stayed at Home* is mentioned in Barry, *Griffith*, 58–59.

21 *BB*, 329.

22 *BB*, 265, 266.

23 *BB*, 162.

24 *BB*, 219.

25 *BB*, 349.

26 Warren I. Titus, *John Fox, Jr.* (New York: Twayne, 1971), 26, 95.

27 *BB*, 44.

28 *BB*, 145.

29 *BB*, 337.

30 *BB*, 351, 444.

31 *BB*, 328. On the tobacco wars see James O. Nall, *The Tobacco Night Riders of Kentucky and Tennessee, 1905–1909* (Lexington: University of Kentucky Press, 1939).

32 *BB, passim*, especially 9, 263, 385, 286, 101, 175.

33 *BB*, 341.

34 *BB*, 237, 11.

35 *BB*, 312, 310; Henderson, *Griffith: Years at Biograph*, 79, 92; Thomas Jefferson, *Notes on the State of Virginia* (New York: Harper & Row, 1964 ed.), 131–35.

36 *BB*, 31, 185, 289.

37 *BB*, 453.

38 Barry, *Griffith*, 47.

39 *Ibid.*, 56–57; Seymour Stern, "The Cold War Against David Wark Griffith," *Films in Review*, VII (February, 1956), 49–59.

CHAPTER II

1 Holman Hamilton and Gayle Thornbrough (eds.) *Indianapolis in the "Gay Nineties": High School Diaries of Claude G. Bowers* (Indianapolis: Indiana Historical Society, 1964), 1–10, 100–103, and *passim*: Claude G. Bowers, *My Life: The Memoirs of Claude Bowers* (New York: Simon and Schuster, 1962), *passim*.

2 Hamilton and Thornbrough (eds.), *High School Diaries*, 68–72, 98–100, 162–164, 202.

3 *Ibid.*, 1–10, 57–60, 68–72, 152.

4 Bowers, *My Life*, 48, 57–60. See also campaign clippings in Claude G. Bowers Papers II, Lilly Library, Indiana University.

5 Bowers, *My Life*, 90–106.
6 *Ibid.*, 107–319.
7 *Ibid.*, 249–319.
8 Hamilton and Thornbrough (eds.), *High School Diaries, passim*; Bowers, *My Life*, esp. 290; Bowers, "Jeffersonian Democracy," pamphlet of speech delivered December 7, 1900, at Plymouth Church, Indianapolis, in Bowers Papers II; Merrill D. Peterson, "Bowers, Roosevelt, and the 'New Jefferson,'" *Virginia Quarterly Review*, XXXIV (Autumn, 1958), 530–43.
9 Richard Hofstadter, *The Progressive Historians; Turner, Beard, Parrington* (New York: Alfred A. Knopf, 1968), *passim*, esp. 3–46. See also John Higham, *History; Professional Scholarship in America* (1965; New York: Harper Torchbook ed., 1973), 171–97. "Establishment" historians included John Bach McMaster, James Schouler, James Ford Rhodes, and Hermann von Holst.
10 Bowers, *My Life*, 102–103.
11 In addition to Bowers' *Jefferson and Hamilton: The Struggle for Democracy in America* (New York: Houghton Mifflin, 1925), see Peterson, "Bowers, Roosevelt, and the 'New Jefferson'"; and Peterson, *The Jefferson Image in the American Mind*, 347–55.
12 On Reconstruction historiography see Bernard Weisberger, "The Dark and Bloody Ground of Reconstruction Historiography," *Journal of Southern History*, XXV (November 1959), 427–47. On the racial settlement and political uses of history, see Jack Temple Kirby, *Darkness at the Dawning: Race and Reform in the Progressive South* (Philadelphia: J. B. Lippincott, 1972), Chaps. 1 and 5.
13 Claude G. Bowers Diary, January 24, 1930, p. 239, in Bowers Papers II.
14 Claude G. Bowers, *The Tragic Era: The Revolution After Lincoln* (1929; Cambridge, Mass.: Houghton Mifflin Sentry ed., 1962), 541–47; Bowers, *My Life*, 141–43, 208–10.
15 Bowers, *My Life*, 209–10; *Tragic Era*, v.
16 On sectional reconciliation see Buck, *Road to Reunion*, and Gaston, *New South Creed*; also Rollin G. Osterweis, *The Myth of the Lost Cause, 1865–1900* (Hamden, Conn.: Archon Books, 1973). Bowers, pamphlet speech, "The Duty of the Sons," June 6, 1905, in Bowers Papers II. In 1898, it might be noted, Bowers was angered that white judges of the Indiana collegiate oratory contest placed a black student from Butler College fourth, when he was "easily the victor." Bowers' protest remained private, in his diary, however. Hamilton and Thornbrough (eds.), *High School Diaries*, 143.
17 Bowers Diary, May 12, 1930, and review files, in Bowers Papers II.
18 Bowers, *My Life*, 103–104, 210; Bowers Diary, January 16, 1930, p. 237, clippings files on commencement speeches, in Bowers Papers II.
19 Bowers, *My Life*, 210; Byrd to Bowers, September 27, 1929, Fletcher to Bowers, September 11, 1929, and Bowers Diary, October 29, 1929, p. 224, in Bowers Papers II; Krock in New York *Times*, September 8, 1929; Lewis in New York *Evening Post*, September 7, 1929.
20 Muzzey review, *Current History*, XXXI (November, 1929), 212, 216, 218; Dodd review, New York *Herald Tribune*, September 8, 1929; Pringle review, *Outlook*, CLIII (September 11, 1929), 66; Kendrick review, *Political Science Quarterly*, XLV (June, 1930), 288.
21 Stephenson review, *Yale Review*, XIX (Spring, 1930), 382; Lingley review, *American Historical Review*, XXXV (January, 1930), 382; Schlesinger review, *New Republic*, LX (October 9, 1929), 210–11.

22 *Journal of Negro History*, XV (January, 1930), 117–19.
23 Lynch letter, "The Tragic Era," *ibid.*, XVI (January, 1931), 103–20.
24 Vernon L. Wharton, "Reconstruction," in Arthur Link and Rembert Patrick (eds.), *Writing Southern History* (Baton Rouge: Louisiana State University Press, 1965), 265–315; Bowers, copy of "The Aftermath of the Civil War" in Bowers Papers II; Bowers, *My Life*, 326.
25 Hamilton and Thornbrough (eds.), *High School Diaries*, 202; Bowers, *My Life*, 14, 19, 24, 26–28, 44, 60, 64–65, 95–99, 102–106, 126–128, 218.
26 Bowers, *My Life*, 200–201; see also files of his *World* columns in Bowers Papers II.
27 Bowers, *My Life*, 265–84, 326–27, 330; Claude G. Bowers, *Pierre Vergniaud: Voice of the French Revolution* (New York: Macmillan, 1950); clippings file on Vergniaud, Bowers Papers II; Claude G. Bowers, " 'History's Warming Finger,' " *Indiana Magazine of History*, L (March, 1954), esp. 7.

CHAPTER III

1 W. J. Cash, *The Mind of the South* (1941; Vintage Books ed., 1960), 387.
2 On Page see his collections in the libraries at the College of William and Mary (which contain many photographs) and at Duke University; also Theodore L. Gross, *Thomas Nelson Page* (New York: Twayne, 1967).
3 On Fox see Edward L. Tucker, "John Fox, Jr., Bon Vivant and Mountain Chronicler," *Virginia Cavalcade*, XXI (Spring, 1972), 18–29; Grant C. Knight, *The Strenuous Age in American Literature* (Chapel Hill: University of North Carolina Press, 1954), 130–31; and esp. Warren I. Titus, *John Fox, Jr.* (New York: Twayne, 1971). Also Alice Payne Hackett, *70 Years of Best Sellers* (New York: R. R. Bowker, 1967), 22, 103–104, 109.
4 John Fox, Jr., *Trail of the Lonesome Pine* (New York: Scribners, 1908), 415–16.
5 George S. Friedman, "Reconstruction and Redemption in Selected American Novels, 1878–1915" (Ph.D. dissertation, Duke University, 1972); E. Stanly Godbold, Jr., *Ellen Glasgow and the Woman Within* (Baton Rouge: Louisiana State University Press, 1972), 241–42.
6 See Thomas Nelson Page, *Red Rock* (New York: Macmillan, 1898); Ernest E. Leisy, *The American Historical Novel* (Norman: University of Oklahoma Press, 1950), 179–88; Harriet R. Holman, "The Literary Career of Thomas Nelson Page, 1884–1910" (Ph.D. dissertation, Duke University, 1947), 74–86.
7 See Page to Arthur Hobson Quinn, in Quinn, *American Fiction: An Historical and Critical Survey* (New York: Scribners, 1936), 300; Page to Henry Simms Hartzog, February 4, 1900, quoted by Holman, "Literary Career," 76–77; Owen F. Oldes to Page, November 10, 1898 and Alfred M. Waddell to Page, December 1, 1898, in Thomas Nelson Page Papers, Duke University.
8 Gross, *Thomas Nelson Page*, 98–99.
9 Fox to Page, October 16, 1891, and April 22, 1895, quoted by Harriet R. Holman (ed.), *John Fox and Tom Page as They Were: Letters, an Address, and an Essay* (Miami, Fla.: Field Research Projects, n.d.), 13, 24.
10 John Fox, Jr., *Crittenden* (New York: Scribners, 1900), 231.
11 John Fox, Jr., *Little Shepherd of Kingdom Come* (New York: Scribners, 1903), 403–404.
12 See John M. Bradbury, *Renaissance in the South: A Critical History of the Literature, 1920–1960* (Chapel Hill: University of North Carolina Press, 1963), 75–79.

13 Shields McIlwaine, *The Southern Poor White: From Lubberland to Tobacco Road* (Baton Rouge: Louisiana State University Press, 1939), 184–92; Godbold, *Ellen Glasgow*, 243–50.

14 See as examples: *Time*, XI (April 9, 1928), 27; (May 14, 1928), 23; XIV (October 21, 1929), 56; XXI (February 14, 1938), 26; XI (May 7, 1928), 5.

15 Bradbury, *Renaissance in the South*, 75–79; McIlwaine, *Southern Poor White*, 193–99.

16 See George B. Tindall, *The Emergence of the New South, 1913–1945*, History of the South Series, X (Baton Rouge: Louisiana State University Press, 1967), 416–21.

17 Cash, *Mind of the South*, 388–89.

18 McIlwaine, *Southern Poor White*, 80–84; Bradbury, *Renaissance in the South*, 97–104.

19 In addition to the films, see Leo Braudy, *Jean Renoir: The World of His Films* (New York: Doubleday, 1972), 32–39, 251–52, 254–55; and James Agee, *Agee on Film* (2 vols; New York: McDowell Obolensky, 1958), I, 166–68.

20 Ellen Glasgow, "Heroes and Monsters," *Saturday Review of Literature*, XII (May 4, 1935), 34.

21 In addition to the novels see Bradbury, *Renaissance in the South*, 102–103.

22 William Faulkner, *The Hamlet* (New York: Random House, 1964 ed.), 4–5.

23 Merrill Maguire Skaggs, in *The Folk in Southern Fiction* (Athens: University of Georgia Press, 1972), 219–34, emphasizes Faulkner's treatment of social mobility and the closeness of poor and rich whites.

24 McIlwaine, *Southern Poor White*, 221–23.

25 Hackett (comp.), *70 Years of Best Sellers*, 12–30.

26 *Ibid.*,

27 See Carl Bode, *The Half-World of American Culture* (Carbondale: Southern Illinois University Press, 1965), 170. Bode reported that Caldwell's works had sold 46 million copies.

28 In addition to *Georgia Boy*, see Erskine Caldwell, *Deep South: Memory and Observation* (New York: Weybright and Talley, 1968), which emphasizes southern white and black religious practice; but see esp. *Call It Experience* (New York: Duell, Sloan and Pearce, 1951), 23–25, 102–103 on his boyhood and paternal influences. Also, Robert Cantwell (ed.), *The Humorous Side of Erskine Caldwell* (New York: Duell, Sloan and Pearce, 1951), ix–xxxiii.

29 Caldwell, *Call It Experience*, 39–142.

30 *Ibid.*, 150–65.

31 Glasgow, "Heroes and Monsters," 3–4.

32 Burke, *The Philosophy of Literary Form* (1941; Baton Rouge: Louisiana State University Press, 1967 ed.), 350–60.

33 McIlwaine, *Southern Poor White*, 217–40.

34 James Korges, *Erskine Caldwell* (Minneapolis: University of Minnesota Press, 1969), 38.

35 Malcolm Cowley, "The Two Erskine Caldwells," *New Republic*, CXI (November 6, 1944), 599–600.

36 Caldwell, *Call It Experience*, 172.

37 John M. Maclachlan, "Folk and Culture in the Novels of Erskine Caldwell," *Southern Folklore Quarterly*, IX (1945), 93–101.

38 Fred C. Hobson, *Serpent in Eden: H. L. Mencken and the South* (Chapel Hill: University of North Carolina Press, 1974); and John L. Stewart, *The Burden of*

Time: The Fugitives and Agrarians (Princeton: Princeton University Press, 1965), 91–205.

39 John Donald Wade, "Sweet Are the Uses of Degeneracy," *Southern Review*, I (1936), 449–66.

40 William Stott, *Documentary Expression and Thirties America* (New York: Oxford University Press, 1973), 33–35, 41–44, 173–74, 183–86; Andrew Bergman, *We're in the Money: Depression America and Its Films* (1971; New York: Harper Colophon, 1972 ed.), 92–98, 102–103; Peter A. Soderbergh, "Hollywood and the South," *Mississippi Quarterly*, XIX (Winter, 1965–66), 1–19.

41 See Stott, *Documentary Expression*, 136, 216–19.

42 Tindall, *Emergence of the New South*, 594–95.

43 Stott, *Documentary Expression*, 165–66; Gilbert Seldes, "Pare Lorentz's *The River*," in Lewis Jacobs (ed.), *The Documentary Tradition* (New York: Hopkinson and Blake, 1971), 123–25.

44 A new edition is available from the Yale University Press, 1969.

45 In addition to the picture book see Stott, *Documentary Expression*, 218–23; and James Agee and Walker Evans, *Let Us Now Praise Famous Men* (1941; Boston: Houghton Mifflin, 1961 ed.), 450–54. It should be added that Bourke-White was quite sensitive to other people—at least on one other assignment, in British Honduras. See Michael J. Arlen, "Green Days and Photojournalism, and the Old Man in the Room," *Atlantic*, CCXXX (August, 1972), 58–66.

46 Donald Davidson, "Erskine Caldwell's Picture Book," *Southern Review*, IV (1938–39), 15–25.

47 In addition to Nixon's book see Stott, *Documentary Expression*, 223–24.

48 See Agee and Walker, *Let Us Now Praise*, passim; Stott, *Documentary Expression*, 222–23, 261–314; Hilton Kramer, "Walker Evans: A Devious Giant," *New York Times*, April 20, 1975, Sec. D., pp. 1, 33.

49 C. Vann Woodward, *Tom Watson: Agrarian Rebel* (New York: Macmillan, 1938). John D. Hicks, *The Populist Revolt* (Minneapolis: University of Minnesota Press, 1930), is usually credited with originating the historical interest in the subject.

50 Frank L. Owsley, *Plain Folk of the Old South* (Baton Rouge: Louisiana State University Press, 1949). See also James C. Bonner, "Plantation and Farm: The Agricultural South," in Arthur S. Link and Rembert W. Patrick (eds.), *Writing Southern History: Essays in Honor of Fletcher M. Green* (Baton Rouge: Louisiana State University Press, 1966), 147–74.

CHAPTER IV

1 W. C. Fields, "Anything for a Laugh" (1934), in Donald Dreschner (ed.), *The Films of W. C. Fields* (New York: Citadel Press, 1966), 29–30.

2 Ellen Glasgow to James Branch Cabell, September 30, 1934, in James Branch Cabell Papers, University of Virginia Library.

3 Andrew Bergman, *We're in the Money: Depression America and Its Films* (New York: Harper Colophon ed., 1971), Pt. 2.

4 H. L. Mencken, "The Sahara of the Bozart," in *Prejudices: Second Series* (New York: Alfred A. Knopf, 1920), 136–54.

5 Fred C. Hobson, *Serpent in Eden: H. L. Mencken and the South* (Chapel Hill: University of North Carolina Press, 1974), 3–120; George Brown Tindall, *Emergence of the New South, 1913–1945*, Vol. X of Wendell Holmes Stephenson and E. Merton Coulter (eds.), *A History of the South* (Baton Rouge: Louisiana State University Press, 1967), 285–317.

6 Hobson, *Serpent in Eden*, 3, 16–18, 177–78.

7 See Bessie Pierce, *Civic Attitudes in American School Textbooks* (Chicago: University of Chicago Press, 1930), 89–91.

8 Donald Bogle, *Toms, Coons, Mulattoes, Mammies, and Bucks: An Interpretive History of Blacks in American Films* (New York: Viking, 1973), 26–33, 53–101.

9 *Ibid.*, 40–50; Peter Sodenbergh, "Hollywood and the South," *Mississippi Quarterly*, XIX (Winter, 1965–66), 1–19.

10 Soderbergh, "Hollywood and the South," 1–19; Ernest E. Leisy, *The American Historical Novel* (Norman: University of Oklahoma Press, 1950), 170. On *So Red the Rose*'s failure as a film see Rudy Behlmer (ed.), *Memo from David O. Selznick* (New York: Viking, 1972), 143.

11 See Marjorie Rosen, *Popcorn Venus: Women, Movies, and the American Dream* (New York: Coward, McCann, and Geophegan, 1973), 167.

12 Alice Payne Hackett (comp.), *70 Years of Best Sellers* (New York: R. R. Bowker, 1967); Behlmer (ed.), *Memo from Selznick*, 211ff; Tom Dyer, "The Making of G-w-t-W," *Films in Review*, VIII (May, 1957), 205–10; Olivia de Havilland, "The Dream that Never Died," in Arthur F. McClure (ed.), *The Movies: An American Idiom* (Rutherford, N.J.: Fairleigh Dickinson University Press, 1971), 425–29.

13 Behlmer (ed.), *Memo from Selznick*, 151; Dyer, "Making of G-w-t-W," 209.

14 Bob Thomas, *The Story of GWTW* (New York: Metro-Goldwyn-Mayer, 1967); Behlmer (ed.), *Memo from Selznick*, 235; Finis Farr, *Margaret Mitchell of Atlanta* (New York: Morrow, 1965), 131.

15 *Time* (in order of reference): XVI, (November 17, 1930), 43; XXIII, (August 17, 1931), 22; XXVIII (November 30, 1931), 46; XXXI (May 2, 1938), 18; XXXIII (January 15, 1934), 53.

16 *Ibid*: XIV (September 23, 1929), 59; XVIII (September 14, 1931), 49; (September 28, 1931), 57; XXVI (July 1, 1935), 1.

17 *Ibid*: XXIV (July 2, 1934), 5; (August 13, 1934), 43; XXVI (August 26, 1935), 57; XXIV (September 3, 1934), 55; XVI (July 1, 1935), 56; (July 8, 1935), 46.

18 See Vernon L. Wharton, "Reconstruction," in Arthur Link and Rembert W. Patrick (eds.), *Writing Southern History* (Baton Rouge: Louisiana State University Press, 1965) 265–315; C. Vann Woodward, *Reunion and Reaction: The Crisis and Compromise of 1877* (Boston: Little, Brown, 1951); Woodward, *Origins of the New South, 1877–1913* (Baton Rouge: Louisiana State University Press, 1951).

19 William Edwin Hemphill, Marvin Wilson Schlegel, and Sadie Ethel Engelberg, *Cavalier Commonwealth: History and Government of Virginia* (New York: McGraw-Hill, 1957), 72–73, 95–96, 119–21, 126–27, 131, 211, 233–35, 262, 267–70, 333, 347–56, 410–16.

CHAPTER V

1 Quoted in New York *Times*, October 20, 1974, Sec. D, p. 19. Dunaway, an "Army brat" born in Florida, was playing Blanche Du Bois in Tennessee Williams' *Streetcar Named Desire* when she uttered this line.

2 David Hackett Fischer, *Historians' Fallacies: Toward a Logic of Historical Thought* (New York: Harper & Row, 1970), 220.

3 Tennessee Williams, "Introduction: 'Something Wild,'" in *Twenty-Seven Wagons Full of Cotton and Other One-Act Plays* (Norfolk, Conn.: New Directions, 1945), n.p.

4 David Bertelson, *The Lazy South* (New York: Oxford University Press, 1967), *passim*.

5 On laziness among Old South gentry and the contrast to work-ethic yankees, see William R. Taylor, *Cavalier and Yankee: The Old South and American National Character* (1960; New York: Harper Torchbook ed., 1973), *passim*.

6 See W. J. Cash, *Mind of the South* (New York: Alfred A. Knopf, 1941), iv; Joseph L. Morrison, *W. J. Cash, Southern Prophet* (New York: Alfred A. Knopf, 1967), 3; C. Vann Woodward, *American Counterpoint: Slavery and Racism in the North-South Dialogue* (Boston: Little, Brown, 1971), 261–83 (esp. 263 on Cash's influence); Arthur S. Link and Rembert W. Patrick (eds.), *Writing Southern History*, 150, 350, 375, 384, 442.

7 See Morrison, *Cash*, 3–106.

8 In addition to Cash, on herrenvolk democracy see George M. Fredrickson, *The Black Image in the White Mind: The Debate on Afro-American Character and Destiny, 1817–1914* (New York: Harper & Row, 1971), 61, 64, 66, 68, 84, 90, 93–94, 190, 226, 267, 322; and Pierre L. van den Berghe, *Race and Racism* (New York: Wiley, 1967), *passim*. Also Ulrich Bonnell Phillips, "The Central Theme of Southern History," *American Historical Review*, XXXIV (October, 1928), 30–43.

9 Cash, *Mind of the South*, esp. 133–137.

10 C. Vann Woodward, "White Man, White Mind," *New Republic*, CLVII (December 9, 1967), 28–30. The chapter in Woodward's collection of essays cited above, *American Counterpoint*, is an enlarged and revised version of the *New Republic* article.

11 Woodward, *American Counterpoint*, 264–67.

12 Morrison, *Cash*, 27–28.

13 Fischer, *Historians' Fallacies*, 219–20.

14 See Woodward, *American Counterpoint*, 273–79. *Strange Career of Jim Crow* was published by the Oxford University Press.

15 Cash liked classical music and made himself conspicuous in Charlotte in protesting against "pop" songs, especially when played loud in his apartment house. See Morrison, *Cash*, 76–77.

16 An excellent survey is Bill C. Malone, *Country Music, U.S.A.: A Fifty-Year History* (Austin: University of Texas Press, 1968), esp. 33–238. Black influences on white country music are noted by Harry Oster, *Living Country Blues* (Detroit: Folklore Associates, 1969), 11–31. See also Roger M. Williams, *Sing a Sad Song: The Life of Hank Williams* (Garden City, N.Y.: Doubleday, 1970).

17 An excellent example of Williams' work is *Moanin' the Blues*, MGM #E3330 (n.d.)

18 Malone, *Country Music*, 136–43.

19 See Nancy M. Tischler, *Tennessee Williams: Rebellious Puritan* (New York: Citadel, 1961); Ester Merle Jackson, *The Broken World of Tennessee Willians* (Madison: University of Wisconsin Press, 1966); Signi Lenea Falk, *Tennessee Williams* (New York: Hawthorn, 1969). In his *Memoirs* (New York: Putnam, 1975), Williams explores his own sexuality at considerable length, but does not make the explicit sexual metaphoric connections to "old" and "new" Souths offered by biographer Falk. Williams does, however, accept "Blanche" as a sobriquet for himself.

20 Falk, *Tennessee Williams*, esp. 163–90.

21 On the *Baby Doll* controversy see the review of "H.H." in *Films in Review*,VIII

(January, 1957), 32–37. On Williams' Italian fetish, see the *Memoirs*, 132, 141 and *passim*. Frank Merlo, a Sicilian-American, was Williams' lover for fourteen years.

CHAPTER VI

1 In addition to Stark Young's and Margaret Mitchell's novels mentioned above, see Laura Krey's best seller, *And Tell of a Time* (Boston: Houghton Mifflin) (number eight in 1938), a pro-Confederate tale of Reconstruction in Texas.
2 See Chaps. 4 and 5 above, and Virginia van Benschoten, "Changes in Best Sellers Since World War One," *Journal of Popular Culture*, I (Spring, 1968), 379–88; and James M. Mellard, "Racism, Formula, and Popular Fiction," *ibid.*, V (Summer, 1971), 10–37.
3 On the above discussion see the films and Thomas R. Cripps, "The Death of Rastus: Negroes in American Films Since 1945," *Phylon*, XXVIII (Fall, 1967), 267–75; Edward Mapp, *Blacks in American Films, Today and Yesterday* (Metucken, N.J.: Scarecrow Press, 1972), 37–38; Donald Bogle, *Toms, Coons, Mulattoes, Mammies, and Bucks: An Interpretive History of Blacks in American Films* (New York: Viking, 1973), 150–54, 158–71; Dorothy B. Jones, "William Faulkner: Novel into Film," *The Quarterly of Film, Radio, and Television*, VIII (1953–54), 51–71.
4 See Robert Penn Warren, *All the King's Men* (New York: Modern Library ed., 1953); and Crowther's review of the film, *New York Times*, November 9, 1949, p. 53.
5 Nora Sayre, "A 1957 Film Speaks of Watergate," *New York Times*, September 8, 1974, Sec. D., pp. 1, 21.
6 Margaret Long, *Louisville Saturday* (New York: Random House, 1950).
7 Samuel Eliot Morison and Henry Steele Commager, *Growth of the American Republic* (2 vols.; New York: Oxford University Press, 1930), I, 415; 2nd ed., 1942, p. 473; 4th ed., 1950, p. 537. Emphasis added.
8 Dumas Malone and Basil Rauch, *Empire for Liberty: The Genesis and Growth of the United States of America* (2 vols.; New York: Appleton-Century-Crofts, 1960), I, 45.
9 Material on Yerby is based upon: Hoyt W. Fuller, "Famous Writer Faces a Challenge," *Ebony*, XXI (June, 1966), 188–90; Frank Yerby, "How and Why I Write the Costume Novel," *Harper's*, CCXIX (October, 1959), 145–50; "The Golden Corn: He Writes to Please," *Time*, LXIV (November 29, 1954), 97; "Talk with the Author," *Newsweek*, LIV (November 30, 1959), 110; J. Lynn Cooper, "Blacks and American Best-Selling Fiction Since World War II," *HST 300*, Miami University, May 20, 1974; and Yerby's fiction, published by Dial Press, New York.
10 See the 1958 films and the following printed sources: Jerry Wald, "Faulkner and Hollywood," *Films in Review*, X (March, 1959), 129–33; Albert Johnson, review of *Cat on a Hot Tin Roof*, in *Film Quarterly*, XII (Fall 1958-Summer 1959), 54–55; Henry Hart, "1958's Ten Best," *Films in Review*, X (January, 1959), 1; Courtland Phipp, review of *Long Hot Summer* in *Films in Review*, IX (April, 1958), 201–203; Joseph Kostalefsky, review of *The Sound and the Fury*, in *Film Quarterly*, XII (Fall 1958–Summer 1959), 47–49; Courtland Phipp, review of *God's Little Acre*, in *Films in Review*, IX (May, 1958), 270–71; Ellen Fitzpatrick, review of *Hot Spell*, in *Films in Review* (June–July, 1958), 336–37.
11 Nancy Tischler, *Tennessee Williams: Rebellious Puritan* (New York: Citadel,

1961), 241–43; Parker Tyler, review of *The Fugitive Kind*, in *Film Quarterly*, XII (Fall, 1958–Summer, 1959), 47–49.

12 Tischler, *Tennessee Williams*, 257–58; Albert Johnson, review of *Suddenly, Last Summer*, in *Film Quarterly*, XIII (Fall, 1959–Summer, 1960), 40–42; Elain Rothschild, review of *Sweet Bird of Youth* in *Films in Review*, XIII (April, 1962), 233–34.

13 Henry Hart, "1960's Ten Best," *Films in Review*, XII (January, 1961), 1, 3.

14 Virginia Cary Hudson, *O Ye Jigs & Juleps* (New York: Macmillan, 1962), 45, 46.

15 Jerry Bledsoe, "Richard Petty: A Cool, Careful Superstar," *New York Times*, March 9, 1975, Sec. 5, p. 2. On *Thunder Road* see Nancy Wharton's review in *Films in Review*, IX (June–July, 1958), 336.

16 I spent many hours listening to and watching Dizzy Dean's broadcasts. He died in July, 1974, and obituaries outlined his career. See: "Colorful Dizzy Dean Dies," *Chicago Tribune*, July 18, 1974, p. 36; and Joseph Durso, "A Modern Folk Hero," *New York Times*, July 18, 1974, p. 42.

CHAPTER VII

1 John Cohen (ed.), *The Essential Lenny Bruce* (New York: Ballantine Books, 1967), 97.

2 See *ibid.*, 52–75, 97–100; and hear *The Sick Humor of Lenny Bruce*, Fantasy #7003 (*ca.* 1960).

3 Terry Southern, "Twirling at Ole Miss," *Esquire*, LIX (February, 1963), 100, 102–103, 105, 121.

4 In addition to Onstott's novels see: "The Best-Seller Breed," *Newsweek*, XLIX (May 13, 1957), 122; John McCarthy, "The Laddie's Not for Boiling," *New Yorker*, XXXVII (June 3, 1961) 91; Alice Payne Hackett (comp.), *70 Years of Best Sellers* (New York: R. R. Bowker, 1967).

5 In addition to the films see Edward Mapp, *Blacks in American Films, Today and Yesterday* (Metucken, N.J.: Scarecrow Press, 1972), 47, 74–75; and Jack Temple Kirby, "Clarence Poe's Campaign for a Segregated 'Great Rural Civilization,'" *South Atlantic Quarterly*, LXVIII (Winter, 1969), 27–37.

6 Donald Bogle, *Toms, Coons, Mulattoes, Mammies and Bucks: An Interpretive History of Blacks in American Films* (New York: Viking, 1973), 199–200; Albert Johnson, "The Negro in American Film: Some Recent Works," *Film Quarterly*, XVIII (Fall, 1964–Summer, 1965), 24.

7 Bogle, *Toms, Coons, Mulattoes*, 202; Mapp, *Blacks in American Films*, 98–101.

8 On "militant" films of the sixties see Mapp, *Blacks in American Films*, 172–235. An interesting review of *Easy Rider* is Harriet R. Palt's in *Film Quarterly*, XXIII (Fall, 1969–Summer, 1970), 22–24.

9 William Styron, *The Confessions of Nat Turner* (New York: Random House, 1967), author's note; Styron, "This Quiet Dust," in Willie Morris (ed.), *The South Today* (New York: Harper & Row, 1965), 15–38.

10 John W. Blassingame, in *The Slave Community: Plantation Life in the Ante-Bellum South* (New York: Oxford University Press, 1972), counts seven revolts.

11 C. Vann Woodward, "Confessions of a Rebel: 1831," *New Republic*, CLVII (October 7, 1967), 25–28.

12 John Henrik Clarke (ed.), *William Styron's Nat Turner: Ten Black Writers Respond* (Boston: Beacon Press, 1968). See also John B. Duff and Peter M. Mitchell (eds.), *The Nat Turner Rebellion: The Historical Event and the Modern Contro-*

versy (New York: Harper & Row, 1971), especially Eugene D. Genovese's "The Nat Turner Case," 203–16, a devastating review of the Black Writers originally published in 1968 in the *New York Review of Books*.

CHAPTER VIII

1 Nixon quoted by Frye Gaillard, "Sour Notes at the Grand Ole Opry," *Southern Voices*, I (May–June, 1974), 50.
2 Percy quoted by Barbara King, "Walker Percy Prevails," *ibid.*, 23.
3 Leon Litwack, *North of Slavery: The Negro in the Free States* (Chicago: University of Chicago Press, 1960); Willie Morris, *Yazoo: Integration in a Deep-Southern Town* (New York: Harper's Magazine Press, 1971); Southern Regional Council, *The South and Her Children* (Atlanta: Southern Regional Council, 1971).
4 Alvin Tofler, *The Culture Consumers: A Study of Art and Affluence in America* (1964; New York: Vintage, 1973), 99–100; *Time*, LXI (January 5, 1953), 67; LXXVII (March 3, 1961), 36; LXXXII (July 12, 1963), 102–103; C (July 3, 1972), 3; XCIC (March 13, 1972), 34–35.
5 George Gallup, "True, South More 'Livable' for Blacks, Voters Decide," New York *Times*, August 15, 1971, p. 2. See Also *Ebony*, XXVI (August, 1971).
6 John Grissim, *White Man's Blues* (New York: Paperback Library, 1970); Patrick Anderson, "The Real Nashville," New York *Times Sunday Magazine* (August 31, 1975), 42.
7 Wayne King, "Some Things You May Not Know About Possums, Including Their Value as Food," New York *Times*, March 16, 1975, p. 49; Howard La Fay, "Alabama, Dixie to a Different Tune," *National Geographic*, CXLVIII (October, 1975), 534–36.
8 Robert Fogel and Stanley Engerman, *Time on the Cross: The Economics of American Negro Slavery* (Boston: Little, Brown, 1974); Herbert G. Gutman, "*Time on the Cross: The Economics of American Negro Slavery*: The World Two Cliometricians Made," *Journal of Negro History*, LX (January, 1975), 53–227; and Herbert Gutman, *Slavery and the Numbers Game: A Critique of "Time on the Cross"* (Urbana: University of Illinois Press, 1975). See also Communist Herbert Aptheker's spirited critique: *Heavenly Days in Dixie, Or: The Time of Their Lives*, pamphlet published by *Political Affairs* (from the June and July, 1974, issues).
9 Tom Wicker, "The Watergate Committee Chairman's New Clothes," *Southern Voices*, I (March–April, 1974), 7–8; "The Dick Cavett Show," ABC-TV, April 18, 1974.
10 Kathleen M. McKenna, "'Good Night, John-Boy,'" *HST 300*, Miami University, May 20, 1974; "Celebrating His Love for Virginia," Norfolk *Virginia-Pilot*, April 6, 1973, p. 48 and also Michael Robbins, "The Waltons Bring Changes to Schuyler," September 29, 1974, Sec. F-1, p. 7.
11 See William F. Heald, "The Appeal of Southern Literature," *Mississippi Quarterly*, XVIII (Winter, 1963–64), 208–18, on "community." NBC-TV sprang into this business, too, in mid-1975 with a pilot movie followed by a fall series (canceled in November) called "The Family Holvak," starring Glenn Ford as preacher and patriarch of a humble southern rural family during the Depression.
12 Joseph B. Cumming, "Slumbering Greene County, a Remote Sliver of Alabama Where Blacks and Whites May Realize the Highest Hope for the South and America," *Southern Voices*, I (March–April, 1974), 22–30.

13 See Mapp, *Blacks in American Films*, 228–29.
14 On blacks in the Old West, see Philip Durham and Everett L. Jones, *The Negro Cowboys* (New York: Dodd, Mead, 1965).
15 Eugenia Collier, review of *Conrak*, New York *Times,* April 21, 1974, Sec. D, p. 11.
16 In addition to the film see Judith Crist's remarks on box office receipts and the significance of the film in *TV Guide*, XXIII (March 1, 1975), A-9; also Charles Higham, "A Mild and Modest Man and His Very Violent Movie," New York *Times*, May 12, 1975, Sec. D, p. 13.
17 Moonshining remained a distinctly southern enterprise in 1975, although the volume of federal business in wrecking stills was on the decline. *U.S. News and World Report*, LXXIX (July 28, 1975), 62.
18 Observations about the hippie and middle-class discovery of the South at the end of the sixties are my own. On country music since 1945 see Bill C. Malone, *Country Music, USA: A Fifty-Year History* (Austin: University of Texas Press, 1968), 239–358; Ed Kahn, "Hillbillie Music: Source and Resource," *Journal of American Folklore*, LXXVIII (July–September, 1965), 257–66; Grissim, *White Man's Blues*, 82–100; L. Mayne Smith, "An Introduction to Bluegrass," *Journal of American Folklore*, LXXVIII (July–September, 1965), 245–56.
19 Grissim, *White Man's Blues*, 34–43, 57–60, 175–76, 183, 216; Gaillard, "Sour Notes," 50.
20 Gaillard, "Sour Notes," 49–50.
21 Chet Flippo, "Country and Western: Some New-Fangled Ideas," *American Libraries*, V (April, 1974), 185–90; Jan Reid, *The Improbable Rise of Redneck Rock* (Austin: Heidelberg Press, 1974); Anderson, "The Real Nashville," 36, 42.
22 Anderson, "The Real Nashville," 36, 42.
23 *Ibid.*, 42.
24 Marshall Frady, "*Gone with the Wind*," *Newsweek*, LIII (July 28, 1975), 11.
25 John Bradbury, "Absurd Insurrection: The Barth-Percy Affair," *South Atlantic Quarterly*, LXVIII (Summer, 1969), 319–29; Barbara King, "Walker Percy Prevails," 23.
26 John Shelton Reed, *The Enduring South: Subcultural Persistence in Mass Society* (Lexington, Mass.: Lexington Books/Heath, 1972), esp. Chaps. 4, 5, 6; Reed, *Southerners: The Social Psychology of Sectionalism* (Chapel Hill: University of North Carolina Press, 1983); Reed, "Life and Leisure in the New South," *North Carolina Historical Review*, LX (April, 1983), 172–82. See also Robert G. Healy, *Competition for Land in the American South* (Washington, D.C.: Conservation Foundation, 1985), on southerners' different residential patterns.

CHAPTER IX

1 Eric Peter Verschuure, "Stumble, Bumble, Mumble: TV's Image of the South," *Journal of Popular Culture*, XVI (Winter, 1982), 92–96. In *Southern Folk, Plain and Fancy: Native White Social Types* (Athens: University of Georgia Press, 1986), Chap. 2, John Shelton Reed conceives the application of the "lord of the lash" type to Ted Turner. It applies to "Dallas" and "Flamingo Road," too.
2 Reed, *Southern Folk, Plain and Fancy*, Chap. 2.
3 "Playboy Interview: Alex Haley," *Playboy*, XXIV (January, 1977), 58; New York *Times*, January 23, 1977, Sec. D, p. 23, January 31, 1977, Sec. D, p. 43; "After Haley's Comet," *Newsweek*, LXXXVI (February 14, 1977), 97.

4 Haley prefers to call his book nonfiction, and best-seller compilers complied, listing *Roots* under "general" rather than "fiction." The book's lack of formal docu-
mentation and its inventive scenes, conversations, and thoughts, render it fiction
in my opinion. But good fiction is sometimes also good history. Haley should take
no offense. Haley's genealogical research, on the other hand, has not withstood
close scrutiny. See esp. Gary B. and Elizabeth Shown Mills, "*Roots* and the New
'Faction': A Legitimate Tool for Clio?" *Virginia Magazine of History and Biography,* LXXXIX (January, 1981), 3–26.

5 The historical validity of the survival of the black family is convincingly documented in a scholarly book that appeared about the same time as *Roots:* Herbert G.
Gutman, *The Black Family in Slavery and Freedom, 1750–1925* (New York: Pan-
theon, 1976).

6 Jimmy Carter, *Why Not the Best?* (New York: Bantam Books, 1975), esp. 7–40.

7 See Doris Kearns, *Lyndon Johnson and the American Dream* (New York: Harper
and Row, 1976), 230–32. Kearns insists, nonetheless, upon Johnson's sincerity.

8 Richard N. Ostling, "Power, Glory—and Politics," *Time,* CXXVII (February 17,
1986), 62–69.

9 Mark Trost, "VCR Sales Explosion Shakes Up Industry," *Advertising Age,* January
9, 1986, p. 14.

10 Sylvia Cooper, "Lowndes Tape Rental Stores Popular," Valdosta (Georgia) *Times,*
January 20, 1986 (clipping supplied by Thomas Newsom of Valdosta).

11 Gantt quoted in John Shelton Reed, "Up from Segregation," *Virginia Quarterly
Review,* LX (Summer, 1984), 377–93.

12 John B. Boles, *Black Southerners, 1619–1869* (Lexington: University Press of Kentucky, 1984).

13 I am especially indebted for this story and interpretation (and for a copy of the
button) to Hardy Jackson of Morrow, Georgia.

14 CBS Evening News with Dan Rather, February 24, 1986.

15 Jack Temple Kirby, *Rural Worlds Lost: The American South, 1920–1960* (Baton
Rouge: Louisiana State University Press, 1986), Chap. 5.

16 Vincent Canby, "From a Palette of Cliches Comes 'The Color Purple,'" New York
Times, January 5, 1986, Sec. H, pp. 17, 30.

Essay on Sources

Preface: History High and Low

Occasional essays on the problem of defining popular culture may be found in the *Journal of Popular Culture*. There is no literature on "popular historiography," however. The preface to this book is intended partly as a step toward defining clearly this branch of popular culture.

Although now dated, Arthur S. Link and Rembert Patrick (eds.), *Writing Southern History: Essays in Historiography in Honor of Fletcher M. Green* (Baton Rouge: Louisiana State University Press, 1965), remains standard, for academic works. Gene Wise, *American Historical Explanations: A Strategy for Grounded Inquiry* (Homewood, Ill.: Dorsey, 1973), applies Thomas Kuhn's theory of interpretive change to academic history—as have I in studying popular history. Professional historians officially acknowledged the difficulty of achieving the ideal of objectivity in Social Science Research Council, Committee on Historiography, *Theory and Practice in Historical Study*, Bulletin 54 (New York: Social Science Research Council, 1946).

Helpful in understanding patterns of knowledge transmission through the popular media is Andrew Tudor, *Image and Influence: Studies in the Sociology of Film* (London: George Allen, 1974).

203

Chapter I: Griffith, Dunning, and "the Great Fact of Race"

Both the literature and politics of sectional reconciliation are well surveyed in: Paul H. Buck, *The Road to Reunion, 1865–1900* (New York: Alfred A. Knopf, 1937), and Paul M. Gaston, *The New South Creed: A Study in Southern Mythmaking* (Baton Rouge: Louisiana State University Press, 1976).

On D. W. Griffith and early film history see: Terry Ramsaye, *A Million and One Nights: A History of the Motion Picture* (New York: Simon and Schuster, 1926); Robert Sklar, *Movie-Made America: A Social History of American Movies* (Random House, 1975), 3–66; Sergei Eisenstein, *The Film Sense*, trans. and ed. by Jay Layda (New York: Harcourt, Brace, 1942); Robert M. Henderson, *D. W. Griffith: His Life and Work* (New York: Farrar, Straus & Giroux, 1972); Iris Barry, *D. W. Griffith: American Film Master* (New York: Museum of Modern Art, 1940); James Hart (ed.), *The Man Who Invented Hollywood: The Autobiography of D. W. Griffith* (Louisville, Ky.: Touchstone, 1972); Karl Brown, *Adventures with D. W. Griffith* (New York: Da Capo Press, 1976); Paul O'Dell, *Griffith and the Rise of Hollywood* (Cranbury, N.J.: A. S. Barnes, 1970); Billy Bitzer, *Billy Bitzer: His Story* (New York: Farrar, Straus & Giroux, 1973).

Griffith's *Birth of a Nation* is much written about. See the above and: Theodore Huff, *A Shot Analysis of D. W. Griffith's "The Birth of a Nation"* (New York: Museum of Modern Art, 1961); Thomas R. Cripps, "The Negro Reaction to the Motion Picture Birth of a Nation," *Historian*, XXV (May, 1963), 344–62; Raymond A. Cook, "The Man Behind *The Birth of a Nation*," *North Carolina Historical Review*, XXXIX (October, 1962), 519–41.

The best essays on Reconstruction historiography are: Bernard A. Weisberger, "The Dark and Bloody Ground of Reconstruction Historiography," *Journal of Southern History*, XXV (November, 1959), 427–47; and Vernon L. Wharton, "Reconstruction," in Link and Patrick (eds.), *Writing Southern History*, 265–315. On the significance of Reconstruction in race relations during the early twentieth century, see Jack Temple Kirby, *Darkness at the Dawning: Race and Reform in the Progressive South* (Philadelphia: J. B. Lippincott, 1972), Chap. 6; see also Wendell Holmes Stephenson, *The South Lives in History: Southern Historians and Their Legacy* (Baton Rouge:

Louisiana State University Press, 1955). The 1901 essays on Reconstruction by prominent Americans appeared in the *Atlantic Monthly*, January through October.

Throughout the book, statistics on best-selling books are drawn from Alice Payne Hackett (comp.), *70 Years of Best Sellers, 1895– 1965* (New York: R. R. Bowker, 1967).

Many of Griffith's Biograph films have been preserved at the Museum of Modern Art (New York) and in the Paper Print Collection at the Library of Congress. These and the large number which no longer exist may still be studied, however, because Eileen Bowser of the Museum of Modern Art rescued and published the *Biograph Bulletins, 1908–1912* (New York: Octagon Books, 1973). The *Bulletins* supplied plot outlines sufficient for my study of regional and ethnic stereotypes, when I was unable to view a film. Robert M. Henderson, *D. W. Griffith: The Years at Biograph* (New York: Farrar, Straus & Giroux, 1970) also has an appendix listing Griffith's early movies, sometimes with the names of scenarists.

Chapter II: Claude Bowers and the Establishment

Naturally, Claude G. Bowers wrote an autobiography, *My Life: The Memoirs of Claude Bowers* (New York: Simon and Schuster, 1962), although it reveals little and lacks Bowers' characteristic zest. Holman Hamilton and Gayle Thornbrough (eds.), *Indianapolis in the "Gay Nineties": High School Diaries of Claude G. Bowers* (Indianapolis: Indiana Historical Society, 1964), on the other hand, is a marvelous young man's self-portrait. Much of the chapter is based upon research in the Claude G. Bowers Papers II at the Lilly Library, Indiana University. (The Bowers Papers I are closed.)

Bowers wrote about the South in *Jefferson and Hamilton: The Struggle for Democracy in America* (New York: Houghton Mifflin, 1925), and especially in *The Tragic Era: The Revolution After Lincoln* (1929; Cambridge, Massachusetts: Houghton Mifflin Sentry Edition, 1962). Merrill Peterson wrote about Bowers' perspective on Jefferson in "Bowers, Roosevelt, and the 'New Jefferson,'" *Virginia Quarterly Review*, XXXIV (Autumn, 1958), 530–43; and *The Jefferson Image in the American Mind* (New York: Oxford University Press, 1960). An excellent study of the progressive historians (with whom I include Bowers) is Richard Hofstadter, *The Progressive Historians: Turner, Beard, Parrington* (New York: Alfred A. Knopf, 1968).

Much of my critique of *Tragic Era* is based upon contemporary reviews of the book. For specific citations, see the notes.

Chapter III: The Embarrassing New South

In addition to the cited works of Thomas Nelson Page and John Fox, Jr., material on the two writers is based upon: Theodore L. Gross, *Thomas Nelson Page* (New York: Twayne, 1967); Warren I. Titus, *John Fox, Jr.* (New York: Twayne, 1971); Edward L. Tucker, "John Fox, Jr., *Bon Vivant* and Mountain Chronicler," *Virginia Cavalcade*, XXI (Spring, 1972), 18–29; the Thomas Nelson Page Papers at Duke University Library and the library of the College of William and Mary; Grant C. Knight, *The Strenuous Age in American Literature* (Chapel Hill: University of North Carolina Press, 1954); Ernest E. Leisy, *The American Historical Novel* (Norman: University of Oklahoma Press, 1950); Harriet R. Holman, "The Literary Career of Thomas Nelson Page, 1884–1910" (Ph.D. dissertation, Duke University, 1947); Arthur Hobson Quinn, *American Fiction: An Historical and Critical Survey* (New York: Scribners, 1936), 300; Harriet R. Holman (ed.), *John Fox and Tom Page as They Were: Letters, an Address, and an Essay* (Miami, Fla.: Field Research Projects, n.d.), 13, 24. John M. Bradbury, *Renaissance in the South: A Critical History of the Literature, 1920–1960* (Chapel Hill: University of North Carolina Press, 1963) is a useful catelog of the broad subject.

E. Stanly Godbold, Jr., *Ellen Glasgow and the Woman Within* (Baton Rouge: Louisiana State University Press, 1972) is an excellent literary biography, but one may still consult with profit the Ellen Glasgow Papers at the University of Virginia Library for Glasgow's and James Branch Cabell's marvelous letters. See also the Cabell Papers at the same library.

The subject of southern poor whites is treated in surveys of literature (such as Bradbury's, above) as well as in three able special studies: Shields McIlwaine, *The Southern Poor White: From Lubberland to Tobacco Road* (Baton Rouge: Louisiana State University Press, 1939); Merrill Maguire Skaggs, *The Folk in Southern Fiction*

(Athens: University of Georgia Press, 1972); and Sylvia Jenkins Cook, *From Tobacco Road to Route 66: The Southern Poor White in Fiction* (Chapel Hill: University of North Carolina Press, 1976).

In addition to Erskine Caldwell's books, I consulted the following sources: his two autobiographies, the useful *Call It Experience* (New York: Duell, Sloan and Pearce, 1951) and the rather uninformative *Deep South: Memory and Observation* (New York: Weybright and Talley, 1968); Robert Cantwell (ed.), *The Humorous Side of Erskine Caldwell* (New York: Duell, Sloan and Pearce, 1951); Kenneth Burke, *The Philosophy of Literary Form* (1941; Baton Rouge: Louisiana State University Press, 1967 edition), 350–60; James Korges, *Erskine Caldwell* (Minneapolis: University of Minnesota Press, 1969); Malcolm Cowley, "The Two Erskine Caldwells," *New Republic*, CXI (November 6, 1944), 599–600; John M. Maclachlan, "Folk and Culture in the Novels of Erskine Caldwell," *Southern Folklore Quarterly*, IX (1945), 93–101. Southern Agrarian outrage at Caldwell's work is well represented in: John Donald Wade, "Sweet Are the Uses of Degeneracy," *Southern Review*, I (1936), 449–66; and Donald Davidson, "Erskine Caldwell's Picture Book," *ibid.*, IV (1938–39), 15–25.

Fred C. Hobson's *Serpent in Eden: H. L. Mencken and the South* (Chapel Hill: University of North Carolina Press, 1974) is a fine monograph on the subject's peculiar relationship to the South. In addition to the Vanderbilt Agrarians' *I'll Take My Stand*, see John L. Stewart, *The Burden of Time: The Fugitives and Agrarians* (Princeton: Princeton University Press, 1965).

On Hollywood's treatment of the South during the 1930s see: Peter A. Soderbergh, "Hollywood and the South," *Mississippi Quarterly*, XIX (Winter, 1965–66), 1–19; and Andrew Bergman, *We're in the Money: Depression America and Its Films* (1971; New York: Harper Colophon 1972 edition), 92–98, 102–103. On documentary treatments of the region see William Stott's excellent *Documentary Expression and Thirties America* (New York: Oxford University Press, 1973); Gilbert Seldes, "Pare Lorentz's *The River*" in Lewis Jacobs (ed.), *The Documentary Tradition* (New York: Hopkinson and Blake, 1971), 123–25; in addition to the picture books cited (by Agee and Evans, Bourke-White and Caldwell, and H. C. Nixon).

Chapter IV: The Grand Old South

Material on H. L. Mencken's and Ellen Glasgow's paradoxical late-life views of the Old South is based upon sources cited above for Chapter III, plus Mencken's "The Sahara of the Bozart," in *Prejudices: Second Series* (New York: Alfred A. Knopf, 1920), 136–54. Excellent for the context of the 1920s and 1930s is George Brown Tindall, *Emergence of the New South, 1913–1945* (Baton Rouge: Louisiana State University Press, 1967). A pioneering study (which badly needs a sequel) on school-book bias is Bessie Louise Pierce, *Civic Attitudes in American School Textbooks* (Chicago: University of Chicago Press, 1930), especially 89–91. Two able books on Hollywood's black imagery are: Donald Bogle, *Toms, Coons, Mulattoes, Mammies, and Bucks: An Interpretive History of Blacks in American Films* (New York: Viking, 1973); and the briefer Edward Mapp, *Blacks in American Films: Today and Yesterday* (Metucken, N.J.: Scarecrow Press, 1972). On women in films see Marjorie Rosen, *Popcorn Venus: Women, Movies, and the American Dream* (New York: Coward, McCann, and Geophegan, 1973).

In addition to the novel and film, *Gone with the Wind*, I found the following printed sources useful: Rudy Behlmer (ed.), *Memo from David O. Selznick* (New York: Viking, 1972); Tom Dyer, "The Making of G-w-t-W," *Films in Review*, VIII (May, 1957), 205–10; Olivia de Havilland, "The Dream that Never Died," in Arthur F. McClure (ed.), *The Movies: An American Idiom* (Rutherford, N.J.: Fairleigh Dickinson University Press, 1971), 425–29; Bob Thomas, *The Story of GWTW* (New York: Metro-Goldwyn-Mayer, 1967); and Finis Farr, *Margaret Mitchell of Atlanta* (New York: Morrow, 1965).

My survey of advertising in *Time* is based upon a thorough perusal of the magazine's issues, 1929–1939. The issues cited in the notes are but representative samples.

Chapter V: The Visceral South

Among many good sources on southern white laziness and violence are David Bertelson, *The Lazy South* (New York: Oxford University Press, 1967); William R. Taylor, *Cavalier and Yankee: The Old South and American National Character* (1960; New York: Harper Torchbook edition, 1973); and Wilbur J. Cash's classic *Mind of the South* (New York: Alfred A. Knopf, 1941). Cash's biographer, Joseph L. Morrison, in *W. J. Cash: Southern Prophet* (New York: Alfred A. Knopf, 1967), adds perspective.

Morrison's biography is uncritical of Cash's history, however; and one should consult instead C. Vann Woodward, "White Man, White Mind," *New Republic*, CLVII (December 9, 1967), 28–30, and an expansion of this brief essay in Woodward's *American Counterpoint: Slavery and Racism in the North-South Dialogue* (Boston: Little, Brown, 1971), 261–83; as well as David Hackett Fischer's delightful *Historians' Fallacies: Toward a Logic of Historical Thought* (New York: Harper & Row, 1970), 220.

Among many excellent scholarly sources on Cash's Proto-Dorian bond among white men are Pierre L. van den Berghe, *Race and Racism* (New York: Wiley, 1967); George M. Fredrickson, *The Black Image in the White Mind: The Debate on Afro-American Character and Destiny, 1817–1914* (New York: Harper & Row, 1971); and the works of C. Vann Woodward.

On Tennessee Williams, one should read his "southern" plays and see the films based upon them. Also in print are: Nancy M. Tischler, *Tennessee Williams: Rebellious Puritan* (New York: Citadel, 1961), the most useful of the biographical-literary studies; Ester Merle Jackson, *The Broken World of Tennessee Williams* (Madison: University of Wisconsin Press, 1966); Signi Lenea Falk, *Tennessee Williams* (New York: Twayne, 1961); Mike Steen (ed.), *A Look at Tennessee Williams* (New York: Hawthorn, 1969); and Williams' *Memoirs* (New York: Putnam, 1975). Williams does not explicitly concede the sexual-metaphoric connections to Old and New Souths offered by biographer Falk, but he does accept Blanche as a sobriquet for himself.

Studying country music necessitates much listening, a mixed blessing. An excellent survey of the subject in print, however, is Bill C. Malone, *Country Music, U.S.A.: A Fifty-Year History* (Austin: University of Texas Press, 1968). See also Roger M. Williams, *Sing a Sad Song: The Life of Hank Williams* (Garden City, N.Y.: Doubleday, 1970), a popular biography of the 1940s star.

Chapter VI: Dixie Mellow

This chapter surveys southern novels and movies of the 1950s, for the most part, and there is little literature on the subject. I read the books and viewed the films cited; when I profited from book and film reviews, I cited them also. On southern blacks and whites in film and fiction, one might consult Donald Bogle's and Edward Mapp's books on blacks in the movies; also Thomas R. Cripps, "The Death of Rastus: Negroes in American Films Since 1945," *Phylon*, XXVIII (Fall, 1967), 267–75; Virginia van Benschoten, "Changes in Best Sellers Since World War One," *Journal of Popular Culture*, I (Spring, 1968), 379–88; James M. Mellard, "Racism, Formula, and Popular Fiction," *Journal of Popular Culture*, V (Summer, 1971), 10–37; Dorothy B. Jones, "William Faulkner: Novel into Film," *Quarterly of Film, Radio, and Television*, VIII (1953–54), 51–71; and Jerry Wald, "Faulkner and Hollywood," *Films in Review*, X (March, 1959), 129–33.

On Frank Yerby, in addition to his novels cited, I relied upon: Hoyt W. Fuller, "Famous Writer Faces a Challenge," *Ebony*, XXI (June, 1966), 188–90; "The Golden Corn: He Writes to Please," *Time*, LXIV (November 29, 1954), 97; "Talk With The Author," *Newsweek*, LIV (November 30, 1959), 110; J. Lynn Cooper, "Blacks and American Best-Selling Fiction Since World War II," HST 300, Miami University, May 20, 1974 (in my possession); and the invaluable Frank Yerby, "How and Why I Write the Costume Novel," *Harper's*, CCXIX (October, 1959), 145–50.

Chapter VII: The Devilish South

As with the previous chapter, this study of southern imagery in the 1960s is a survey and analysis of the books and films cited; helpful reviews are also cited in the notes.

Ingenious pillorying of the South may be found in John Cohen (ed.), *The Essential Lenny Bruce* (New York: Ballantine Books, 1967), 97; *The Sick Humor of Lenny Bruce*, Fantasy #7003 (*ca.* 1960); and Terry Southern, "Twirling at Ole Miss," *Esquire*, LIX (February, 1963), 100, 102–103, 105, 121.

Donald Bogle's and Edward Mapp's previously mentioned histories of blacks in American films are particularly useful on changes in the 1960s. See also Albert Johnson, "The Negro in American Film: Some Recent Works," *Film Quarterly*, XVIII (Fall, 1964–Summer, 1965), 24.

The only secondary information on Kyle Onstott I discovered was "The Best-Seller Breed," *Newsweek*, XLIX (May 13, 1957), 122, and John McCarthy's derisive review of the stage version of *Mandingo*, "The Laddie's Not for Boiling," *New Yorker*, XXXVII (June 3, 1961), 91.

William Styron wrote about his quest for Nat Turner before the appearance of the novel in "This Quiet Dust," in Willie Morris (ed.), *The South Today* (New York: Harper & Row, 1965), 15–38. C. Vann Woodward's favorable review, "Confessions of a Rebel, 1831," appeared in *New Republic*, CLVII (October 7, 1967), 25–28, nearly a year before the publication of the militant black reaction, John Henrik Clarke (ed.), *William Styron's Nat Turner: Ten Black Writers Respond* (Boston: Beacon Press, 1968). Professor Eugene D. Genovese's devastating review of the black writers' response may be found in John B. Duff and Peter M. Mitchell (eds.), *The Nat Turner Rebellion: The Historical Event and the Modern Controversy* (New York: Harper & Row, 1971), 203–16.

Chapter VIII: Dixie Redux and Demise

Evidence of the emergence of southern chic about 1971 is scattered about in printed sources: Willie Morris, *Yazoo: Integration in a Deep-Southern Town* (New York: Harper's Magazine Press, 1971); George Gallup, "True, South More 'Livable' for Blacks, Voters Decide," New York *Times*, August 15, 1971, p. 2; the entire issue of *Ebony*, XXVI (August, 1971); Wayne King, "Some Things You May Not Know About Possums, Including Their Value as Food," New York *Times*, March 16, 1975, p. 49; Howard La Fay, "Alabama, Dixie to a Different Tune," *National Geographic*, CXLVIII (October, 1975), 534–36; and Joseph B. Cumming, "Slumbering Greene County, A Remote Sliver of Alabama Where Blacks and Whites May Realize the Highest Hope for the South and America," *Southern Voices*, I (March–April, 1974), 22–30.

Among many useful sources on country music are Bill Malone's previously cited survey; John Grissum, *White Man's Blues* (New

York: Paperback Library, 1970); Patrick Anderson, "The Real Nashville," New York *Times Sunday Magazine* (August 31, 1975), 42; Frye Gaillard, "Sour Notes at the Grand Ole Opry," *Southern Voices*, I (May–June, 1974), 50; Ed Kahn, "Hillbillie Music, Source and Resource," *Journal of American Folklore*, LXXVIII (July–September, 1965), 257–66; L. Mayne Smith, "An Introduction to Bluegrass," *ibid.*, 245–56; Chet Flippo, "Country and Western: Some New-Fangled Ideas," *American Libraries*, V (April, 1974), 185–90; and Jan Reid, *The Improbable Rise of Redneck Rock* (Austin, Tex.: Heidelberg Press, 1974).

On recent southern fiction and the future of regional distinctiveness one should read Walker Percy's and James Dickey's works, and: William F. Heald, "The Appeal of Southern Literature," *Mississippi Quarterly*, XVII (Winter, 1963–64), 208–18; Barbara King, "Walker Percy Prevails," *Southern Voices*, I (May–June, 1974), 23; John Bradbury, "Absurd Insurrection: The Barth-Percy Affair," *South Atlantic Quarterly*, LXVIII (Summer, 1969), 319–29; and C. Vann Woodward, *The Burden of Southern History* (1960; New York: Vintage edition, 1961), 3–26, 167–92. A most valuable empirical study of southern whites' regional identity (which should be repeated in a few years) is John Shelton Reed, *The Enduring South: Subcultural Persistence in Mass Society* (Lexington, Mass.: Lexington Books/Heath, 1972), especially Chaps. 4–6.

Index

213